ANY
CHILD
CAN
READ
BETTER

ANY CHILD CAN READ BETTER

HARVEY S. WIENER

OXFORD UNIVERSITY PRESS
NEW YORK   OXFORD

Oxford University Press

Oxford   New York
Athens   Auckland   Bangkok
Calcutta   Cape Town   Dar es Salaam   Delhi
Florence   Hong Kong   Istanbul   Karachi
Kuala Lumpur   Madras   Madrid   Melbourne
Mexico City   Nairobi   Paris   Singapore
Taipei   Tokyo   Toronto

and associated companies in
Berlin   Ibadan

Copyright © 1990, 1996 by Harvey S. Wiener, Ph.D.

First published in 1990 by Bantam Books,
666 Fifth Avenue, New York, New York 10103

Revised edition first published in paperback by Oxford University
Press, 1996, 198 Madison Avenue, New York, New York 10016-4314

Oxford is a registered trademark of Oxford University Press

Library of Congress Cataloging-in-Publication Data
Wiener, Harvey S.
Any child can read better : developing your child's reading
skills outside the classroom / Harvey S. Wiener. — Rev. ed.
p.   cm.
Includes index.
ISBN 0-19-510218-5 (pbk.)
1. Reading—Parent participation.   2. Reading (Elementary)
I. Title.
LB1050.W437   1996
649'.58—dc2   95-33331

2 4 6 8 10 9 7 5 3 1

Printed in the United States of America

TEXT CREDITS

ART CREDITS

The end, at last, to the mystery—
I learned to read
When you read with me
When
you
read with me.

For

Blanche Koster Gold
We miss you, Mom

Contents

Acknowledgments

I am blessed with loyal family and friends who support my work spiritually and intellectually, and I want to thank them lovingly for their efforts.

Thank you, Barbara Wiener, for teaching me so much about beginning readers and how to reach them through print. Thanks, too, for listening and for answering all my questions with your usual sensitivity and for helping me make this a better book. Thank you, Melissa Wiener, now a wonderful teacher yourself of second-graders in Pleasantville, New York, for keeping me up-to-date on new ideas in teaching reading.

Thank you, Joseph Wiener and Saul Wiener, for letting me test out my ideas on you and for allowing me to share your private thoughts with people you don't know. Saul, thanks for your terrific drawings and your keen insights.

Thank you, Rosalie Bean, Kit, across the country in Seattle, for being a loving, sensitive librarian and for helping me identify just which books make kids happy. Thanks too for your excellent summaries and suggestions for book talk.

Thank you, Janet Lieberman, for showing me a schema for teaching reading. You helped me find order in a chaotic universe. You deserved the Dana Award you received.

Thank you, Chuck Bazerman, for working with me over the years to develop some of my ideas for beginning readers.

Thank you, Nora Eisenberg and Karen Greenberg, mothers and first-rate scholars of language, for looking at previous versions of *Any Child Can Read Better* and for tender, indispensable advice about it.

Thank you, Dee Shedd and Sheila Byers, for your long hours working with me on the manuscript in its sundry forms. How could I get by without you?

ANY
CHILD
CAN
READ
BETTER

Introduction

YOUR CHILD CAN READ BETTER WITH YOUR HELP

■ — ■

The Home Reading Option

Today's parents have a lively interest in assisting their children as learners, and this interest has spawned a plethora of books on home reading programs. It's natural to raise this question, then: why yet *another* book for helping children read at home? Surely the bookstore and library shelves are groaning with volumes that can help you create a "home schoolroom," enough to produce a nation of advanced readers. Why yet another book?

For good reasons, believe me.

Obviously, most parents want to help their children learn. A couple of years ago, Professor Joyce Epstein at Johns Hopkins surveyed the parents of more than 250 Baltimore children. Her findings, reported in *The New York Times*, showed that kids had higher reading scores if parents supported their youngsters' efforts at home. What's even more interesting is that although mothers and fathers wanted to involve themselves actively in their children's learning, very few knew just what to do. A shocking eighty per cent reported that they didn't have a clue about where to begin in helping their children succeed in school. With this apparent insecurity, many moms and dads are reaching for books in an effort to learn what they don't know. Hence, all the how-to-help-your-child read productions.

However, unlike *Any Child Can Read Better*, most "home learning" books address parents of toddlers and preschoolers and attempt to create a race of superkids who can read almost before they can walk. Teach-your-child-to-read books concentrate on turning the home nursery into a classroom—reading drills with flash cards, oversized words pinned as labels on familiar objects, interminable sessions on alphabet skills, phonetics, sight vocabulary, and sounding-out words. Too many books for parents of young learners have turned on the pressure and have turned off the pleasure for mothers and fathers as guiders and shapers of learning experiences.

Moms and dads are not drill sergeants. Home isn't boot camp.

If you're the mother or father of a preschooler, unless you're home learning parents who won't send your children to school in any case, *don't* teach your son or daughter how to read. Leave that job for preschool classrooms, kindergartens, and the primary grades. Sure, create a home environment in which words are important, in which reading is cherished, in which pencil and paper are available and fun to use. Read to and with your child whenever you can; talk with your child about words and books—about anything. I've laid out my position on these issues in other books, particularly *Any Child Can Write* (revised edition, Oxford, 1990), and *Talk with Your Child* (Viking, 1988).

Why shouldn't you teach your baby to read? First, the job is tough to do properly. Teachers and scholars give their lives to instructing children in the mechanics of reading: how to use the alphabet, how to say letters alone and in combinations, how to pronounce words, how to distill meaning from print. No matter how dedicated you are, it's difficult to achieve in your living room what teachers try to achieve throughout the grades. Home learning moms and dads, who for philosophical, religious, and social reasons provide all instruction at home, really have their work cut out for them!

Second, if you become more of your child's teacher, you risk being less of a parent, and you can strain the already delicate relations in a household. It's awfully tough to make your child feel that you love him when you're seething with impatience at his restlessness, at his off-and-on attitude toward books, at his stubborn refusal to sound out a word some days. Simply living with our families can create pressures; burdening often fragile home environments with classroom tactics can make everyone miserable.

I'm not denying that innumerable opportunities exist for teaching and learning at home. In my books I advocate and endorse the contributions moms and dads can make to learning. Yet you must remember that your primary role in your child's life is as a loving parent, not as a teacher of school skills. Being a parent and a subject skills teacher for your own child is like oil and water: they don't mix even under very good conditions.

The third and most important reason to resist teaching your child the rudiments of reading is that she's probably going to learn them pretty well without your help. Why waste your energies here when you could be stimulating more productive learning? She'll get the letter combinations and the alphabet; she'll learn useful sight vocabulary; she'll read successfully on a basic level.

As I've suggested, what many parents try to do at home, teachers do pretty well in the formal classroom setting.

Besides, little scientific data support the claim that kids who learn to read at a very young age are, in the long run, any better off than their later-learning peers. Youngsters level off: by the time they reach the third grade, those who learned to read early, before experiencing school, and those who learned only through classroom instruction, are very much in the same ball park.

Here from David Elkind, Professor of Child Study at Tufts University, and a leading authority on young people's learning, is food for thought on teaching school subjects to kids at home. Elkind is shocked at how teachers, parents, administrators, and legislators are developing for infants and young children the kinds of educational programs aimed quite specifically at school-age youngsters. "When we instruct children in academic subjects at too early an age," he says in his landmark book *Miseducation: Preschoolers at Risk*, "we miseducate them; we put them at risk for short-term stress and long-term personality damage for no useful purpose. There is no evidence that such early instruction has lasting benefits, and considerable evidence that it can do lasting harm."

In light of all these observations, let me repeat the question I posed earlier: Why yet *another* reading book?

When elementary school teachers across the grades complain that youngsters don't know how to read, they don't mean that children cannot decode words or unpuzzle basic syntax. Rather, they mean that children cannot extract vital meanings, cannot generalize, classify, predict outcomes, decipher figurative expressions— in short, cannot perform the kinds of intellectual tasks that mark the critical reader.

That's where you come in. And that's why I've written this book for you. Very few among the countless how-to-help-your-child-read-and-learn books intelligently address the parents of school-age children who are trying to make their way through the maze of assignments and exercises related to classroom reading. I've written this book to help you help your child as she's learning and practicing reading at school where your efforts can supplement daily academic instruction. You won't find any information here on how to teach alphabet sounds and phonics for the very young. You will find information about assisting your child as she reads a classroom textbook or some other class assignment.

That's one reason for *Any Child Can Read Better*.

Another is that children of the many young families of the mid-eighties are now growing up. Yesterday's toddlers and preschoolers now are filling the primary-grade classrooms of America. What you might have learned from other books about helping preschoolers will not stretch far enough as your son or daughter advances through the grades. Still, if you are a parent of one of these grade-school youngsters, you're probably no less anxious today about your child's success than you were when he or she attended nursery school, day care programs, or courses at the museum, the music center, or the sports academy. If at this moment you're a parent of an infant or a toddler, it won't be long before you're looking for ways to help her with her school learning.

As a parent, you need a book on how to help your maturing child survive as a reader in school and out. Learning to read well and for different purposes is an ongoing, organic process. Every page your child reads provides an opportunity to sharpen reading skills, and kids need help in extracting the most possible meaning from print. To complicate matters, once kids have to spend six hours a day at a classroom desk, teachers start piling on homework. Very often the assignments involve language activities, vocabulary building, and reading comprehension. These home activities regularly mystify children. "Reading" homework—especially when the disciplines expand to such areas as science and social studies—invariably draws parents into its web when kids wonder aloud: How do I do this? What does the teacher want? What does this mean?

I want to restate an important point I made earlier. Many of today's elementary school youngsters have mastered the rudiments of reading. By that I mean that they know how to recognize basic words, and they know the phonetic and syntactical rules for identifying many unfamiliar words. Those who do not know how to "decode" when they enter kindergarten or first grade generally learn the skill in a reasonable amount of time. That is, they meet the goals set by the school for reading progress.

Once kids know the basics of reading, a teacher's work really begins. Yet, try as they may, teachers cannot provide the guidance and stimulation that will advance every child's reading excellence. Classes are too large. Too much content in too many disciplines veers classes off the reading track. Kids' learning experiences vary so widely that typical front-of-class teaching can put off many youngsters. Thus, you, the parent, serve a valuable role as reading support agent, and your home and surrounding community, even more than the school, serve as reading laboratories for advancing skills.

Building Home Reading

This book will show you how to make your child a critical reader in school, at home, and in the society at large. As I've said, this is not a how-to-teach-your-child-to-read book. Too many of these painfully prescriptive volumes already strain our bookshelves. I intend to help you, concerned mothers and fathers, move to the next stage of your child's intellectual development, in which your home or the preschool setting is not the primary learning environment.

I offer here practical steps for forming essential skills. I'm building on almost thirty years' experience as a teacher of reading and writing from elementary school through college and as a parent for eighteen years. Three lively, inquisitive kids helped me understand the needs of learners at home, as my kids' teachers gave formal classroom instruction, hewing to required hours and mandated curriculum.

I have identified for you the skills that I believe contribute most to critical reading and have organized the chapters of *Any Child Can Read Better* according to those skills. Thus, I'll give you a brief overview of some basic strategy that a novice reader must master; and then I will show you how to use home conversation and relaxed questioning to lead your child to gain command of the essential skills. I'll also show you some typical reading materials that children are likely to bring home in elementary school, and I'll show you how to direct your child's attention to a text's core meaning.

As I point out the necessary skills, I'll draw regularly on the nonverbal world, the world of pictures, signs, advertisements, and supermarket products to assert the potential and power of visual literacy in helping your child master reading. Knowing how your youngster applies an important skill in nonlinear print settings makes your role as reading coach much easier than you might have thought. By connecting those skills with a book's demands, you can use creative, relaxed discussion to draw meanings out of print material. By talking with your child about school-based home readings, you can tease out the careful, intelligent exploration that teachers expect from their pupils but have little opportunity to nurture.

If you have a school-age child at home, I'll bet you've been wondering about what you can do to help your child learn. What, for example, do you do when your first grader brings home a worksheet on word families, when your second grader brings home a photocopied story with questions, when your fifth-grader brings home a science book with a reading assignment to complete by the next morning? How can you help your son or daughter understand the words and ideas and to build on them to advance thought and comprehension? What books can you steer your child toward as interest in reading expands? How can you talk about key books at home in order to heighten both your child's competence as a reader and his or her love for the printed page?

If you're a parent who wants to see her child succeed in today's classroom, *Any Child Can Read Better* will help you answer those questions. It will help you continue to influence your child's learning without increasing stress or anxiety in the home. I do not believe in high-pressured teaching. I do not believe in transforming parents into professors. With comfortable conversation and enjoyable exercises that tap children's native abilities, you can help your child practice the critical thinking and reading skills that guarantee success in the classroom and beyond.

Let's have fun. And what better place to begin than with words, the currency of our language and reading kingdom?

2

Mining Word Meanings

■──────■

Quick now, what's your knee-jerk advice when your child is reading and he asks you the definition of a tough word he can't figure out?

"Look it up in a dictionary," right?

It's bad advice. It's particularly bad advice for developing readers struggling through a thorny selection and trying to make sense of it.

Don't get me wrong—I have nothing against dictionaries. I love dictionaries. They are indispensable language-learning, language-checking tools. Writers, always aiming for precision amid perplexing word choices, could not survive long without dictionaries. For readers, too, dictionaries are important, but not in the ways we typically advise children to use them.

Certainly, researchers and very sophisticated readers do use dictionaries as side-by-side companions to books. Watch a thoughtful poetry student reading something by Milton or Housman or Browning and you'll see regular expeditions into a dictionary to check nuances and alternative meanings. For the most part, though, established readers will use a dictionary to check an unfamiliar

11

word *after* they read a selection and can't figure out the word's meaning.

Unfortunately, most classroom dictionary work focuses on having kids look up lists of words. Most often, those words are not connected to any reading exercise; and without a context for word exploration, the activity is an utter waste of time. When the words do relate to content, children are asked to look up the lists of words before reading. Sure, knowing definitions of potentially difficult words can remove some obstacles to comprehension, and I support telling youngsters in advance what a few really difficult or technical *key* words mean—words whose definitions cannot easily be derived from the context (more on this later) but whose meanings are essential for understanding. Still, you don't want your child slaving over a list of tough words, looking them up and writing definitions, as a necessary precursor to a reading activity. He'll be bored and exhausted by the time he starts the first sentence!

In fact, most of us don't often take the advice we give freely to our children. When was the last time that you looked up words prior to reading? When was the last time you stopped reading a novel or an article—just closed the book or the newspaper—to look up a word that puzzled you? I'm willing to bet that you can't remember. In fact, odds are you don't use a dictionary much to check uncommon words that pop up as you read.

And for good reason. You don't want to stop reading because you risk losing your own train of thought as well as the writer's. If you're engrossed in a good book, you don't want to interrupt your pleasure to hunt meanings in a dictionary. And often a hunt it really is—checking guide words, figuring out alphabetical placements, reading numbered definitions, testing a few out in the sentence containing the unfamiliar word. Although most of us can survive occasional sidetracking steps like these with just minor annoyance and can reenter our reading relatively unblemished, youngsters are enormously taxed by the process. It's so difficult for them to return to their text after they've taken a dictionary detour.

Stop telling your child to use a dictionary if he asks about an unfamiliar word. Instead, show him how to use one of the strategies you really do use for determining meanings when you meet an unfamiliar word.

In this chapter, I want to uncover some of those strategies. By now, you are using them almost instinctively and probably have not brought them to conscious awareness. I also want to explore realistic ways to help your sons and daughters learn and use new vocabulary to sharpen their reading skills.

Learning Words from the Beginning

Let's first go back to your child's preprint word learning for a moment. You should know that your youngster starts to accumulate vocabulary from the earliest moments of wakefulness in the crib. You determine your baby's meaning by interpreting and explaining the sounds she makes. As your infant grows in years, you probably engage in what speech experts call *self-talk*, where you describe what you're doing as you're doing it; and *parallel-talk*, where you describe action by action what your child is doing. You enhance your child's word knowledge by bringing linguistic meaning to the disparate sensory experiences surrounding him.

Regular sustained conversation with children even as young as six weeks starts the all-important process of language socialization—but it also begins the lifelong lesson of learning words and what they mean. Thus, talking with your child regularly and listening to her share thoughts, ideas, and impressions lay the cornerstone for the vocabulary storehouse that a healthy learner builds and develops straight into adulthood.

Another influence on word knowledge is the reading you do with your child as she grows. Another is your child's independent reading of books at home and in the library. Here, too, we're talking about the earliest stages of contact with print as well as the later, more sustained contact with books.

Even your supermarket shopping excursions with your baby sitting in the grocery cart is a word-building exercise as you drift up and down the aisles reading signs of sale items and labels from cans and boxes on the shelves. "Yes, those are the cookies that are on sale. See the sign?"—here you're pointing to the letters that make the word *cookies*. "And this word, *SALE*. Let's pick out the Hydroxes from all the others on the shelf." Your baby is reading when she pulls that box of cookies into her lap. She may be using only the visual clues—familiar colors or packaging, even graphic print layouts—without really reading the letters to make out the words *Hydrox* or *Oreos*. But she is reading nonetheless, and your encouragement in these informal settings go further than any drill exercises designed to teach words and their meanings.

The sooner that books enter your child's life, the sooner you direct her down the road to advanced word knowledge.

The all-picture, no-word cloth books in the nursery contribute to vocabulary growth as you and your baby construct stories from the illustrations, pointing to a truck or a rose or a blue jay, for example, and naming it. When you pore over a newspaper or magazine with your son or daughter in your lap and together identify what you see in the photographs and drawings, you are establishing the vital connection between print and meaning.

Families that emphasize reading's joy and value

from infancy onward are families that send youngsters to school ready to learn from their teachers the all-important decoding strategies—that is, the basic technical skills for making meaning from print. As I've stated before, these include being able to recognize the letters as well as knowing the sounds made by letters individually and in groups, and the words produced when sounds are strung together. The skills also include knowing the object or idea that the sound clusters refer to. Regarding this last point, of course, the more experiences you can expose your child to, the easier it will be for her to connect a word with its referent. A child who had never seen a blimp might be able to read the word with ease, but she might not have the slightest notion of what the object being signified by the letters was.

My point in reviewing some of these principles of language growth is once again to assure you that most children—yours included, certainly—have the basic equipment to learn reading mechanics. It's the rare child who does not enter school with sufficient command of words for describing and explaining her immediate world and her inner imaginings. And I'll bet that your child's vocabulary is strong enough to help her read the primers and other available reading materials, no matter what instructional method her classroom teacher uses. Those of you teaching your children at home will find the same issues true with your youngsters. Despite its apparent complexity as an intellectual and conceptual task, learning to read in its early manifestations is not an overwhelming problem for most young children.

Getting Unhooked on Phonics

No doubt you've seen and heard the incredible assertions for *Hooked on Phonics*, a home reading program that claims to teach your child to read in record time through a series of audiotapes and print short stories. For $229.95, promotional materials state, your child learns the ABC's and moves to phonics to learn reading—all this to musical accompaniment that will hold your youngster's attention. He practices by reading 100 brief fictional works and answering multiple choice questions about the readings. Sales for *Hooked on Phonics* have reached extraordinary heights; and, if your community library is like mine, it has weeks of backlogged reserve orders on the program for home borrowing.

Wait. Before you write a check for the miracle snake oil, let's have a look at the complaints about *Hooked on Phonics*. In the first place, the company's claims are extravagant and apparently unjustified, at least as far as the law is concerned. The ads have said that the program can

> quickly and easily teach those with reading problems or disabilities to read, regardless of the problem, and will enable those users to improve significantly their reading levels and classroom grades; that the program can teach those with dyslexia, attention deficit disorder, and other learning disabilities to read; that the program can teach reading in a home setting without a teacher or tutor; that the program effectively teaches reading comprehension skills; and that the program has helped nearly one million students to learn at home.

Would you buy such unrestrained allegations? Well, the Federal Trade Commission (FTC) didn't. In December 1994, the FTC reached a settlement with Gateway Educational Products Ltd., distributor of the materials—no more misleading claims about educational profit for kids unless Gateway "can substantiate the claims with competent and reliable evidence." As I write this, no convincing evidence has yet emerged.

A number of teacher organization representatives and other experts testified at FTC hearings against *Hooked on Phonics*, arguing—and I believe in this point deeply—that although learning letter combinations and the sounds they make may be an important reading skill, they are simply insufficient to serve as the main building blocks for teaching youngsters the complex task of reading. As I've indicated before, why waste your time (and money) teaching your child the rudimentary skills that she'll probably pick up anyway without your help? The last thing a parent should do is concentrate on letter sounds and phonics at home! You have much more important work to accomplish if you truly wish to help your child succeed as a reader. Read to and with your child. Talk about books and pictures. Allow freewheeling conversations about print to fill your home discussions. But don't become one of Elkind's "miseducators"!

Many enlightened reading teachers abhor the phonics-first approach—not because they see the skill as inconsequential but because they see it as only a tiny sapling in the reading arbor. Phonics is not mysterious (this letter says this, these letters say that), is relatively simple to teach and test, and is easily understood by ordinary people in the way many other reading maneuvers are not. Therefore, the leafy and prodigious phonics tree easily can overshadow other key strategies in the reading forest, strategies much more complex in leading a child to the essential skill, comprehension. Kids don't have to know how to sound out every word in a sentence and paragraph to know what the word means. And just because a child *can* say correctly every word in a sentence or paragraph is no assurance that he understands what he has read.

The latest in a long line of theories about children and how they best learn to read is the "whole language" approach, now extremely popular in the schools and largely responsible for the general antagonism to what critics see as an atomistic, phonics-based, basal-reader approach to reading instruction. (In the 1950s Rudolph Flesch's *Why Johnny Can't Read* blasted the then-current reading philosophy—the "meaning-first" approach, which also warred with phonics—and led to a resurgence in phonics instruction. Ah, well.) Trying to avoid what they see as murdering kids' interest in reading and to use "literature"—interesting stories and poems instead of canned stuff prepared for primers—as well as regular practice in writing and lots of discussion and read-alongs, whole language teachers believe that a print-rich atmosphere builds necessary skills only when a child explores whole texts. Resolute whole language teachers eschew instruction in phonics and word recognition; these skills are learned anyway, the teachers believe, as actual reading ensues. By helping children build meaning from an entire text, whole language teachers discourage accuracy of word-by-word sounding-out exercises and allow children to proceed at their own speed. Skill and drill are out; natural learning is in.

Don't think whole language is without its critics, however. In a recent article in *The Atlantic Monthly*, "The Great Debate Revisited," Art Levine traces the war between the "meaning-first" and the "phonics-first" advocates and highlights the position that despite the wide acceptance of whole language tenets among teachers and schools of education, "research and experience not only fail to demonstrate its superiority but also make a persuasive case for the importance of phonics." Many whole language adherents reject the conventional methods of judging success in reading as misleading and irrelevant; meaning-first supporters argue that reading tests and controlled studies are narrow, unhelpful in telling what children actually do when they read, and a reflection of an outdated paradigm of educational beliefs. Some people argue further that phonics is completely irrelevant and that the need for methodical instruction in phonics is a myth.

As in many educational debates, the arguments become reductive because of the passions of the arguers. Good sense rarely prevails when, having chosen sides, hostile camps meet on the educational battlefield. But some educators do see the point. Kids are so varied in their demands as readers and so impossible to fit into theories that a mix of approaches, based on each child's needs, always seems to make the most sense.

Some academics criticize this belief, particularly Professor Kenneth Goodman, a renowned reading educator and proponent of whole language at the University of Arizona, whom you'll hear about later in our discussion of context and "miscues" in reading. Goodman believes that an eclectic use-what-works approach is stupid: "We're not going to solve anything by trying a little of this and a little of that." But consistency of theory and pedagogy is less important to me than meeting the particular learning demands each child brings to the reading environment.

I believe passionately that a phonics-first approach is wrong and is torture for most children aching to read. Surround your child with print and, more than any other strategy, you'll help her move quickly down the road to reading success. Stay away from *Hooked on Phonics* because through meaningless alphabet drill and word sounds you risk turning your youngster away from the joys of reading forever. However, as many school districts and programs now advocate, a skillful blend of whole language exercises and activities and discerning phonics instruction shows much promise.

Unless you're a home-learning parent, continue to avoid formal reading instruction at home. Keep the flame of reading alive for your preschoolers and early-grade youngsters by reading together and talking about print wherever you can.

Home-learning folks, use your common sense. Establish a rewarding home program that draws first on actual reading experiences from lively and challenging books. Expect your child to pick up phonics and other skills as she reads and writes, trusting her skills at natural learning. Avoid targeting one word at a time for sound and meaning focus; help your child use surrounding words and sentences for educated guesses. It's all right for a child NOT to know what every individual word means as long as he can grasp the idea from context. (We'll look at context in more detail later in this chapter.) But since phonics is part of reading—"just one part of the reading process," cautions Karen Smith, Executive Director of the National Council of Teachers of English (NCTE)—be prepared, when necessary, to help with word recognition through alphabet sounds.

Context Leads the Way

When reading materials grow more difficult and when content-based reading matter—a social studies book, the science section of the weekly reader, a mystery novel from the library—enters your child's life, print makes more challenging linguistic demands. It's obvious that your child needs to know more and more words if she's going to respond successfully to the various adventures that a growing young reader faces each time she turns to print.

We use the term *context* to indicate the power of surrounding words and sentences to inform the meaning of a single word or set of words. In this section we'll examine the range of contextual clues readers rely on to derive meaning. Context clues are the most frequently used tools to help determine an unknown word's definition.

But before you start focusing on the meanings of single words your child may not know on a page, remember that it's possible to gather the meaning of a whole print entity without knowing exactly what each piece means precisely. In reading, the whole is always greater than the sum of the parts.

Important research by Professors Kenneth and Yetta Goodman of Arizona State suggests that even if your child is somewhat off the mark in guessing an unknown word's definition, the contextual imperative, if he uses it, can help him understand the sentence anyway. A wrong definition for a word will not eclipse meaning totally. All other things being equal—the difficulty level of materials, your child's interest in the content, the physical setting in which the reading takes place—even if your child takes a miscue from the print environment, he still can construct meaning from what he's read in order to make sense. Thus, knowing the exact definition of every word in every paragraph is not essential.

The trick is to learn how to use available information to determine meaning even when some of the words stump you. What's most compelling about applications of the Goodmans' work is that primary school kids can learn not to labor over every difficult word they see. If you've ever watched a below-grade-level reader struggling to decipher each word in a sentence as she reads, you'll know how unproductive that process can be. Instead, we want to encourage young readers to use the total print environment—surrounding words, sentences, and paragraphs; pictures, drawings, and illustrations; captions, charts, and typography—whatever features on a page that are available as aids to meaning. More on this later.

As a well-practiced reader, you know by now that words have multiple meanings. You can't count on a dictionary to tell you a definition easily each time you have doubts, because one word can mean many different things, depending on how the writer uses it in a sentence.

Here, I want to consider the fairly obvious notion that if one word has a variety of meanings, you can't tell which meaning is appropriate unless you ground the word in its surrounding environment.

As an example, consider the word *ground*, the verb in the final clause of the last sentence above. What would you say if your child asked you what it meant? If you're like most parents, without much thought you'd probably respond with the most familiar definition—"Ground? Oh, that's the earth, you know, the solid surface on top." But I'll bet that the definition would get you into trouble—especially if it appeared in a sentence like the one we're talking about.

Did you know that *ground* has almost thirty—that's right, thirty—different meanings enumerated in a dictionary? Without knowing which definition the writer might have intended, you shouldn't even try to guess at an answer to your child's question. You've got to know what the context is. Let me show you some of the various uses for the word *ground*.

- The submarine moved slowly along the ground.
- The farmer leveled the ground and then tilled it for planting potatoes.
- Speak softly when you approach the Indian burial grounds.
- His strange behavior gave us grounds for suspecting that he stole Manny's wallet.
- I poured the coffee grounds down the sink.
- Father grounded the wire before plugging in the old hair drier.
- He grounded his opinion in many years of research by scientists all over the world.

- His eyesight was weak, and as a result the company grounded the pilot permanently.
- The batter grounded out to the shortstop.
- During our trip out west we covered lots of ground.

Unless you had a clue about the intended meaning, guessing at the word *ground* in the abstract makes no sense. You need to consider the context. I've simplified this presentation somewhat by building pretty clear clues into the ten sentences containing the word *ground*, but the print environment does not always create such conditions. Often you have to consider information in surrounding sentences, paragraphs, sometimes even pages in order to know the writer's intended meaning.

In talking over the concept of multiple meanings, consider the many words your child knows that have more than one definition. Start with these; then ask your son or daughter to expand the list by adding other familiar words. (You might want to check these out in a dictionary just so you yourself know the range of options.)

1. bear
2. floor
3. light
4. book
5. free

6. black
7. leaf
8. match
9. pin
10. ring

I believe that of all the tips you can give your child about determining the meaning of an unfamiliar word, the most important is: figure out what the word means from the sentence it's in and the other sentences around it.

Of course, none of the work I mentioned before on "miscue analysis," as the researchers call it, challenges the importance and value of teaching children how to make educated guesses at meaning for new words. Once you acknowledge the power of context over meaning, you can consider some strategies that most good readers use to figure out what unfamiliar words mean from the surrounding print environment. I think that you'll find these columns useful as you investigate word meanings

How to Use Sentence Hints for Word Meanings

Hint	Example	Explanation
Some sentences set off the definition for a difficult word by means of punctuation.	The *principal*—money he put in his savings account to earn interest—was safe even though the bank was closed by the police.	The pair of dashes sets off the definition of *principal*, here used to mean "sum of money." Other punctuation that may set off meanings includes commas, parentheses ( ), and brackets [ ].
Sometimes helping words, along with punctuation, provide important clues.	Carlos looked *dazed*, that is, stunned, as if someone had shocked him with bad news or with a heavy blow to the head.	Helping words: *that is, meaning, such as, or, is called.*
Some sentences tell the opposite of what a new word means. From its opposite, you can figure out the meaning of the word.	During office hours he looked very *tense* and anxious, but on weekends he was quite relaxed.	The word *but* helps you understand that *relaxed* is the opposite of *tense*. If you know that *relaxed* means "at ease," you can figure out that *tense* means "tight" or "at attention."

Hint	Example	Explanation
Sometimes you can use your own experiences to figure out the definition of a word.	Martha's husband and mother died within a month of each other, and she cried often at her terrible *sorrows*.	You know that family tragedy would fill a person with great sadness, the meaning of *sorrows*.
Sentences before or after a sentence containing a difficult word sometimes explain the meaning of the word.	The lovely wooden tray had grown *brittle*. It was dry and hard and cracked easily.	Anything dry, hard, and easily cracked may be called *brittle*.
Some sentences are written just to give the definitions of difficult words—words that readers will need to know in order to understand what they are reading.	She wanted baked clams for her *appetizer*. An appetizer is the first course of a meal.	The second sentence defines the word *appetizer*.
Because some sentences give examples for a new word, you can build a definition.	*Legumes*, such as string beans, lima beans, and green peas, are important in your diet.	The sentence doesn't say that *legume* is a name for a group of vegetables with pods, but you can figure out some of that meaning from the examples.
Some sentences use a word that you do know to help explain a word that you do not know.	The mayor wanted *privacy* because he knew that being alone would help him solve his problems.	You can tell from the sentence clues that *privacy* means "being alone."

with your child. First, check yourself to see how to use the different hints often embedded in sentences as aids to meaning. Next, go over these illustrations to point out some of the valuable techniques your sons and daughters can be using as they read.

You're well armed now to answer questions about what words mean when your child presents you with an unknown creature in a sentence! Draw on these varied context clues to see if you can engage your youngster in educated guesswork.

For starters, let's try out some strategies for using context clues, by examining a selection from *Mystery Cat and the Monkey Business* and the word in italics, *reappeared:*

> (1) Kelly Ann and Sara watched from the Darbys' as the silver ladder slid up into the maple tree. (2) A fireman climbed up the ladder and disappeared from sight among the leaves. (3) There was a pitiful cry from M.C. (4) "The fireman has pulled him off the branch," Kelly Ann explained to Sara. (5) Then the fireman *reappeared*, backing down the ladder.

Do you see how the whole paragraph helps your child guess at the meaning of the word *reappeared*— and gives you the tools for helping her make that guess correctly? What does the context say about *reappeared*?

After saying the word in his mind, your child might connect it with an experience that will help him supply the meaning quickly. Perhaps you had used the word to describe the family pet goldfish weaving through the fish tank's ceramic castle; perhaps a magician at the library used the word in one of his vanishing tricks; perhaps a newscaster said that the governor *reappeared* after a meeting behind closed doors and your child watched as he showed up again on your television screen. In any case, the sound of the word and its echoes in personal experience are key elements in producing meaning as a child reads words.

Using experience further for the *Monkey Business* sentences, we know that when a person ascends a ladder into a tree we may not be able to see him for all the foliage. Sure enough, sentences one and two reflect that experience. A child who didn't know what disappeared meant could probably guess at the meaning from the phrases at the end of sentence 2, "from sight among the leaves." Your child would know by the end of sentence 2 that if she were part of this scene, she couldn't see the fire fighter any longer. Your conversation could draw out those conclusions.

Sentences 3 and 4 provide more narrative detail; then, in sentence 5 we read about the fireman again, this time "backing down the ladder." You could guide a child who didn't know what *reappeared* meant to use surrounding clues in the paragraph. These include the actions in sentences 1 and 2, the last four words in sentence 5, her own experience, and the fact that *disappeared* and *reappeared* are opposites.

See if your child can use context clues again in the paragraph, this time to guess at the letters "M.C." What do the letters refer to? Prompt your youngster with questions.

Be alert for a connection with the popular abbreviation for Master of Ceremonies, "emcee." Here your child's knowledge would not help her if she knew the term "emcee" and tried to apply it in this sentence. Praise her effort, of course; then start prompting her with questions.

What could possibly be in a tree, giving off a pitiful cry? The writer uses the word *him*, so that your child should be able to guess that the object is a male animal of some kind. Might it be a human baby, who certainly could give off a sorrowful wail? Not likely—experience convinces us that babies usually don't get into a tree's high branches. Could it be an older boy child? Possible, but not probable. A young boy who could make his ways high up into a maple probably wouldn't need rescuing in such a fashion. If your child recalled the name of the book from which the excerpt came, she might have a logical guess at the identity of M.C., a cat. Cats do get stuck in trees, emit powerful cries, and submit to rescuing by fire fighters.

Ready for another example? Let's go to a four paragraph sequence in an article from *The New York Times*. We're going to focus on the words *plummeted* and *eradicated* here. These are not words found typically in an eight- to eleven-year-old's vocabulary, but you can guide your son or daughter to use context clues and come up with appropriate meanings.

1. The elephant population in Africa has been halved in the last ten years.

2. The African Wildlife Foundation, a conservation group based in Kenya and in Washington, estimates the numbers have *plummeted* from 1.3 million to 750,000, with the largest population in Zaire.

3. At the present rate of decline, the elephant will disappear from the continent within 10 years, according to an international conference held in Nairobi last November and attended by African and Western governments, including the United States.

4. Kenya has upward of 20,000 elephants, with Tsavo holding the largest concentration. (5) The elephant has been all but *eradicated* in neighboring

Uganda, according to the East African Wildlife Society.

6. But for the Kenyans, the slaughter of the elephants is particularly alarming.

You can help your child determine the meaning of *plummeted* by exploring the example in sentence 2, the sentence in which the word appears. When numbers of elephants go from over a million to 750,000 they drop sharply, an excellent definition for *plummet*. Sentence 1 sets the framework for the total falloff: of the elephants alive ten years ago only half remain alive today. If your child has trouble attaching value to numbers in the millions and hundred thousands, don't fret. Clues lie elsewhere. The next sentence, 3, similarly talks about reduced numbers. Here's a perfect example of how adjoining sentences contribute to shaping the context for an unfamiliar word.

Now, your child might not offer "fell steeply" or "plunged" straight off as the definition for *plummeted*, but with your help in pointing out how to use context clues, he very well could make sense from the unfamiliar word and its paragraph environment.

My nine-year-old son Saul produced "changed" as a definition for *plummeted* when we talked about this selection. As I probed for a more exact meaning, encouraging his use of context clues, he at first suggested that the word meant "changed for a higher number." The 1.3 beside the 750,000 threw him off track; he thought that the first number was smaller than the second. When you see the word million and the absence of the word thousand—only the place-holding zeroes provide the number clue here—you can understand his difficulty. With all those zeros the 750,000 does look much bigger than the 1.3. Saul had some trouble with those big numbers, not realizing until he started explaining aloud that 1.3 *mil-*

lion (his saying the word aloud made all the difference!) was in fact larger than 750,000. *Plummeted*, he then explained, meant "changed by dropping lower."

You can use similar strategies in exploring *eradicated*, a more difficult word to unpuzzle than *plummeted*. Our old friend *disappear* in sentence 3 continues to focus our attention on the vanishing elephants. Sentence 4 provides a count for one of the African regions considered here. But *eradicated* does not release its meaning easily in sentence 5. After the numbers provided in 4, you could say "saved" as a synonym for *eradicated*. Kenya has twenty thousand elephants, a large number remaining in one particular area of that country. With no knowledge of the word's denotation and without an effort to look further for clues, a child could propose that Uganda had saved many elephants.

What prevents such a reading? Again, the context. First, the peculiar syntax "all but" implies a negative, perhaps desperate, setting for the concept it introduces here. But this is a subtle issue, and don't be surprised if your child struggles with it. Saul and I had to spend some time with the idea here. We examined other clues, noting the words "rate of decline" and "disappear." The idea of slaughter in sentence 6 also suggested features of the meaning. These synonyms and experiential clues ultimately helped Saul realize that *eradicated* meant "got rid of."

But the syntax of sentence 5 did throw him a curve. At first he thought from "all but" that *eradicated* meant that you had to have a little left and that those were then being wiped out. It's a perfectly legitimate conclusion to draw here, but the word's meaning itself does not necessarily require that provision. With some easy conversation, we soon worked out the true definition. Even if we hadn't, Saul would have gathered all he needed to determine the meaning of the passage, even without an exact definition for the word in question.

Word Part Clues for Meaning

When thoughtful readers discover an unfamiliar word, they can draw on a number of strategies—some individual, some overlapping—to produce meaning. We've already looked at the power of context in producing comprehension in the mind of a reader when a new word appears. You've also seen how not knowing a word's meaning does not necessarily impede understanding of a selection: You can make your way to the end of a thought, grasping it fully without knowing either the pronunciation or the definition of a strange word—even misreading the word completely or substituting another word in its place.

Yet among the complex talents we bring to words in our effort to extract their meaning is a set of techniques that help us deal with individual words as we frame them in contextual settings. Look again at our selection from Saunders' *Mystery Cat and the Monkey Business* and the word *reappeared*.

> Kelly Ann and Sara watched from the Darbys' as the silver ladder slid up into the maple tree. A fireman climbed up the ladder and disappeared from sight among the leaves. There was a pitiful cry from M.C. "The fireman has pulled him off the branch," Kelly Ann explained to Sara. Then the fireman *reappeared*, backing down the ladder.

What will your child do to figure out the word *reappeared* if it's unfamiliar, if the context provides insufficient clues to meaning for him, and if he wants to know what that word *reappears* means exactly?

If he has the skills to determine the sounds made by the letter combinations, he'll probably try to say the word in his mind, even aloud perhaps. Understand, this task is fraught with complexity. For instance, the first two letters here *(re)* must not be combined with the next two *(ap)* following it. We say the first four letters *(reap)* to rhyme with *knee cap.* Under ordinary circumstances—as if anything in reading is ordinary!—the *e* and *a* beside each other signal a diphthong, meaning that the first vowel in a two-vowel combination gets a long sound and the second vowel is silent. If the letter combination were simply *reap* with no letters after it, you'd have to pronounce it to rhyme with *sleep.* (You can see the diphthong rule at work if you glance at the next side-by vowels—also *ea*—further on in the word *reappeared*. The *ea* in *pear* rhymes with *fear*: long sound (e) for the *e,* silence for the *a.*)

And now to complicate this already complex issue even further. The ordinary diphthong rule that guides so much of our pronunciation, here appropriately used in the final syllable of reap*pear* (again—to rhyme with *fear*) is immediately challenged by the stand-alone word *pear,* which rhymes with *hair.* Now as for *hair* . . . well, enough.

Do you see the point of this digression? I'm trying to illustrate more than just the tough, often unpredictable, rule-defying nature of English and its challenges to any language learner. I'm trying to point out how smart your youngster is if, in fact, she can read the word *reappeared*—even if she doesn't know what it means. Just consider all the difficult operations her brain performs in a flash to translate the letter clusters into recognizable sounds and to put all of them together as a legitimate word in our language. There's a young genius in your family—and don't forget it!

Many experienced readers as part of their general attack on unfamiliar words through context will use word-part clues to help determine word meanings.

In some cases readers draw on known meanings for familiar letter combinations. These combinations are not words themselves, but are discrete entities with identifiable definitions. A *prefix* is a cluster of letters with special meaning at the beginning of a word. A *suffix* is a cluster of letters with special meaning at the end of a word. A *root*, generally derived from Latin or Greek, is the base of a word, a group of letters endowed with meaning and influenced by other elements (like prefixes and suffixes) added to it. With prefixes, suffixes, and roots we rely on our ability to recognize stable meanings for certain letter combinations, which may occasionally change their form.

In our example, *reappeared*, the prefix *re,* meaning *again*, adds on to the base word *appear*, meaning *to come into view*. *Appear* itself comes from the Latin *apparere*, made from the root *parere*, meaning *to show,* and the prefix *ad*, meaning *to*. (Languages absorbed into each other keep adding and changing parts.) The *-ed* ending on *reappeared*, strictly speaking, is not a suffix— it has no identifiable definition—but is instead an *affix*, a letter combination that signals something about a word. The affix *-ed* on a verb signals the past tense; *-s* at the end of a verb signals the third person singular; *-s* at the end of a noun signals plural. ("The girl reappears," for example, as opposed to "The girls reappear.")

Before we take this discussion of word parts as clues to meaning any further, you should know that not all educators believe that prefixes, roots, and suffixes are major players in the vocabulary building game for children. Unfortunately, many of us use the word-part skill only a posteriori. That is, only *after* we learn what an unfamiliar word means do we say, "I see it now! The *re* at the beginning means *again*. Of course, *reappear* has to mean *to become visible again."*

As we read, it's not easy to make the connection between word parts—like prefixes and suffixes that are not themselves legitimate words—and the words to which these parts are attached. In addition, knowing prefixes, roots, and suffixes does not assure that you can spot them appropriately in a word. The first two letters in *reap* (rhyming with *sleep*), for example, have nothing to do with the prefix *re*, and you'd be off target if you tried to determine what the word meant from the two letters. Finally, methods of learning prefixes and suffixes generally have taken the form of requiring kids to memorize long alphabetical lists—a torture for most youngsters.

Nevertheless, learning to look at meaningful units within unfamiliar words is yet another tool for figuring out what words mean. When you check the charts below, you'll see that I've presented word-part clusters in related groups so that you can help your child use them efficiently. In print material that you examine when reading with your youngster, call attention to words that have recognizable prefixes, suffixes, or roots. Both the negative prefixes (*a, non, ex, anti*, and so on) and the time prefixes (*re, ex, pre*, and so on) are so common and accessible that you will find it easy to pay some attention to them.

Prefixes That Say No
a-: not (asocial)
an-: not (anarchy)
un-: not (unattractive)
im-: not (impossible)
in-: not (insecure)
non-: not (nonviolent)
mis-: wrongly (mistreated)
ir-: without, not (irresponsible)
il-: not (illiberal)
mal-: bad or wrongful (maladjustment)
anti-: against (antimissile)
contra-: against (contradict)

Prefixes That Show Placement
ab-: from or away from (abstain)
circum-: around (circumference)
com-: with, together (commission)
trans-: across (transport)

dis-: away (displace)
sub-: under (submarine)
inter-: among or between (interlocking)
intra-: within, inwardly (intramurals, introvert)
in-: in or on (invest)
de-: down from (deflect)

Prefixes That Tell Time and Amount
ante-: before (antedate)
pre-: before (predict)
post-: after (postdate)
ex-: former or out of (exconvict)
re-: again, back (repeat)
hyper-: too much (hypertension)
super-: above or highest (superman)
poly-: many (polyangular)
pro-: in favor (proponent)
semi-: half (semicircle)
extra-: beyond, outside (extracurricular)

Prefixes That Mean One
uni-: single, one (uniform)
homo-: same (homogenize)
self-: one's own person (self-propelled)
mono-: one (monologue)
auto-: self, same (autograph)

Suffixes to Signal Meanings

RELATING TO OR PERTAINING TO   SOMEONE WHO
-al (formal)   -er (speaker)
-ic (tonic)   -or (debtor)
-ance (performance)   -ist (florist)
-ence (permanence)

Able to Be
-ible (terrible)
-able (capable)
-ful (sorrowful)

Filled with
-ous (joyous)
-y (juicy)

State or Quality of
-ship (statesmanship)
-ment (management)
-ion (tension)
-ness (happiness)
-ism (terrorism)
-hood (manhood)
-tude (aptitude)

Without
-less (mindless)

Useful Roots for Building Word Knowledge

Roots of the Senses		Example
spect, spic	means "look"	spectator
loqu, locut	means "speak"	eloquent
tang, tact	means "touch"	tangent
vid, vis	means "see"	vision
voc, vok	means "call"	vocal

Roots of Action		
vers, vert	means "turn"	divert
pos	means "place"	position
port	means "carry"	porter
mor, mort	means "die"	moratorium
mit, mis	means "send" or "put"	admit

Let's go back to our selection from *Mystery Cat* to see how to help a child struggling with the word *reappear* or some other word with a recognizable prefix, suffix, or root. With *reappear*, spend some time examining the prefix *re*. If it means *again*, you might say, and *appear* means *to become seen*, what does *reappear* mean? Talk with your child about any other "re" words she might know, like *retell, reread, reorder,* and *recharge.* If your youngster says *relax, regret,* or *repair,* praise the effort, but as you can see, knowing the prefix in those cases doesn't help a jot in guessing at the meaning. Make lists of *re* words, *a* words, *ex* words, for example. Examine a page in a newspaper or magazine and see how many prefix, suffix, or root words you can find together.

In the paragraph from which we've extracted *reappear* (see page 31), do you see any other words in which knowledge of word parts can help? You spotted *pitiful,* didn't you? Help your youngster split the word into its two parts: *pity* (the *y* becomes an *i* when parts are added to the word) and the suffix *-ful.* Share the *-ful* words you both know: *delightful, beautiful, helpful,* so many others. What does each word mean? Ask your daughter or son to use each word in an original sentence.

You should be aware of other word-part hints for readers. A word may be *compound.* In a compound word, two words together form a new word whose meaning might not be immediately apparent. By considering what the two words mean separately and what they might mean when put together, you sometimes can generate a definition. Look at these examples:

treehouse	tree + house
bookmark	book + mark
offshore	off + shore
notepad	note + pad

The words in the first column might stump a young reader confronting them in print for the first time and not recalling any immediate personal experience with them. Breaking *treehouse* into *tree* and *house,* your child could determine the meaning: a house in a tree. She could come up with that definition even though she might not know the reality of such an object first hand. Similarly, she might figure out meanings for *bookmark, offshore,* and *notepad.*

Go back again to the paragraph on *Mystery Cat*. Did you see the compound word *fireman?* The two parts, obviously, are *fire* and *man* and you could draw on what you know of each word individually to make an educated guess at what the compound word means. Despite what some readers see as the inherent sexism in such combinations, the word *man* helps create many words that your child must learn to read—even if you should be teaching him to avoid those words in his own writing in favor of words with neuter gender, like *fire fighter* instead of *fireman*, for example. Unfortunately, language takes many years to respond to social awareness, and like it or not your child will be reading about firemen, policemen, repairmen, and salesmen well into the next century.

What other *-man* words can you and your youngster generate? What more neutral substitutes can you propose? What other compound words can you identify together from your everyday vocabulary? Have some fun by making up your own compounds and defining them: *snackchild, funmom, applechomper, videovictim*, for example.

As your youngster turns to you for help in reading, be aware of compound words and call them to your child's attention. Your talk of word-part clues can solve pieces of the reading puzzle. By calling them to your child's attention, you can expand her options for getting at the heart of a word.

Making Educated Guesses

So far we've looked at some major areas of reading designed to help your child mine word meanings. This list of pointers will help your youngster approach a sentence or paragraph with unfamiliar words.

Mining Meanings: What to Do When You're Stumped

1. Skip the unfamiliar word and read on.

2. Use the surrounding words and sentences to help you figure out what the word means.

3. Think of a word you know that might make sense in place of the word you can't read.

4. If you need more help in reading the word, look at its parts.

5. If you're really stuck, ask for help.

Using these guidelines, let's practice some more with discovering meaning in selections containing unfamiliar words.

Depending on your own energy (always an important consideration when helping children!) and your son's or daughter's age and level of interest, look at these other words from the selection about the vanishing elephants (page 28) and see how many meanings your youngster can determine through word-part clues or context clues. Realize that the five short paragraphs are an excerpt from a longer newspaper story. For which words is a dictionary absolutely essential?

wildlife	international
conservation	Nairobi
estimates	Tsavo
Zaire	concentration
decline	neighboring
continent	slaughter

You'll have lots of practice focusing your youngster on context when she brings home pages of her textbooks or other readings and asks for your assistance. Nevertheless, I've selected some examples that you might like to try out. In each case, help your child use clues in the surrounding print environment to determine meanings. No dictionaries, now—unless you are completely convinced that the context provides little help.

The company behind the project, Space Biospheres Ventures (SBV), has brought in scientists from around the world to help. The people at SBV are, in a sense, model builders. They're trying to build a model of one of the most elaborate systems in the universe.

SBV scientists refer to Earth as "Biosphere I." Biosphere is another word for ecosystem, the complex network of nature that has a niche for every living thing.

Biosphere II, if successful, will be a working model of Biosphere I. The structure, about 600 feet long and 85 feet high, will cover an area larger than two football fields. Inside will be seven different Earth zones, or "biomes." At the south end of the building will be the desert biome, complete with a 50-foot-high mountain. . . . The scientists living inside, who will be called "biospherians," will have to work together as a team. Each will be a specialist in his own field. . . .

—*Boy's Life Magazine*

Words to Define

ecosystem	niche
biome	biospherian

Have you ever heard of insects called fleas? Some types of fleas live on dogs. Fleas suck blood from a dog's body. They depend on the dog for their food. This can be very harmful to the dog. Some fleas even carry diseases that can make dogs very sick.

Living things that depend on and harm other living things are called *parasites*. Fleas are parasites. Living things that parasites depend on are called *hosts*. A dog is a flea's host.

—*Third-grade science textbook*

Words to Define

flea   parasite
disease   host
harmful

Animals that eat other animals are called carnivores. Some carnivores can also be called predators. A predator is an animal that hunts other animals for food. The animal that a predator hunts is called a prey.

—Third-grade science textbook

Words to Define

carnivore   prey
predator

How could the Texas ranchers get their cattle to the railroad towns? They decided to walk their cattle there. In those days very few people lived in the Southwestern United States. There were no fences. The cattle could travel for days along trails through open spaces. It was the job of the cowhands to move the cattle along the trails. The trip was called a cattle drive. . . .

Sometimes the cattle were frightened by a loud or strange noise. Then the whole herd stampeded, or ran wildly.

—Third-grade social studies textbook

Words to Define

rancher   southwestern
trails   cowhand
stampede   cattle drive

Now, when the cry "What does this word mean?" echoes through your living room, you'll be able to say, "Let me help you figure it out on your own."

Mothers and fathers of school-age kids are not dictionaries.

Here are a few final words of summary, in poetry, from Jill Marie Warner, a reading specialist in Ithaca, New York.

Independent Strategies

When I get stuck on a word in a book,
There are lots of things to do.
I can do them all, please, by myself;
I don't need help from you.

I can look at the picture to get a hint,
Or think what the story's about.
I can "get my mouth ready" to say the first letter,
A kind of "sounding out."
I can chop the word into smaller parts,
Like *on* and *ing* and *ly*,
Or find smaller words in compound words
Like *raincoat* and *bumblebee*.
I can think of a word that makes sense in that place,
Guess or say "blank" and read on
Until the sentence has reached its end,
Then go back and try these on:
   "Does it make sense?"
   "Can we say it that way?"
   "Does it *look* right to me?"
Chances are the right word will pop out like the sun
In my *own* mind, can't you see?

If I've thought of and tried out most of these things
And I *still* do not know what to do,
Then I may turn around and ask
For some help to get me through.

                               —Jill Marie Warner

3

Words, The Magic Kingdom

■————————■

When Alice faces the extraordinary Wonderland notions of saying what you mean and meaning what you say, she confronts language's great potential and disappointment. Words should, but do not always, mean what they say; and we who use them do not always produce what we mean. If only we could point to a direct correspondence between each word and only one exact meaning! Reading would simplify in a flash. Ah, but what we might gain in exactness and dazzling clarity, surely we would lose in flexibility, nuance, suggestiveness, and contextual richness. It's good that words have such a wide range of meanings and uses; as such they enrich our capabilities as earth's highest life forms and its most competent communicators.

Knowing the possibilities of language, understanding the many qualities of words and how our language depends on them, can enhance your child's attempts to determine meaning from print.

In the long climb up the mountain to word mastery, a major feature of language that you can help your youngster understand is that words often mean more than they say.

Meaning—and Meaning

Certainly, words have *denotative* meanings. That is, words have exact definitions that you could check easily in a dictionary.

A *jeep* is a heavy-duty, four-wheeled vehicle.

A *communist* is someone who believes in a social and political system characterized by common owner-ship and labor organized for the common good.

A *frigate* is a high-speed, medium-sized war vessel of the 17th, 18th, and 19th centuries.

Yet each of these words has *connotative* meanings as well. What a word connotes is what it suggests or implies beyond its actual meaning—including the asso-ciations and feelings aroused by the word. A *jeep* is more than a motor vehicle with four-wheel drive; its connection with the military and rugged outdoor life suggests certain associations—rough riding, speed, even danger perhaps. Your son or daughter might like to ride to school in a jeep just for the fun of it, but you'd have been puzzled (to say nothing of your par-ents!) if your date for the senior prom honked the jeep horn outside your front door when he arrived to pick you up.

Similarly, the word *communist* carries connotations not at all part of its dictionary meaning. Depending on your own political and economic viewpoint, of course, you might think of a communist as a traitor, an innova-tor, a hopeless dreamer, a third-world revolutionary, or a modern-day savior.

And as you consider the word *frigate*, you soon real-ize that it says more than its essential denotative mean-ing as a warship. Its connection with swashbucklers, gun runners, and pirates, with red-blazing cannons amid the spume of waves, brings an inescapably roman-tic connotation. (By *romantic* I mean the sense of great deeds and exploits in past ages.) Frigates mean high adventure, open seas, stolen treasures, and captured loves.

Denotation and connotation underlie word choice, conscious and unconscious, especially for good writers. Look at how William Safire deals with the issue in this brief excerpt from his column in *The New York Times Magazine*:

> At the start of a new Administration, the *short list* is the place for an officeseeker to be. It is a kind of honor to be on the lips of the Great Mentioners of the media, enabling the mentionee to bask in the attention without having to fill out the onerous ethics forms.
>
> A synonymous phrase for *on the short list* is among the *final contenders*, each meaning "small group of those under consideration," though *contender* imputes to the mentionee his or her active solicitation of the job. Although *finalist* is sometimes used, that word carries too much of a beauty-contest connotation, and *competitor*, even more than *contender*, shows not the proper deference to the fiction that "the office seeks the man."

Had you ever stopped to consider the shades of meaning among those very closely related words in italics? Safire openly points out the denotative and connotative differences because he wants you to reflect on the words as words. Generally, however, writers expect readers themselves to acknowledge explicit and implicit meanings thoughtfully. Rarely will a writer point out the exact meanings she expects you to bring to her words. That's part of the reading process itself.

All writers, but especially poets, labor to choose words with appropriate denotative and connotative meanings that advance the writer's intentions. Consider how this first stanza of Emily Dickinson's famous poem compels us essentially through word choice to see reading poetry as a supremely adventurous and romantic activity. Pay special attention to the words in italics.

> There is no *Frigate* like a Book
> To Take us *Lands* away
> Nor any *Coursers* like a Page
> of *prancing* Poetry.

This poem provides a mini-study in denotation and connotation. You know about the associations for the word *frigate* from our previous discussion: excitement, daring, romance. Dickinson's point is to make us see how reading, especially reading poetry, is a quintessentially romantic act. Choosing the word *frigate* instead of *ship*, say, or *boat* or *launch* or *steamer* helps establish conditions of romance, immediately connecting us to an adventurous past. (For street-smart high-school kids, *frigate* sounds like the familiar contraction, the "F-curse" followed by the word *it*. No doubt Dickinson would not appreciate street language connotations imposed on her word choice, but if you're talking about this poem with adolescents, you've got to know that they're snickering at "Friggit!" not *frigate*.)

Dickinson's word *lands* similarly heightens the drama and distance traveled by this bold sea vessel, the frigate—which stands for a book of poetry in the comparison here. Think of how different an effect we'd have if Dickinson had said in line 2, "To take us *miles* (or *streets* or *blocks* or *yards* or even *countries*) away."

In case you didn't know, a *courser* is a swift, spirited horse used as a charger in battle. How the word packs the line with meaning! A page of poetry has the vigor, the courage, the passion of a soldier-carrying horse in a war. Consider how different an idea the poet would have produced with a word like *horse* or *mare* or *colt* or even *stallion*. And the word *prancing*, too, reinforces the lively imagery that Dickinson connects so strongly with reading a poem. Like a horse that struts about full of life, so is a page of poetry. Every word I placed in italics in the poem reinforces the desired sense of adventure.

To mine the riches of anything we read, we must be alive to denotation and connotation, and you should help your child acknowledge these qualities of words and to probe deeply when he or she considers meanings. Critical readers do not rely simply upon hasty or superficial definitions. Writers depend on connotations as much as denotations to shape intended meaning, and readers can lose powerful insights in a piece of writing if they don't stop to think, "Hmmm. Why did she use *that* word instead of another with the same or similar definition?"

Have some fun at home with your youngster of eight or nine, even younger. After you've considered what *denotation* and *connotation* mean as concepts, talk with your child about what words like those below denote— and then what they connote to her.

- grandmother
- smoking
- jet plane
- black cat
- college

Then, look at the groups of words below and talk together about their denotative and connotative meanings. Your child will sense rather quickly that all the words in each group have roughly the same denotative meanings, but that the connotations are different in each case. You might start by placing words in categories of positive and negative connotations. Soon, however, you will realize that those categories are overly simplistic. Weighing the subtleties is all the fun. Try to draw out details in the manner that I presented them in the discussion of *jeep, communist,* and *frigate* on page 44.

How Are These Grouped Words Alike? Different?

1. thin, skinny, slender, shapely

2. male, manly, masculine, *macho*

3. smart, shrewd, brilliant

4. unpleasant, mean, nasty

5. light, lamp, chandelier

6. scared, frightened, anxious, cowardly, yellow

7. tired, exhausted, weary, pooped, drained

8. grin, smile, smirk

9. firm, stubborn, unyielding

10. overweight, heavy, chubby, fat, obese

Another excellent source for addressing important language issues like multiple meanings, denotation, and connotation is the advertisements in newspapers and magazines to which you and your child have access. You know how carefully advertising agencies struggle to choose language designed to create effects and, ultimately, to get readers to buy a product. Look with your child at familiar ads. Talk about word choice. Try substituting for a word another word with similar meaning. Is the effect the same? Why or why not?

Children and Figures

Much of the riches and diversity in our language use resides in *figurative expressions.* Before I define the term, here's a short, composite conversation between Saul, our ten-year old, and his older brother Joseph, thirteen.

> SAUL: Ma, I'm trying to watch Cosby. Get him out of here. *He's bugging me.*
> JOSEPH: *If you weren't such a little rat . . .* We're not watching Cosby. We're watching *Police Academy.*
> SAUL: Oh, no we're not.
> JOSEPH: You always have to get your way. *You act like a baby.*

Sound familiar? The argument, certainly, is typical—and so is some of the language. In this little verbal battle between two headstrong kids you see three examples of figurative language, all in italics: He's bugging me, if you weren't such a little rat, you act like a baby.

What is figurative language? Simply, language that compares. Using figurative language is a need shared by all human beings: We explain, refer to, understand objects and ideas in terms of other objects and ideas. To make our language clearer, more interesting, even more poetic, we make statements that are not literally true. When we try to create images; to paint pictures with words, we often rely on figurative language.

None of the highlighted expressions that I repeated from my two boys' conversation is literal—they do not mean exactly what they say. Joseph and Saul were not talking about bugs, rats, and babies. Looking at the first instance, for example, we see that Saul was comparing Joseph to an insect—even though he was really talking about Joseph. The phrase "bugging me" means that a person is behaving annoyingly—like a fly, a mosquito, or a bee perhaps. But with trite figurative expressions like "bugging," we've lost the freshness of the visual connection. We no longer see the pictures that the words originally intended to create. I'll bet that if I hadn't explained the image that "bugging" aimed for, the words would not have produced any picture in your mind. The figures start off originally, of course, but with overuse they become vapid.

Good writers who use figures, however, aim for surprise and delight, and they expect vivid pictures to leap to mind when you read them. An original figure always puts together unlikely objects or ideas. On first thought, you wouldn't imagine that the two are actually related, but as you weigh the comparison you see the relation between the terms and the new idea delights and enlightens you for its clarity and freshness.

A sentence in the first paragraph of George Orwell's brilliant essay, "A Hanging," is so rich in figurative language that the image is unmistakable. Look at the two versions below, the first without the figures, the second just as Orwell wrote it (the italics are mine):

> A yellow light was slanting over the high walls into the jail yard.

> A *sickly* light, *like yellow tinfoil*, was slanting over the high walls into the jail yard.

The first sentence above does provide a picture, certainly. We see the jail yard, the high walls, and the slanting yellow light over them. The description is completely literal—no comparisons here. The second sentence, on the other hand, is figurative, and as a result indelibly vivid. We know that light cannot be ill (only living things can have good or bad health); yet by calling the light *sickly* and thereby comparing it to a living entity, Orwell establishes the moment's pervasive infirmity. Another original figure fills our minds with picture: The light is so densely yellow it looks like tinfoil. No tinfoil actually appears high above the prison walls, of course. And what an unusual pair of objects to relate; light and yellow tinfoil. Yet by means of this comparison between unlikely partners, Orwell paints a highly original picture. If you have seen or can imagine yellow tinfoil, you can picture the kind of bright, textured, reflective light he wants you to see slanting over the jail yard walls.

In making comparisons, writers draw on a wide range of rhetorical techniques identified and named by the early Greeks. The most familiar—the figures your children are most apt to find in their reading at school and at home—are simile, metaphor, and personification. (If you're interested in helping your child use original figurative language in his own writing, see my book *Any Child Can Write.*)

A *simile* is a comparison in which one object is said to be like another. The words *like* or *as* usually signal this kind of figurative expression. Orwell's comparison of light to yellow tinfoil is a simile: The word *like* says that the one object is similar to the other. Here are some others I've drawn from writers you may know:

O, my luve is like a red, red rose
That's newly sprung in June.
O my luve is like the melodie
That's sweetly played in tune.

—*Robert Burns*

In the sky the sun hung like an apricot.

—*J. Ernest Wright*

What happens to a dream deferred?
Does it dry up
like a raisin in the sun?

—*Langston Hughes*

The mysterious East faced me, perfumed like
a flower, silent like death, dark like a grave.
                              —*Joseph Conrad*

His face was white as pie-dough and his arms
were lank and white as peeled sticks.
                              —*Robert Smith*

A *metaphor* is an implied comparison. That is, one
object is said to *be* another object. When the objects are
quite different, the equation is striking.

Her hand, a withered brown leaf, fluttered to
her side.

Here, someone's hand is compared to a leaf, suggesting frailty and age. But the hand is not said to be *like* a
leaf—the hand *is* the leaf. If we rewrite Orwell's simile to
make it a metaphor, it would read: A sickly light, yellow
tinfoil, was slanting over the high walls into the jail
yard. In this sentence, the light and the tinfoil are one.
More metaphors:

If dreams die,
Life is a broken-winged bird that cannot fly.
                              —*Langston Hughes*

An aged man is but a paltry thing,
a tattered coat upon a stick.
                              —*William Butler Yeats*

My father's body was a globe of fear
His body was a town we never knew.
                              —*Michael Ondaatje*

In *personification*, nonhuman things are given the
qualities of living, usually human, beings. When Orwell

calls the light *sickly*, he endows it with a human trait. Here are some other examples of personification:

> Why should I let the toad work
> Squat on my life?
>
> —*Philip Larkin*

> Scarlett saw a thin tongue of flame lick up over the roof of the warehouse in whose sheltering shadow they sat.
>
> —*Margaret Mitchell*

> Hope is the thing with feathers
> That perches on the soul
>
> —*Emily Dickinson*

> When duty whispers low, *Thou must*
> The youth replies, *I can.*
>
> —*Ralph Waldo Emerson*

> Love walked alone
> The rocks cut her tender feet
> And the branches tore her fair limbs.
>
> —*Stephen Crane*

Helping Your Child with Figurative Language

Why have I taken all this time to remind you of figurative language? My first point was to show you how deepseated the instinct for comparison lies in your child's mind and in his or her language. We, children and adults, generate our own figures—some trite, some original—in regular conversation. So natural a method of thought and expression, figurative language is a mainstay in written work, too. Yet when children read figures, they are often mystified, seeing metaphor or personification, for example, as a kind of sidetracking. You can see puzzlement in their eyes; what's going on here, they wonder? A page of literal information makes a sudden foray into figure's territory and we have confusion.

Writers in newspapers, magazines, and books, writers of poetry, fiction, and nonfiction, draw regularly on figures to make a point clearer or more lively, and often both. Children need guidance in negotiating the figures that appear regularly in their reading material. You'll find these pointers useful:

Helping Your Child Understand Figurative Language

• Be sure that your child is aware that the writer is making a comparison and is not merely sidetracking. In the example above, *Her hand, a withered brown leaf, fluttered to her side*, the writer is describing a woman's hand. By introducing the leaf, he is not suddenly shifting gears to describe an autumnal scene. He merely is sharpening a picture by drawing together two unlikely companions in a fresh and satisfying manner.

• Make sure that your child, in concentrating on the figure, doesn't lose the writer's point. Reading figurative language often requires a high degree of attentiveness, especially regarding metaphor, which can be very subtle for a child. Look at this example in a poem by Robert Frost. Frost, setting a scene for us to appreciate his narrator's loneliness in the poem "Bereft," writes

Out in the porch's sagging floor
Leaves got up in a coil and hissed,
Blindly struck at my knee and missed.

• It takes a few minutes to realize the metaphor here: a pile of leaves are a sinister snake. This is an unlikely comparison, to be sure, but a highly original one and brilliant in its precision for the moment's mood. The metaphor is just a comparison: nothing further about snakes will appear here. You should be able to help your child understand the figurative language he meets when he reads, assisting him to return to the main idea of the text.

• Help your child look for words like *like, as, seems, similar to, resembles,* or *than* as signals for figurative language.

• Help your child state the comparison in his or her own language.

• Talk with your child about *why* the writer has made the comparison. If we ask ourselves, for example, why Frost compares the leaves to a snake or why Orwell calls the light sickly, the answers reveal much about the writer's tone and purpose.

How would some of these tips work practically when your child consults with you about reading? Let's examine a line from a paragraph on popcorn that appears in a second-grade workbook.

The corn used to make popcorn has a hard shell. The white part we like to eat is inside. Also inside the hard shell is a little water. The popcorn is heated up. The heat changes the water to steam. The steam pushes so hard that the shell blows up. It pops! All at once the white part pops out. It gets much bigger. It almost covers the old shell. *The old shell seems to peek out of a white cloud.*

Why, in this paragraph on how corn pops, does the writer suddenly talk about a cloud? We have a comparison here. How do you know? Can your child state the comparison—what is being compared to what? And why?

The clue "seems to" tells the alert reader that this is a simile, an explicit comparison between a kernel of popped corn and a cloud. The writer is counting on a young child's ability to envision the sun peeking out from behind a cloud. He hopes that your child will transfer that mental picture to the heated kernel, whose yellow shell, like the sun, is just barely visible within the white mass of popped corn.

Why has the writer provided a simile? Certainly to create a sharp mental picture. Anyone who hasn't seen a popped kernel can visualize it through the connection to sun and clouds. We're not expecting a sudden treatise on meteorology here. The picture drawn, the writer can continue his story.

I want to call your attention in passing to the context for the simile we just looked at. It wasn't poetry or fiction, the two most available written sources for regular use of figurative language. The value of comparisons is unassailable: Even in this "science" lesson, the importance of the figure asserts itself. I point this out for you to see that comparisons will appear regularly in the reading that your son or daughter does for school and on his or her own.

Let's examine some other examples drawn from writing for children in various grade levels. How would you deal with these if you and your youngster uncovered them in a joint reading session?

Social Studies: Grade Three

The rice raised near Konduru grows on land covered with water. It is grown in paddies. A rice paddy is a piece of land with low walls of dirt around it. *It is like a pool that gets filled up with rain water.*

Poetry: Second Grade

CLOUDS

> *If I had a spoon*
> *As tall as the sky*
> I'd *dish out* the clouds
> That go *slip-sliding by*
>
> —*Dorothy Aldis*

Science Reading: Fourth Grade

"What's happening?" asked Mr. Rose.

"Justin was pushing. He stepped on my foot," Richard answered.

"But it was an accident!" Justin insisted.

Mr. Rose said, *"Put the brakes on,* Justin. There's plenty of room in the van. Let's go."

> —*Harriet Ziefert*

Young Boy's Magazine

For two years, the scientists expect to depend on their own little world, known as Biosphere II, for survival. Their air, water, and food will be produced inside the *green-house-like* building, with no supplies coming in from the outside world.

> —*William R. Forstchen*

Science Textbook: Third Grade

Conifers either have *needle-shaped leaves or scalelike leaves.*

Weekly Reader: Grade Four

Sounds enter the inner ear and go into a tube that has tiny *hairlike* cells.

Fiction: Third Grade

And all the while that strange feeling of wanting to be good, of wanting to be perfect, *washed over him like a big splash of warm bath water.*

Children's Magazine

Rossini's music is often difficult to perform because it's usually very fast. The notes, when they're sung, have to *trip and jump off the tongue,* more rapidly than a tongue can handle them unless that tongue happens to belong to a very good singer.

We've looked at the magic kingdom of words, and weighed many of its possibilities. We're just about ready to jump on the reading track to explore words as consecutive entities on a printed page. But before racing forward, we have to take an important detour.

4

Reading Warm-Ups

I've told you that this book will help you help your child be a better reader. After our discussion of the power and glory of words, you're probably expecting me to gun the accelerator across the vast reading roadways beckoning your son or daughter.

But no, not yet. We're still not ready to talk about reading as you probably think of it, the moment that your youngster opens a science or social studies or "reading" book and starts her journey through the pages.

Why the delay? We have some troubleshooting to do. You have to be able to *prepare* for those times at home when your guidance can improve comprehension dramatically. You have to stimulate your child to read with the highest possible degree of attention and to get the most from his or her print experience with minimal frustration.

To reach those goals, before we do anything else we need to talk about warm-up activities, essential but often neglected areas of reading's domain. *Warm-up* is a familiar phrase: When you warm up, you prepare to achieve something you want to do well. Runners push against a fence or wall to stretch their muscles before an early morning jog. Pitchers toss a few practice shots before flinging the first ball to the opposing batter. On land swimmers shake their arms and wriggle their legs before taking the big plunge. Mentally, competitive athletes warm up by "imaging," a technique in which they picture all the details of the upcoming meet, project themselves into it, and try to feel all the attendant sensory responses.

Warming up is as important and as useful an activity for readers as it is for exercisers and athletes. The warm-up session is one that teachers pay little attention to at school; although they may show the whole class some of the strategies I'm about to recommend, they don't often help children apply some of these warm-up techniques on their own. And yet of all the areas in which you can contribute to your youngster's growth as a reader, this one strikes me as one of the easiest to achieve and one of the most significant in its potential for long-range success.

Previewing

Children, and many adults, too, unfortunately, often leap into a reading selection without much advance thinking about the awaiting territory. As a result, they can stumble easily before they make much progress, simply because the ideas, details, and vocabulary strike no familiar chords in their minds and imaginations. You can help your child enormously by prodding him to find out as much as he can about what he's reading—*before reading it.*

Sound strange? Perhaps—but even before a child reads a few pages, she can learn a great deal about what awaits her simply by *previewing*. Previewing means "viewing beforehand." In other words, you look ahead before you read in order to learn as much as you can *in advance* from the various clues that leap out at you.

What clues? If you examine any of your child's school books—I'm talking mostly about recently published ones here—you'll see what a careful job of layout and design the publisher performed to entice your youngster to read. Lavish pictures and illustrations, perky chapter titles and subtitles, two-color ink and other lively typographical elements, running heads, embedded definitions of new vocabulary, special sections like glossaries and appendixes in the back of the book, detailed indexes and tables of contents—a cornucopia of reading aides for the modern reader. Unfortunately, many youngsters ignore these features and, as a result, miss out on powerful guides that help navigate the occasionally rough seas of an unfamiliar reading selection.

You can help your child learn to preview both whole books and individual selections in books—chapters, sections, a few consecutive pages—by calling attention to the various features of the books he uses regularly at home and school.

Let's look at some of the helpful features of books in general.

Tips for Previewing Books

• **Look at the table of contents.** Found in the front of the book, the table of contents is a list of the *names of the chapters* and the pages on which they begin. If the book is divided into parts, that information also appears in the table of contents. If you study the names of the chapters you can get an idea of what each section of the book deals with, of how the topics relate to each other. Sometimes a table of contents is very detailed: You might find a listing of the topics treated in each chapter.

- **Look at the preface.** Coming before the table of contents, the *preface*, sometimes also called the *foreword*, is a brief essay in which an author gives reasons for writing the book. From the preface you get an idea of the kind of reader the author is writing for, of the aims the author has for the book, what she expects you to learn as a result of reading it, and of the topics in the book and the approaches to those topics. The preface is a personal message to the reader. Often the author will thank the people who helped to prepare the book. Not all books will have a preface, as you may know; and sometimes a preface will deal with matters that interest the author but may not have much to do with the specific ideas in the book. Still, it's good to look the preface over, even if you just skim it, so that you can judge for yourself whether or not to read it carefully.

- **Look briefly at the index.** At the end of a book you may find an alphabetical listing of the topics, subjects, ideas, and names mentioned within. A quick look at the index will suggest some of the points the writer deals with and how detailed the book might be.

- **Look at one of these special features that sometimes appear in books:**

  - After the last chapter a writer sometimes provides a glossary, which is a list of difficult words or terms in regard to the book's subject. The words are listed in alphabetical order; their definitions appear also. The fact that a book has a glossary may indicate that the subject is technical but that the author does try to explain the difficulties.

  - An *appendix* (plural *appendixes* or *appendices*) at the end of the book presents additional information that is interesting and useful. However, the book is complete without the appendix, and the information we find there is only extra. An appendix may include charts and graphs, special letters or documents, or facts about the lives of the people mentioned in the book. It may just give information to explain something the author felt needed more attention. A look at the appendix, if the book has one, will indicate how a writer deals with special problems.

• **Read the introduction.** Often the first chapter of the book, the introduction states the basic problem the author will deal with. It gives background information or discusses the history of the topic. It may summarize what others have said about the subject. It may even explain the method of research the author used. Sometimes—especially in a work of fiction like a novel, a collection of short stories, or a play—someone other than the author writes the introduction. Such an introduction often explains the book to the readers, pointing out key scenes or ideas worth noting.

• **Look at the bibliography.** At the back of the book an author sometimes gives a *bibliography*—a list, in alphabetical order, of some or all the books that helped the author to write this book. The bibliography (sometimes called *works cited* or *references*) can tell you the author's range of knowledge and basic interests.

• **Think about what parts the book has and doesn't have.** A book with a detailed index, a long bibliography, and a number of appendixes may be more appropriate for research than a book with only a short table of contents. Books with glossaries often provide helpful introductions to difficult subjects.

Once you've spent some time reviewing these features with your child, examine together any book from her book bag or home library shelf. Keep reminding your youngster to preview the books she needs for school. Her teacher may have introduced the general concept of previewing early in the school year, but, believe me, once is not enough. Books vary greatly in the support they offer readers, and unless you know exactly what the book you're using has to offer, you could be missing out on lots of help. When I discovered that even my college students failed to consult their end-of-text glossary in a poetry course, or when my colleague in the math department told me that she realized from poor homework grades that her students never knew their textbook provided all the answers to problems—it was then that I began previewing all books that I assign in the courses I teach.

Confident of the various parts of her books, your child also needs your guidance in learning how to preview a typical book selection or a selection in any of the magazines or special readers that teacher assigns.

Previewing a Reading Selection

- **Look at the title.** Titles often given the main idea of the selection. Does the title tell what you will be reading about? If so, you can then set a purpose for your reading.

- **Look for subtitles or headings.** Essays, newspapers articles, and other longer readings include print subtitles or headings. Appearing below titles in heavy, dark print or in italics, subtitles suggest the kind of information that you will find in a small portion of the reading.

- **Look at lists of goals or objectives.** Sometimes a selection gives a list of goals for a chapter. Here, the writer tells you what you should get out of it. Check the goals before you read so that you'll know what to read for.

- **Look at the pictures, charts, or drawings.** Often an illustration helps you figure out in advance what your reading will deal with.

- **Look at the first sentence of each paragraph.** This gives you a quick idea of what the reading involves before you begin to read carefully.

- **Look at the first paragraph.** The first paragraph

usually tells just what the reading will be about. Read it, and then try to say in your own words what you think you will be reading about.

• **Look at any questions that appear after the reading.** If you look at the questions *before* you read, you then have an idea of what's important. Questions tell you what to expect from a passage. When you read with a knowledge of the questions, you know in advance what kind of information to look for.

• **Look for key words in different print.** Sometimes heavy bold letters, italics, or even colored ink calls your attention to important words or ideas. Titles of books, for example, appear in italics. Noting these in advance can give you important information.

• **Look for a summary.** At the end of a piece, a writer sometimes summarizes the main points. Look at the summary before you read a selection. The summary can help you see more clearly what the selection deals with.

On pages 66–69 is an excerpt from a popular fourth-grade geography book. Which special features would you point out to your youngster?

Did you notice the chapter title in large upper case letters? Did you notice the photograph above the chapter title? Discussing these before your child reads the chapter can stimulate much creative thought about the contents. Note, too, these other elements, which are repeated throughout the book, and which can provide a window on meaning before your child ever reads a single paragraph within:

• The subheadings. "Ways of Living" is a second-level head; "Migration Changes Cities," "Languages of the World," and "Language Families" are third-level heads. The second-level heads, in large upper and lower case letters, appear in black ink. The third-level heads, all in upper case letters, appear in orange ink.

• The table and chart. There's a table on urban

Chapter 3

THE EARTH'S PEOPLE

MIGRATION CHANGES CITIES

If you looked down from an airplane over the United States, you would see cars, trucks, buses, and trains moving along below you. Most of the people in them are not migrating. They are just making short trips to work, stores, or schools. But some of he people *are* migrating–and if you could watch their movements over the entire United States for a long time, you would notice certain patterns. For example, the number of people who are moving south outnumber the people who are moving north. And there are more people moving west than east.

The table below shows the ten largest cities in the United States in 1950 and 1990.
1. What cities on the 1950 list were no longer in the top ten by 1990? In what parts of the country are those cities located?
2. How did the populations of older cities like New York, Baltimore, Philadelphia, and Chicago change during the time between 1950 and 1990?
3. What new cities joined the top ten between 1950 and 1990? What part of the country are they in?

1950		1990	
New York, N.Y.	7,891,957	New York, N.Y.	7,322,564
Chicago, Ill.	3,620,962	Los Angeles, Calif.	3,485,398
Philadelphia, Pa.	2,071,605	Chicago, Ill.	2,783,726
Los Angeles, Calif.	1,970,358	Houston, Tex.	1,630,672
Detroit, Mich.	1,849,568	Philadelphia, Pa.	1,585,577
Baltimore, Md.	949,708	San Diego, Calif	1,110,549
Cleveland, Ohio	914,808	Detroit, Mich.	1,027,974
St. Louis, Mo.	856,798	Dallas, Tex.	1,006,831
Washington, D.C.	802,178	Phoenix, Ariz.	983,403
Boston, Mass.	801,444	San Antonio, Tex.	935,927

CHECKPOINT

1. What is the difference between immigration and emigration?
2. What is the most common reason for moving?
3. On what continents do most people live in cities? On what continents do most people live in rural areas?
4. How has industrialization affected urbanization?

Ways of Living

If you have younger brothers or sisters, have you ever noticed how they imitate you? They may use the same expressions you do or try to dress like you. They are learning your way of living. You, your family, and other people around you are their teachers. Every group of people has its own way of life — ways of speaking, working, making decisions, and so on. All these ways of thinking and doing things are called **culture.**

LANGUAGES OF THE WORLD

Every group of people in the world has a language. Some languages are spoken by millions of people, some by only a few hundred people.

An **anthropologist** (an-thruh-POL-uh-jist) is a scientist who studies human beings and their ways of life.

No one knows how long ago people started talking. But **anthropologists** can tell that speech has been part of human life for a very long time, because people have worked together in ways

---

What Is Culture?

Culture is the way of life developed by people. It is the way people go about the business of living, from day to day and from year to year. One way to describe culture is to divide it into four parts.

1. Every group of people in the word has a *language.* What is your language? How did you learn to speak it?

2. All people use tools to make work easier. *Technology* means tools and the skills needed to make and use them.

3. *Institutions* are long-lasting ways of doing things that are important to people, such as choosing leaders, making laws, educating children, exchanging goods, or raising families.

4. All people have *beliefs* — beliefs about the everyday world, beliefs about what is beautiful, beliefs about right and wrong. People's beliefs influence the way they act and how they live.

82

THE INDO-EUROPEAN LANGUAGE FAMILY

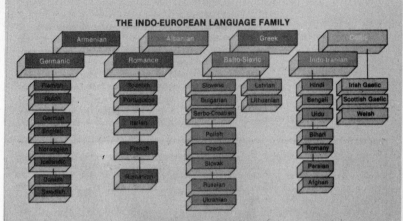

that required communication. For example, **archeologists** have found large pens where early hunters trapped the animals they needed for food. Those hunters must have had a language. Without speech, they could not have planned ahead for the hunt or cooperated to build the pen. Wherever there is evidence that prehistoric people worked and planned together, researchers know those people had a language. But no one today knows what their languages were, because they left no written records.

An **archeologist** (ar-kee-OL-uh-jist) is a scientist who studies the remains of ancient peoples.

LANGUAGE FAMILIES

In the course of human history, many, many languages have disappeared forever. Other languages have changed so much that people who spoke them centuries ago would not understand them now.

The languages people use today are thousands of years old, and each language contains clues that help to trace its history. Some of those clues show that languages are related to one another. Like people, languages come in families. For example, English is part of the Indo-European language family. Look at the diagram on this page. It may surprise you to see how many languages English is related to. What languages are in the same branch of the Indo-European family as English? What is the name of that branch? What branch includes Spanish and French?

populations (which the writers might have labeled more clearly with a title) and an excellent chart called "The Indo-European Language Family." These present complex materials in easy-to-understand visual formats. (You'll read more about visual aids in Chapter 6.) Again, a quick conversation about what a reader can learn from these elements helps prepare for thoughtful reading.

• The questions on reading materials. In this book, one set of questions appears in a regularly repeated section, "Checkpoint," which is identified with the attractive bull's-eye logo in the margin. Questions are also integrated within prose discussions. Considering questions in advance of reading helps focus attention on important points to look for.

• The difficult vocabulary in boldface out in the margin, accompanied by pronunciation clues and definitions. These highlighted words, *anthropologist* and *archeologist*, also appear in a glossary in the back of the book.

• The special display "What Is Culture?" set off in a box, one of its edges a double band of bright orange ink. This display allows the authors to consider an important concept that they do not treat directly in the text. Again, this is a repeated element in the book.

Armed with the skills of previewing, your child will learn a great deal about what he has to read before he reads it and thereby will enhance possibilities for comprehension and retention. Researchers believe that we can prepare our minds for more attentive reading simply by becoming aware of the issues that might arise in a selection. For example, examining some of the text's special vocabulary in boldface print or in headings and subheadings makes it easier to deal with the words in the selection itself, words that otherwise might throw a developing reader off track.

When you preview, you get an advanced look at the action, like a preview of coming attractions in the movies. When you see a snippet of Indiana Jones squirming in a cave of rats or smashing a villain's ugly face, you're primed to see the whole film when it reaches your neighborhood movie house later on. Previewing a book gets you ready in much the same way.

Prereading Warm-Ups

Previewing is not the only kind of before-reading activity that you can help your child practice. Experts in reading now talk of "prereading," and I want to tell you a little about it so that you can encourage your youngster along these lines as soon as possible. *Prereading* means "before reading": When you preread, you brainstorm before you read by trying to think of whatever you know about the topic. You can get a sense of the topic from the title, the subheads, the illustrations, and the other elements I've already pointed out in this chapter.

In prereading, you consider all the possibilities that the ensuing pages might address simply by thinking about the topic in advance. In this way, you improve your ability to understand it better and to get the most out of it. You draw on your personal experiences, your prior reading and knowledge, your imagination, your thoughts—anything that leaps to mind that might in some way relate to the topic. Even if we're about to read something we think we really don't know much about, we can set our brain juices flowing by trying to imagine what the writer will address or what questions we'd like to have answered about the topic or what issues we'd like to read about. By taking that extra step—thinking about the topic before reading begins—a child can enhance comprehension enormously.

Suppose your child is about to read an article on dinosaurs in the *Weekly Reader*. Before reading, set your youngster thinking about whatever she remembers of those huge animals that lumbered across the steamy regions of the earth millions of years ago. Encourage you child's advance thinking on the topic. In that way, you'll be helping her prepare her mind for any new information. When she reads, the warm-up will help her understand new ideas.

Researchers encourage readers to write down their prereading warm-up activities. The process of writing thoughts down allows a reader to make desultory impressions permanent and serves as a good touchpoint for emerging ideas. Encourage your boy or girl to jot prereading ideas down on paper. Don't be concerned with spelling or grammar errors: just get those ideas down!

Your youngster may use one of a number of strategies for writing down and organizing advance thoughts on a reading.

Prereading Warm-Ups

- *Make a List.* With this kind of warm-up exercise, encourage your child to make a list of whatever comes to mind about the topic of the reading, as announced in the title, subtitles, captions, photographs, or any other elements in the text. In the list below, the reader wrote down all her thoughts about a selection she was assigned on dinosaurs:

Dinosaurs

animals early creatures-prehistoric
lay eggs?
huge bodies, little heads
live in swampy places
none left now (extinct?)
big bones left in mts. (Utah, any other place?)
muzeems put bones back together
dinosaur toys very poplar now
dinosaurs not too smart

movies: King Kong?
Some fly: man eaters?

As you can see, the list includes many different impressions, from dinosaurs today back to dinosaurs in early history. And notice the errors: *extinct, museums,* and *popular* are all misspelled. Again, the errors are unimportant. The child tried just to record all the unedited thoughts she had on the subject, just to stimulate mental activity before she reads. When kids have to worry about mistakes, they dam up the flow of their creative juices. Recent research in writing confirms that observation: Writers who attend to correctness too early in the writing process sweep aside considerations of thought and content.

- *Do brainstorming.* You've heard the term brainstorming, haven't you—literally, it means "a storm in the brain." The most productive way to brainstorm is to raise as many questions as you can about the topic of a selection before you read it. Using as many clues as possible—photographs, illustrations, charts, titles and subtitles, and so forth—help your child make a list of questions he might want to answer when he reads. On page 74 are questions that Saul raised in advance brainstorming for the geography book selection that we looked at on pages 66–69.
- *Freewrite.* When your child freewrites, she writes freely about the subject of the piece she's going to read. Producing consecutive sentences on paper, she writes about the topic nonstop without editing her thoughts. She writes whatever comes to her mind about the reading just before she reads it. Here again, visual clues can be very helpful. As with the list-making activity, this one also requires

what religions do ethnic groups follow?

about how many people live in the world today and how has it increased?

how much do populations change per year?

how many acres of land do most rural areas have?

where are rural areas found?

why isn't San Diego Calif. on the first list and is on the second?

what ancient people do archeologists study?

no attention to errors. Discourage spelling or grammar corrections. The point is to get as many ideas as possible on paper, no matter how strange or remote from the topic they may seem. Here's an example of freewriting prepared in advance of reading the selection from the geography text:

The earth's people. I don't know what to think about them. I am an earth's people. I am interested in languages but what is a language family? How is a language a family? Maybe one is like the father and the others are like babies. I can't say some of the words on the chart. Like Bahari and Urdu. My mother speaks German. Her family came over to America many years ago. How come some cities grow and others don't. I visited Baltimore once. It was nice. It's on the chart on p. 81.

Do you see how this reader just put down whatever ideas leaped to mind as she thought about the topic? Note how she drew on her own experiences to help her think about the issue. When she reads, some points in the selection will seem familiar to her.

- *Make a Word Map.* With a word map, your child produces her thoughts in a visual format. This visual scheme is called a map because it represents words and ideas as shapes and connects them—in much the same way that countries or states are connected in the maps we use for geography. Using lines, arrows, circles, boxes, and other shapes, your youngster can map her ideas on a subject she's ready to read about before she begins reading.

Don't think of this word map exercise as having any rules or rigid requirements. For this visual prereading warmup device, you want to help your youngster lay out his thoughts in a picture. The visual joins related information.

Suppose your youngster brought home a reading selection called "The Greatest Tightrope Walker." How could you use a word map to shake loose some ideas? Look at the sample on page 76 prepared by a young reader before she read the piece.

Do you see how the boxed words "tightrope walker" serve as the starting point for the map, all other elements emanating from them? Four major thought clus-

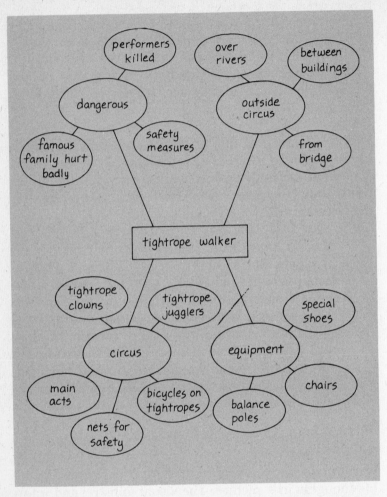

ters develop from the words "tightrope walkers": in large circles, they are "circus," "equipment," "outside circus," and "dangerous." Note, for example, how all the ideas pertaining to the cluster *circus* hang together, each item clearly related to the big top: jugglers, bicycles, nets, main acts, and clowns. No doubt, these words stem from the child's memory of a past circus visit or perhaps to a circus she viewed on television or in the movies.

You can see how this warm-up would help a child ready her mind for the reading she's about to do. On the level of vocabulary alone, this child has generated some words she's apt to confront as she reads. Without knowing it, she put on paper many of the ideas that the selection would deal with. In fact, "The Greatest Tightrope Walker" is about Blondin, a famous Frenchmen who thrilled crowds in daring circus feats on the high wire. In 1859 he walked a tightrope across Niagara Falls.

Next time your youngster arrives home with a textbook assignment, look at the materials in advance of reading. Using whatever available clues you can, ask your child to do some prereading warm-up of the kind I've described here. Then ask your youngster to read the selection. How does he think the exercise helped him as he read?

5

"Just the Facts, Ma'am"

READING FOR INFORMATION

■———————■

In the last chapter, we looked at how examining pages *before* actually reading them provides useful advance preparation for young readers at home. Let's look now at the act of reading itself. How do we get the most out of what we read?

What Is Reading, Anyway?

Researchers now say that we can best understand what happens when someone reads if we think of reading as a process—a process in which a reader and writer transact information.

For the time being, we're going to think of reading exclusively as print-bound. (We'll reconsider this premise later on.) The writer provides words, sentences, and paragraphs. The reader brings to the writer's pages personal experiences and impressions, knowledge of language, individual attitudes, thoughts, and ideas. In reading, both reader and writer engage in a kind of conversation to work out the message together. Not only the

writer, but the reader as well, has considerable responsi-
bility in determining meaning. Most enlightened educators no longer regard the old notion of a single, correct,
absolute meaning for a piece of writing; readers and
writers together shape the ideas captured by the words.

The transactional activities involve sophisticated
skills, such as what we infer from a reading, what generalizations and conclusions we draw, what judgments we
make of the writer's effort—others, too, as you can imagine. We learn the advanced skills as we mature as readers, and I'm going to explore those skills throughout
many of the remaining chapters of this book. Yet our
ability to reach those more advanced regions of thought
rests very much on what we perceive as the writer's
essential idea, the nuggets of vital information con-
tained in what we read. In short, we try to see that
everything comes together in an answer to this question:
"What is the writer trying to say?"

Educators usually refer to a reader's basic ability to
grasp information—facts, if you will—as *literal comprehension*. Literal comprehension means understanding
the main idea that the writer is trying to convey and
knowing the essential details that contribute to and support that main idea. We use the main idea and information basics as a framework for the higher-order skills
that advanced readers draw on to get the most out of
print.

A few important reminders are in order here before
we proceed.

Remember our Chapter 2 discussion of context and
the idea that the whole print environment can contribute
to the meaning of a single *word*? Keep in mind, here, too,
that meaning does not always reside exclusively in tar-
geted phrases, clauses, and sentences either. Reading is
not like a column of numbers where we just total up
everything to yield a neat figure produced only by adding

one item to the next. The nucleus of a sentence often appears only when we consider nearby sentences. Further, we cannot grasp a single paragraph's full range of meaning without considering surrounding paragraphs. And illustrations, drawings, headings and subheadings, photographs, captions, charts and graphs (typical elements in a reading selection that children, and adults too, face regularly)—all these features serve the total meaning. Each is a blossom offering its special scent to the garden. Certainly we can distinguish a particular aroma close up; yet the garden's fragrance is more than the sum of what each individual flower offers separately.

Next, take care not to think of reading only as a linear hierarchy of skills. We don't read first for literal comprehension and then start considering more advanced skills like inferential meanings or generalizations or conclusions. Human minds resist easy classification, and when we read we draw on many skills, talents, and techniques at the same time. For example, in order to reach a literal meaning, sometimes we have to draw on our skills at generalizing or making inferences. To explain them to you and to make it practical for use with children, I've separated these skills, giving them separate chapters, but you should be aware that often we exercise the skills all at once.

Pinpointing Sentence Ideas

None of these complexities (you're used to them by now, aren't you!) should detract you from focusing your child's attention on main ideas and supporting details. These will help you help him tease out the rudimentary meanings in what he reads. A piece of writing often presents many ideas; yet those ideas usually relate to a key point, the main idea. True, a unit of writing may project more than one main idea, several of them perhaps equal in importance.

Still, despite many disclaimers from different schools of thought, the notion of a *main idea* persists as an important element in how educators talk about reading. You can expect your school-age child to know the term from her teacher. If you're a home-schooler, you too should use the term in your conversations about reading with your youngster. When you help your child with a reading selection, you want to convey the sense that the varied ideas in a piece of writing generally relate to a major thought the writer is attempting to convey. To understand how the varied ideas fit together, we have to identify the main idea that provides the overall meaning.

Even if you look at a single sentence you can focus its primary meaning by thinking about the main point. Though many different kinds of information are being conveyed, essentially a sentence names a subject and tells something about it. (It's the old subject-and-verb definition of a sentence.) In other words, a sentence asserts (1) who a person or what an object is and (2) what that person or object does. Look at this sentence:

> Even in the spring a garden filled with fragrant flowers is very hard to find amid the glass and cement buildings of a big city like Boston.

What is the key point here? The sentence tells about a garden. We know that the garden is hard to find. All the information about the time of year, the kind of garden, the physical nature of the city, the name of the city adds details. Certainly the details complete the scene for the reader; and often we need to examine the details carefully to understand the key point more clearly, to flesh out meanings more completely. Nevertheless, the main point of this sentence is *A garden is hard to find*.

If we can get a child to extract that idea from the longer sentence, we are establishing important ground rules for determining meanings. We're saying, "Between the capital letter and the period is a main thought elaborated by details, but nonetheless separable from them."

Children need guidance in identifying sentence meanings; all too often kids get so hung up on individual words and nonessential details that they miss the main point of a sentence. I've seen youngsters stumble on words like *fragrant* and *amid* in our model sentence. In fact, those words bring little to the basic idea of the sentence: It's hard to find a garden in a city.

Consult this box to help your child figure out the main point in a sentence.

Finding the Main Point in a Sentence

- Ask who or what the sentence is about.
- Ask what the person or object is doing or what is being done to the person or object.
- Strip away supporting details. Details that add information without necessarily contributing to the main point of the sentence often answer the questions *where*?, *when*?, *which*?, *how*?, or *why*?

As with most cases regarding language, these otherwise useful questions I've suggested above to help you find details (so that you can focus on the main idea) resist exact responses. You can ask what someone is doing—but if the sentence says that a person feels or understands, for example, or that the person merely is, the question is an imperfect means of arriving at the answer. Sometimes one subject in a sentence does more than one thing and both are equally important in arriving at the main idea.

In many cases you want to sift through details to arrive at the main point. In this example from a fourth-grade *Weekly Reader* piece on Vietnam, you must use details to make sense of the sentence:

> Tet is also the time that everyone in Vietnam celebrates his or her birthday.

If you're a stickler for exact responses to the first two questions in the box on page 82, you get only *Tet is the time* as the key idea, if that. It doesn't seem key at all, does it? Here again, the subject really isn't doing anything. It just is. To make sense of this sentence, you must draw on some of the details; the main point is that *Tet is birthday-celebrating time*. Thus, you see that some details are more important than others. (I'll have more to say about major and minor details later in this chapter.) What you should realize here is that sometimes you need to guide your child to use some of the details in order to state the main point precisely. Be flexible so that you make the questions suit the groups of words you're looking at.

Let's explore ways to help your youngster find key ideas in sentences like the ones he'll meet when he reads. Here's a sentence from a third-grade language arts book:

> Tom dashed away to the store with his dog Spot racing along behind.

Who is this sentence about? *Tom*.
What is Tom doing? Tom *dashed*.

Note the way that the remaining details answer some of the questions posed in the box above.

Where? *to the store*.
Which Tom? The one *with his dog Spot*.
Which Spot? The one *racing along behind*.

All the information other than *Tom dashed* in that sentence adds details to let your child know more about the special conditions surrounding the subject's actions.

Still, the essential meaning here boils down to a boy named Tom who dashed somewhere.

For practice, talk with your child about the main point in each of the sentences below. I've taken them all from current textbooks in use at elementary schools or from library-recommended books and periodicals for youngsters between five and eleven. I've arranged the sentences in the list from lower to upper grades.

1. Airplanes that could fly like birds in the sky were once a dream.

2. Betsy brought some pretty yellow flowers for the room.

3. Every day Thumbelina would wash her beautiful new wings with soap and water.

4. After playing loud music for years, some musicians now wear hearing aids.

5. But no matter when the New Year is celebrated, it is always a joyful time.

6. There, in the middle of a compound of cages, sat a television set, its tangle of extension cords trailing off into the distance.

7. Although scientists have learned a lot about dinosaurs in recent years, the debate over warm- or cold-blooded dinosaurs continues to be a hot one.

8. When Muhammad was about forty years old he had the religious experience that caused him to begin preaching.

9. Either way, no matter what kind of work he does or for which goal, the scientist must first know how to collect detailed data, then interpret it, so it can be put to use.

10. While the skin color of Africans is generally dark, it varies greatly from place to place.

Main Ideas

I want to begin our discussion of main ideas in longer written pieces like paragraphs, stories, and articles by looking at a visual illustration. Here's the delightful cover of Susan Saunders' *Mystery Cat and the Monkey Business*.

If you wanted to explain the main point of this picture, what would you say?

I bet you'd say something like: *Two girls watch in shock as a cat frightens a monkey up a pole.*

How did you determine the main idea here? You drew on the visual clues, you used your own prior experience, you constructed a meaningful sentence from your own linguistic storehouse. You did not simply total up all the visual information. In fact, whether you're aware of it or not, you weeded out some details in this illustration, ignoring them because they did not affect the main idea in any profound way. Your main idea statement probably did not address the fact that the scene takes place at a circus or carnival. You did not acknowledge the elephants standing in the background over to the left— interesting details certainly but relatively unimportant for knowing what the main point of the picture is. Similarly, you don't need to acknowledge the tent, the elaborate circus cart in back of the monkey, the starred border of a circus performance ring behind the girls.

Many of the same cognitive processes used to determine the main point of a picture or illustration pertain to a print selection as well. Get your child to practice framing main idea statements from photographs and illustrations in newspapers and magazines around the house. Have some fun by looking at action-packed family pictures and talking about the main points the pictures suggest.

Now let's see how these cognitive processes work when a reader tries to identify the main idea of a longer selection.

As you know, we use the word *paragraph* to identify a set of consecutive sentences about some related subject. Just as a sentence has a key idea, so does a paragraph. Often a writer will state very clearly what she intends as the main idea of her paragraph; surrounding sentences in the paragraph will expand on the idea by providing support or evidence, through analysis, by making generalizations, or by stating alternate points of view, among other possibilities.

Sometimes writers state their main point as the very first sentence in the paragraph:

> *Aside from all its other problems London's weather is very strange.* It can rain several times a day; each time the rain may come suddenly after the sun is shining brightly. The air is damp and chill right through July. On one March afternoon on Hampton Heath last year it rained three times, there was one hail storm and the sun shone—all this within two hours' time! It is not unusual to see men and women rushing down the street on a sunny morning with umbrellas on their arms. No one knows what the next few moments will bring.

The main idea here is *London's weather is strange.* The sentence I've placed in italics says it very clearly. All the other sentences contribute to the meaning of the paragraph by providing supporting details.

Sometimes a writer will place the main idea in the middle or at the end of the paragraph:

> It's easy to remember to turn off a light if it's not in use. Some people can walk short distances to work instead of driving. Others can use public transportation. *So there are many specific steps to take in order to ease the fuel crisis.* Not too many people are unhappy with house temperatures of 68 degrees. A hot shower is just as good as a hot bath in keeping us clean. We can learn to use dishwashers, washing machines less often. Of course, watching less television would not be too popular, but that too could save valuable oil.

Although the buildings are tall, they do not blot out the sky. People rush about as in New York, but someone always stops to answer a question or give directions. A person will listen when asked a question. Often a sudden smile will flash from the crowds of strangers pushing down State Street. It is a smile of welcome and of happiness at the same time. The traffic is tough and noisy, but a person never feels as if he takes his life in his hands when he crosses the street. Of course, there is always the presence of Lake Michigan shining like an ocean of silver. Something about that lake each time it spreads out around a turn on Lake Shore Drive says, "Hello. It's good to see you again." *Chicago is a friendly city.*

The main ideas in these paragraphs are *There are many steps to take to ease the fuel crisis* and *Chicago is a friendly city*. In the first paragraph the main idea appears in the fourth sentence. In the second paragraph the very last sentence states the main idea.

Here's a paragraph in which the main idea appears in more than one sentence:

Dogs make warm, friendly pets. But they can also be very troublesome. No one will deny the feeling of friendship when, after a long day's work, a wet pink tongue of greeting licks your hand at the door. And watching television or reading a book, you can reach down over the side of the couch and feel a warm furry creature. You can hear the quiet contented breathing of a good friend. However, try to plan a trip without your faithful pet and your life is very difficult. Where will you leave him? Who will feed him? Further, leaving a cozy house in the midst of winter and facing a howling frozen wind so the dog may take his walk is no pleasure at all. I often wonder why people put up with such demands upon their time and energy.

In this instance, the first two sentences state the main point of the paragraph. True, dogs are friendly pets—and several of the sentences back up that idea—but the paragraph also provides details to support the notion that dogs can cause owners some problems too.

It would be easy, wouldn't it, if determining the main idea of every paragraph simply meant adding up the ideas of the individual sentences. But even in these relatively straightforward examples you've just looked at, we didn't arrive at the main idea simply by summation. Unfortunately, the adding machine principle is too simplistic for the act of reading a paragraph. Our minds don't work like calculators producing sums. That transaction—I've used the term before—between the reader and the writer to produce meaning goes beyond the mere sum of the various sentence ideas in a paragraph. What we think, what we know, what the writer says, what the various words mean in terms of their connotations and denotations, what we infer from the words—all these contribute to our definition of the central meaning in a paragraph.

Knowing these factors is especially important when you read paragraphs in which the main idea is only implied. Often, a paragraph does not state the main idea exactly: we ourselves must determine it. The writer suggests it by means of the information, details, analysis, and observations made in the selection. Look at this brief newspaper piece:

Only thirty percent of family businesses survive their founders and make it into the second generation according to most authorities on the subject. The rest are sold or go bankrupt. And the statistics grow grimmer with the passage of time. Only half of those companies that live through the transition to the second generation will survive as a family business into the third or fourth generations.

—*The New York Times*

What is the main idea here? Is it *About thirty percent of family businesses last beyond the lives of their founders*?

No. Although the paragraph certainly makes that point, it's not the *main* point. It's just a detail that contributes to the overall meaning. We'd be narrowing the meaning too much to choose the single issue as the essence of the paragraph.

Is the main point *Family businesses can go bankrupt*? Again, the answer is no. It's true that family businesses can go bankrupt, and indeed the paragraph implies the point. But we couldn't say that the idea of bankruptcies for family businesses rules the meaning of the paragraph. It's too narrow. And you couldn't say, *Family businesses do not succeed* is the main point; The generalization is too sweeping. The paragraph is giving evidence that many family businesses do not succeed beyond a certain time frame, but surely those that do succeed challenge the overly broad generalization provided here.

The main idea of the paragraph is something like, *Over time, family businesses do not have a high survival rate*. To figure it out, you have to muse over the facts presented in the individual sentences, drawing into the hopper what you know about family businesses as well as what the sentences say about them. No single sentence in the paragraph states the main point exactly. You know that relatives can carry on family businesses to the next generation in only about a third of the cases. As time goes on the odds get worse: of those who last into the second generation (already a very small pool) only fifty percent will survive into the third or fourth generation. Maybe you know about a local, mom-and-pop deli or hardware store that closed when sons and daughters chose careers in computer engineering or accounting instead of the family business. You put all that information together to draw the generalization that it's tough for a family business to outlive its founders.

Determining the main idea in a paragraph when the main idea is only implied is a critical skill for your young reader. Much of the reading we do throughout life involves our ability to see implications and to generalize (see Chapter 9) based on specific information the writer provides. Not just paragraphs, certainly, but longer works like stories, book chapters, essays, whole books themselves, regularly challenge us to boil down a kettle of ideas into a soupcon of meaning. Every time you tell a friend the point of something you read or of a film you've seen, you're highlighting a main idea. This is not to say that every entity has a *single* main point or that we can state it succinctly in a simple sentence the way I've tried to do for illustrative purposes here. Nevertheless, we frequently must react to the implications in a larger work and state its essence in our own language.

Use this chart to help you help your child identify main ideas in a paragraph and, by extension, a longer piece:

Stating Main Ideas in Your Own Words

- Make a complete sentence that names a person, an object, or an idea *and* that tells what a person or an object is doing.
- Use the supporting details in the paragraph to help you determine the main point. Don't allow one of the minor points to distract you from what may be a larger issue. You don't want to see a narrow feature as the main idea.
- Do not offer a statement that is too general as the main idea.

Let me explain how Saul and I discussed a paragraph to zero in on its meaning. The paragraph comes from a book that we are reading aloud with him, James Howe's *Morgan's Zoo*. Saul, our ten-year-old, was a little confused about this paragraph, which starts Chapter 4.

(1) Mayor Thayer was a bald-headed man with a gently sloping paunch that evidenced his love for fine food. (2) Aside from his reputation as a gourmand, he was known to be a politician who cared about his constituents and wanted nothing more than to please them. (3) However, recent pressures from the City Council had necessitated his making a number of severe cuts in the city's budget. (4) As a result, his popularity among the people was in decline. (5) Depressed over this, he had taken to hiding away in his office and eating nothing but junk food.

No doubt you've identified some of the difficult vocabulary here, difficult enough to stump many fourth-graders. You know from Chapter 2 how context clues can yield meanings of the tough words like *paunch, gourmand, constituents,* and *depressed,* so I'll leave you on your own with those words if you and your child decide to examine this paragraph. However, even without knowing these words, a child can figure out the paragraph idea.

Even though many paragraphs do not yield their essential meaning if we simply add up the information found in each sentence, in a confusing paragraph it's helpful nonetheless to start by examining the sentences one at a time. Saul used the strategies that I pointed out before for determining key ideas. Here's the way we worked out the meaning of the numbered sentences:

1. Mayor Thayer loved fine food.

2. He cared about his constituents and wanted to please them.

3. Pressures forced him to cut the budget.

4. His popularity declined.

5. Depressed, he hid and ate junk food.

What's the main idea of this paragraph? Using the key ideas from the various sentences, we agreed that the main point here is something like: *Budget cuts decreased Mayor Thayer's popularity and depressed him.* Of course, many other ideas are afloat here—interesting descriptive, narrative, and analytic details—but the sentence in italics states the paragraph's essential point. It's not that the other ideas are unimportant or uninteresting, it's just that we don't need them all in order to state the main idea. Some of the details are more important than others (more on this in the next section). And you'll note that the main idea that we constructed is stated nowhere in this paragraph. Again, it is implied. The various sentences hint at that overall meaning without ever stating it directly.

For more practice, you might want to look at this paragraph with your youngster. It appears in a sixth-grade science book:

(1) The greatest problem facing the Southern farmer was cotton. (2) The once-rich soil had become worn out through constant planting of this single crop. (3) Carver knew that if farmers would rotate cotton crops with crops of peanuts and sweet potatoes, the soil would once again become fertile. (4) But farmers, who depended on sale of their crops for money with which to live, would not plant crops that few people would want to buy.

Let's take them one at a time. In 1, whom is the sentence about? [George Washington] *Carver*. What is he doing? He *knows* something: *the soil again can be fertile*. The responses to the questions tell the main point, although *to know* does not answer the "What is he doing?" question exactly. If you look then at the "detail" question *how*—how could the soil turn fertile again— your answer is that farmers rotating crops would bring about the results Carver hopes for.

In 2, whom is the sentence about? *Farmers*. What are they doing? *Not planting certain crops*. Now ask some of the other questions. *Which* farmers is the sentence talking about? Those farmers who have to sell their crops to make a living. *Which* crops won't they plant? *The crops that people won't buy*. On your own, work out the meanings of sentences 2 and 3 with your child.

Now, what do you believe is the main idea of the paragraph? Can you and your child work it out together, based on the key ideas in the sentences you've already determined? Here's what I'd see as the main idea:

> *Carver knew that cotton farmers would not plant crops that wouldn't sell, even though cotton-only crops ruined the soil.*

Your language might be considerably different from mine here, but the key elements are the need to rotate crops and the cotton farmers' understandable resistance to planting crops that might improve soil but that no one would buy. Here, too, the main idea is not stated exactly in any single sentence but instead is implied by the information in the paragraph.

Look with your child at some paragraphs from his school books or from a library book you're reading together and, using some of the hints I've provided here, work on figuring out the main ideas.

Fact-Finding and Checking Out Details

The main idea of a paragraph or a longer selection provides an overall notion of the writer's point. Other details support the main idea, providing the information base—all the necessary facts and evidence upon which the writer builds the main point she's trying to make. Those facts are our link to knowledge on an issue. They may give a more complete picture than you can gather from the main idea alone, they may prove a point, show how ideas relate to other ideas, provide examples to make ideas clearer. It's not enough to know only the intrinsic concept that a writer is asserting; we've got to know the essential details as well.

You know from your own reading how dense with supporting information some paragraphs can be. And, as I've pointed out before, not all details are created equal. In other words, until we show our children how to weed through the garden of information in a paragraph, we're not helping them learn the necessary skills for retaining vital material.

To make the best use of facts and details in a paragraph, your child should know how to (1) find important facts (2) separate major details from minor details and (3) understand the order or sequence of details as the paragraph presents them.

Help your child be a better reader for factual information by calling his attention to the points in the chart on page 96.

Let's focus on a typical assignment made to a fifth-grade class in their language arts textbook. The children are asked to read an encyclopedia article and then to write a summary. Summary writing helps pinpoint the reader's attention on essential facts, and the textbook acknowledges that in its instruction to children. "When you summarize," the book says, "you tell only the main points. You leave out minor details. Summarizing is a good way to

Locating and Remembering Facts

- **Have a purpose for reading.** When your youngster sits down to read a selection, what is he trying to find out? Review some of the prereading warm-ups I talked to you about in Chapter 4. A purpose stated in advance can rivet the reader's attention to important facts.
- **Read for the main idea.** Once you can state the main idea, facts that support it may stand out more easily.
- **Realize that all facts and details are not created equal.** Some information is more important than other information. Facts that support the main idea are the essential facts.
- **Pay attention to the way information is arranged.** Knowing typical paragraph patterns can help you get a handle on the details.
- **Actively raise questions as you read.** Help your child frame the simple information questions about facts and details as he reads: "What does that mean?" "Why is the writer telling me this?" Also, help your child frame questions that someone else might ask about the reading. Being able to frame those questions relates directly to stating a purpose in advance of reading.
- Use the five W's to ask yourself about important facts.

  Ask the question *who?* and then look for a person's name.

  Ask the question *what?* or what happened and look for an action.

  Ask the question *when?* and look for a date or a time.

  Ask the question *where?* and look for a place.

  Ask the question *why?* and look for an explanation of an action.

review what you have read. It forces you to think about what you have read and helps you understand it."

Good advice. But alas, no information, like the chart I've presented above, assists a child in determining the main facts and distinguishing major from minor details, which, by the book's own admission, are the critical skills involved here. Youngsters need at least some initial help in shrinking the meaning of a paragraph to its core.

So then, how do you help your child gather appropriate information from this piece on Sacagawea? (For discussion's sake, we'll look at the first paragraph on page 98 only.)

First, talk with your child about her purpose in reading. Here, too, the book could provide more guidance. It asks for a summary, but does not address the specific task the selection deals with. (The photograph accompanying the selection will help provide some context if you talk about it in advance with your child as part of regular previewing activities.) If I had written the instructions, I'd say, "Read this encyclopedia article on Sacagawea, an Indian woman who helped guide Lewis and Clark in their Western expedition during the early 1800s. Then write a summary." Instructions like those define the purpose precisely for beginning readers. Absent those specific instructions, you're stuck with just the little bit on writing a summary.

In any case, it's always a good idea to call attention to any directions accompanying assigned reading. With the instructions I've provided, your child, acknowledging the embedded information on Sacagawea, should be reading this piece with an eye toward finding out about Sacagawea's role in the great nineteenth-century Western expedition.

Content established, you might have some fun with a word map or with list-making about the words *Indian*, *expedition*, or *guide*. Don't forget prereading!

After your child reads the selection, talk about the main idea. Encyclopedias aim for density, compressing as many details as possible in small spaces so; this paragraph has a nexus of main points. Let me state them in a single sentence: *Sacagawea, a captured and enslaved Indian woman, was an important guide in Lewis and Clark's expedition.* Once you and your child agree on a main idea statement, you're well armed to consider the

Social Studies

In social studies you are sometimes asked to summarize information. When you summarize, you tell only the main points. You leave out minor details. Summarizing is a good way to review what you have read. It forces you to think about what you have read and helps you to understand it.

▶ Try it. Read this encyclopedia article. Then summarize the article in your own words. Give its most important points in no more than five sentences.

SACAGAWEA, *sak uh juh WEE uh*, Sacajawea, or Sakakawea (1787?-1812?), was the interpreter for the Lewis and Clark Expedition to the Pacific Ocean in 1804 and 1805. Sacagawea's name means *Bird Woman*. She was born among the Shoshoni, or Snake, Indians of Idaho. Enemy Indians captured her, and sold her as a slave to a French-Canadian trader, Toussaint Charbonneau. Charbonneau and Sacagawea joined the Lewis and Clark Expedition as it passed up the Missouri River. Sacagawea was the principal guide of the expedition. While crossing the Continental Divide, the explorers met relatives of Sacagawea among the Shoshoni. She was able to get food and horses that the travelers needed to continue their journey to the Pacific Ocean and back (see Lewis and Clark Expedition).

Almost nothing was known of Sacagawea for a hundred years after the journey. According to one account, she died on the Missouri River in 1812. Others have contended that she died and was buried on the Wind River Reservation in Wyoming in 1884. An entry in Captain Clark's journal of 1825-1828 lists her as dead.

Sacagawea has been honored by having a river, a peak, and a mountain pass named after her. Monuments and memorials to her stand at Portland, Ore., Three Forks, Mont., Bismarck, N. Dak., Lewiston, Ida., and near Dillon, Mont. William H. Gilbert

Readers at Work Librarians help decide what new books a library will order each year. To do this, they read book reviews. A book review gives a summary and an evaluation of a book.

▶ List the kinds of books you would order for a library. For example, you might choose science fiction or biographies of famous athletes. For each kind of book, invent several book titles and authors.

facts and to identify the major details. Major details support the main idea. Details that offer less crucial information within the main idea context are considered minor.

Which details are major? Here's what I propose:

- Sacagawea was interpreter for the Lewis and Clark Expedition in 1804 and 1805.
- As a slave she joined the expedition on the Missouri River with her owner.
- She served as principal guide for Lewis and Clark.
- She obtained needed food and horses from Shoshoni Indian relatives.
- Through her help the travelers continued their journey.

Which details are minor? You can deduce them from what's left out of the above list. For example, the fact that Sacagawea means Bird Woman or that Shoshoni translates as *Snake* are very interesting, no doubt, but certainly are not essential to understanding the main point. We also don't need to know the slave owner's name or the fact that he is French Canadian. These facts contribute little to the main idea.

Want some practice? Here's a variation on an exercise with some open-ended questions from one of my reading textbooks. Try it out with your youngster. Remember to preview and do prereading warm-ups after you read the instructions.

Read the following explanation about two sports used for self-defense to learn their differences and similarities. Then answer the questions that follow.

Judo and Karate

Judo and karate are sports for self-defense. They began in the eastern part of the world, but now many Americans enjoy them too. In fact, schools for teaching them have been opened all over the United States and Canada.

Players in both sports use only their hands, arms, legs, and feet. Aside from that, the two sports are quite different. In karate, players hit each other with the open hand and with the closed fist. They also use the foot for kicking. In judo, players are more likely to throw one another. Then they try to pin each other down. In judo, then, players touch each other. They also move their arms and legs in large circles. Karate moves, on the other hand, are short and quick. Players stand away from each other. They only touch one another with quick punches and kicks.

Can a karate player beat a judo player? It depends on the players. One sport is not better than the other. They are both very good forms of self-defense. Both aim toward control of the mind and body. A wise old man in Japan had a good answer to the question. He said, "We do not say the other martial arts are bad. The mountain does not laugh at the river because it is lowly, nor does the river speak ill of the mountain because it cannot move about."

—*Jeannette Bruce*

1. What is the main idea of the selection?

2. Which details are important in helping you understand how to do judo?

3. Which details are important in helping you understand how to do karate?

4. Which details do you consider minor details in this selection? Why?

Again, I don't mean to oversimplify this ability to

determine the main point and to find essential factual details. Please remember that in my attempts to show you these comprehension strategies, I'm not trying to minimize the complicated and interlocking skills we tap when we try to understand a selection. Nevertheless, by knowing some of the cognitive processes available to readers and exploring them carefully, you can help your child practice for reading power.

Noting the Sequence

Last week was your daughter's birthday party, and you've just taken the rolls of pictures out of the film shop. They're all great—well, maybe one or two don't show your child as the true Hollywood star you know she is. Now you're trying to arrange the photographs attractively in the family album. In what order will you present the delightful color impressions before you?

You have a number of choices. You can stick photos onto album paper any old way. That would surely save time, but it wouldn't give you an orderly sense of the party ten years from now.

You could arrange the pictures chronologically—that is, photos of the first events first, the second next, and so on. Time-order would help you create a narrative so that when you looked at the pictures later on—or if some stranger looked at them—the party's "story" would emerge.

Or, you could arrange those photographs spatially: a couple of shots near the window here, a few beside the parakeet cage near the wall there, on this page a cluster of shots at the dining room table. The spatial arrangement wouldn't give a narrative sequence to the day's events, but it would provide a pleasing order of related photographs.

Then again, you could arrange the pictures by importance, saving the most important for last. In this way you could build up to the main event visually. Let's see, the shot of Julie standing at the door and waiting for her friends, you'd display that one first. Blowing out the birthday cake—those delightful photos would go toward the middle of your arrangement. Ah, but the pictures of your child opening her gifts—especially the new roller skates she'd been begging for all year—those surely would go toward the end of the sequence.

No matter which arrangement you choose, by ordering your pictures you try to create a pattern of meaning. Writers, too, observe the concept of order by the way they arrange paragraph information. Sometimes the patterns are easy to label and recognize and pointing out the most familiar patterns to your child will help her see how various paragraph details fit together. Once she is familiar with the patterns, she'll be able to spot them when she reads, even when writers mix or overlap ordering principles.

Did you notice the chronological arrangement of the details in the piece about Sacagawea? (See page 98.) The writer tells us what happened first, what next, what after that. Time sequence is one of the most familiar ordering principles in writing, and you should help your child recognize it.

As in our album-arranging dilemma, another ordering principle for writers is spatial. A sixth-grader writing a description of his room uses a modest spatial arrangement in this paragraph:

I See the Frost on the Trees

On this February morning in Miss Olson's room in Spokane, Washington, I gaze around and see the frost on the trees outside of the windows. Also I spot the sun shining on the floor and brown desks. My friend, Karen, is sitting by me. She is wearing a golden blouse and a plaid skirt with white socks and black shiny shoes. She has brown hair and hazel eyes. The walls of the room are a soft blue, the ceiling an off-white. The trim of the walls is a beige color. On the wall in front of me is a photo of George Washington. It looks as if he's staring at me with his black eyes. Every once in a while I hear the clock go tick-tock, tick-tock. There are twenty-six classmates in my room.

—*Theresa Carroll*

Note how this child moves from the scene outside the window to the indoor scene. She describes her friend, then the walls, then the wall right in front of her.

Another useful way to arrange information in a paragraph is by order of importance. Here, a writer builds to the most significant point and presents it last.

Robert Hooke's work in science was varied and important through the 1700s in England. In the first place he served as the head of the Royal Society, a group of the day's leading men of science; there he urged new tests and experiments to advance knowledge. He helped provide a means by which people could discuss their ideas with others who shared their concerns. Hooke was also a well-known architect whose advice about the design of buildings was welcome. He designed a large beautiful house in London where the British Museum now stands. Unfortunately Hooke's building burned down; the six long years of work he did on it were wiped out by a careless servant. Of all Hooke's gifts to humanity, however, the most important was his own research in science. He studied the movement of planets and improved tools for looking at the heavens. He invented the spiral watch spring. And, of course, it was Hooke who first described the cell as a basic part of plant tissue.

As I said before, pointing out these ways of ordering details will help your child recognize writing patterns and will ease her understanding of information she reads. This chart will help you review the issue:

HOW TO SEE PARAGRAPH ARRANGEMENT

- Certain words in paragraphs give you hints about how the ideas are arranged.
- For *time order* look for words that tell time, such as *when, then, first, second, next, last, after, before, later, finally.*
- For *place order* look for words that locate, such as *there, beside, near, above, below, next to, under, over, alongside, beneath, by, behind, on.*
- For *order of importance* look for words that help us judge importance, such as *first, next, last, most important, major, greatest, in the first place.*

Just a couple of points here before we move on. First, writers rarely stick to any absolute ordering principle, so expect to see lots of overlap, combinations, and new inventions. Especially in longer pieces you should expect a variety of arrangements, although certainly—as in a narrative story, for example, where chronology may rule—one type often predominates.

Second, several writing strategies have a kind of built-in ordering mechanism that, when acknowledged, can help a reader further absorb content more easily than if he ignored the manner of presentation. For example, if you know that a writer is trying to offer a list of examples, you know to look for several items to support the main point. (Usually a simple listing follows an order-of-importance arrangement of details.) If you know that the writer is comparing or contrasting two objects, you know to expect the objects to be considered side by side. If you know that a writer is trying to explain causes and (or) effects, you know to seek explanations, information telling you why something happened or what happened as the result of something.

I've listed below a few familiar writing patterns we haven't considered yet along with some clues for recognizing them. These clues will help your youngster anticipate the manner of presentation and, hence, will improve his ability to understand information more easily when he reads.

Ready to consider some examples? Here from an elementary school geography book is a paragraph that offers a simple listing.

Pattern	Clues to Recognize Them
Listing of Details	Look for words like "there are many reasons for" early in the selection.
	Look for words like "for example" or "for instance" or "as another example."
	Look for "counting words" like *first, second, third* or *first, next, last.* Look for numbered items in a list.
Comparison and Contrast	Look for key words that help relate the objects to each other: *similarly, also, in addition, further, in the same way.*
	Look for words that suggest differences: *on the other hand, in contrast, but, different from, although, yet, in spite of, even so, nonetheless.*
	Keep in mind the objects or ideas being compared and (or) contrasted.
Cause and Effect	Look for explanations of what happened because of something.
	Look for explanations of what might happen because of something.
	Look for key words: *since, as a result, because, therefore, so, why, consequently.*

There are many reasons for conflict among nations. Some of the most important causes of disagreement are (1) disputes over boundaries; (2) differences in ways of living; (3) disputes over national homelands; (4) economic conflicts over matters such as natural resources and trade; (5) disputes over leadership; and (6) control of strategic places.

You've already examined a comparison-contrast selection. Go back and look at the little piece on judo and karate on page 99.

Here's a paragraph dealing with causes of crime; the paragraph is organized around cause and effect reasoning. Notice some overlap with listing of details as a principle of arrangement.

Why does a person turn to a life of crime? There is no simple answer, but psychologists believe that some clues lie in the early life of the criminal. A child raised in an unhappy home, or by a strict parent or parent substitute, or a child raised in poverty runs the risk more than others of turning against the law. Some investigators believe that there is something in the basic personality which forces someone into crime. Several people suggest that it is a feature of the genes—something within the human cell tissue—that determines criminal action. And, of course, there is solid evidence to suggest that pressures of present day society give rise to crime. Even an unlikely type for crime might turn to it because he or she is unable to face the hectic pace and style of life our present age demands.

Fact or Opinion?

Knowing how to identify main ideas and key supporting details is essential for intelligent, thoughtful reading on the literal level. As we move up the rungs to critical reading skills, however, we must be able to interpret what we read. Interpretation includes skills like drawing inferences, predicting outcomes, drawing conclusions, and generalizing, all topics for later chapters in this book. Here, I want to treat a basic higher-order skill that leads to the sophisticated arena of judging the quality of what we read. That skill requires a child's ability to distinguish fact from opinion.

Not everything we read is pure fact. Simply by excluding certain details from a factual report, for example, a writer subtly exerts her opinion on the material. But there's no shame here; most writing includes a balance between fact and opinion, where the writer presents information and offers commentary on it to explain his or her position on the issues. No writer claims that everything in a written selection is fact. She will stand by the facts, certainly, but she will acknowledge that the opinions are her own and that readers might not necessarily agree with those opinions—although sometimes the writer's purpose is to convince you to agree with her.

The issue I'm trying to address with these comments and with the rest of this chapter is that not everything in print is absolute, verifiable truth, and the sooner your child learns this reality as he moves through the upper grades the sooner he joins the ranks of critical readers.

Consider this statement by someone trying to sell you a new toy:

> The electronic Target A Battleship comes with a mounted laser gun, motorized sailors that walk the deck, and over twenty moving parts. It's the best children's toy around today.

Only certain pieces of information are factual here. The name of the toy, its inclusion of a laser gun and moving sailors, it number of moving parts—these are facts. However, whether this toy is the best on today's market is only a matter of opinion. Other children, parents, consumer groups, or educators might prefer other toys to Battleship A. No doubt, many kids would give the toy highest ratings for fun and excitement.

You're probably aware that keeping fact and opinion apart is not always a simple matter. Just try to get two people in the midst of a hot argument to agree on who fired the first verbal salvo and you'll see that what one person believes as fact is probably just an opinion to the other guy. Writers sometimes will present as fact items that others simply would not acknowledge as true.

In addition, sometimes writers get their facts wrong. The Ptolemaic vision of our solar system, thoroughly erroneous and proven so by the work of Keppler and Galileo in the modern age, for hundreds of years commanded the intellectual imagination of scientists and clergy everywhere. Century after dark century no one challenged Ptolemy's observations and authority.

Sometimes writers do not bother to check their facts. In other cases, writers mix fact and opinion so closely that it's hard to tell where one ends and the other begins. Philosophers and theologians often argue about the intrinsic difference between truth and speculation. Most people do have strong opinions, which they believe to be facts, and represent those opinions *as* facts.

Despite the apparent caveats, we need to help kids tell the difference between fact and opinion. Facts are verifiable truths, statements that tell what really happened or what really is the case. Facts are based on evidence and are known by experience or observation. *Opinions* are statements of evaluations, judgment, belief, or feeling. Opinions show someone's personal views on an issue. Some opinions are based more solidly in facts, or are rooted in more knowledge and awareness and, therefore, are more reliable that other opinions. Nevertheless, an opinion is an opinion is an opinion, simply somebody's point of view and not incontrovertible facts.

Let's examine some statements about American Indians from Dee Brown's *Bury My Heart at Wounded Knee: An Indian History of the American West*.

1. In 1848 gold was discovered in California.

2. In 1860 there were probably 300,000 Indians in the United States and Territories, most of them living west of the Mississippi.

3. Now, in an age without heroes, the Indian leaders are perhaps the most heroic of all Americans.

In sentence 1 we read a statement of fact. We have evidence of the discovery of gold in California in 1848. If we checked sources, we would see that the statement is true.

The use of numbers, dates, and geography in sentence 2 creates a sense of fact. But the word *probably* suggests some doubt, and we cannot accept the statement as completely factual. That doesn't make it wrong or untrue. It just makes it partly an opinion. Because Dee Brown is a scholar in American Indian history, most people would accept his statement as fact. But it is still his educated judgment that 300,000 Indians lived in the United States in 1860. The writer's education and background seem reliable, and we accept his statement as true without much thought. It is possible, though, that some people have other views on this subject.

In sentence 3 we have a clearer example of the author's opinion. The statement is not wrong. Yet it clearly is not a statement of fact. The word *perhaps* tells us that the author himself believes other ideas are possible. It is true that many people would agree that Indian leaders are the most heroic. Others might say, however, that leaders during World War II or leaders in countries in times of crisis were the most heroic. Others would say that leaders on Vietnam battlefields were the most heroic. None of these statements is incorrect. All, however, are opinions.

I think that you'll find this review chart helpful to identify opinions:

Looking for Opinions

- Be aware of "judgment" words. Words like *beautiful, ugly, foolish, smart, expensive, cheap, worthless, productive* always express someone's opinion.
- Be aware of "doubt" words. Some words indicate that doubt exists about a statement's truth and that other opinions on the matter are likely. These are words like *sometimes, often, maybe, usually, perhaps, probably, likely, possibly.*
- Be aware of "opinion" words. Some words clearly state that an opinion will follow. These are words like *in my opinion, I think, I believe, I feel, I suggest.*

Look at this paragraph from the sixth-grade social studies book I've cited from time to time. What are the facts here? What are the opinions?

> Today people are paying more attention than ever before to the thinly settled areas of the world. One reason is that the population of the world is increasing. And, as the population increases, so does the need for food, water, minerals, and other resources. Perhaps some of those "empty" areas can be made useful for people.

In this section you've had your first look at high-order reading and thinking skills. Before taking up other key reading areas, I want to explore the importance of visual language as you stimulate advanced reading at home.

6

Words and Pictures
USING VISUAL AIDS

I want you to expand your definition of reading.

Most people define the word literally: Reading is determining meaning from printed words and sentences.

But I believe that that's too limited a definition. We're always trying to "read" meanings from our physical environments, even when no print is involved. (It's interesting to note the legitimate, though certainly metaphorical, use of the word *read* for actions beyond a page of text.) The point to remember here is that the same skills that we use for a printed page we often apply to nonprint experiences as well. Thus when you try to "read" any situation, you aim to extract meaning from it.

However, the connection between reading print and reading the surrounding world is more than a metaphorical one. The roster of skills in the table of contents for this book, *Any Child Can Read Better*—figuring out the main point, inferring, predicting outcomes, generalizing—are the intellectual processes we use almost everywhere to decipher meanings throughout the day.

As I explain those skills and how to help your son or daughter use them, I'll be showing you the connections you can make between print and nonprint situations. You'll be able to help your child apply to words on a page some of the same mental activities that she draws on to interpret her daily life.

A Thousand Words' Worth

When your child sees a group of youngsters waiting at the school bus, or when she watches an episode of *Captain Kangaroo,* or when she looks at a photograph or a cartoon or an advertisement—as soon as she tries to figure out what's going on, she's reading. Shakespeare reminds us that all the world's a stage; but it's also a book.

As you know, I've been making frequent connections all along between the print world and the world of nonprint experiences that your child tries to read (that word again!) each day. In this chapter I want to concentrate on some of the representational forms that youngsters meet regularly in their lives. By *representational* I mean all those elements that stand for, or represent, experience. I mean words and sentences here, of course—our language represents experience so that others can perceive it in the way we do. But I also mean images, such as drawings, illustrations, photographs, cartoons, tables, graphs, and charts—the visual aids that interact with printed language (or replace it) to convey meanings. You know the familiar contexts in which these interactions occur: package covers, book covers, advertisements, recipes, maps, fix-it manuals, emergency instructions, corporate reports, instructions for assembling toys or appliances. It's a much longer list than I have here.

Page 113 shows just one example, an airline's emergency escape card:

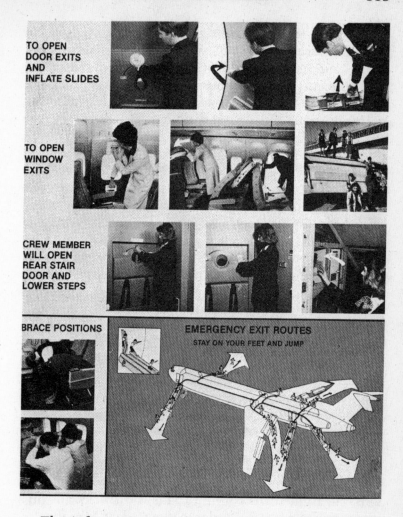

The information is critical—everyone on the plane must understand what to do in case of emergency. But note how few words appear. The explicit photographs and drawings carry the message's essence. You have to "read" the visuals to know what to do.

On their own, many of the visual forms I've mentioned express complex meanings quite independent of any accompanying language. As language props, on the other hand, they clarify and supplement meanings we derive from the words and sentences surrounding the images. I'm especially interested in the way that language and visuals interrelate in print, points at which the two forms work together in the universe of our reading experiences. Calling attention to these meeting points in your child's reading can help her develop advanced skills as a reader.

Why do communicators use visuals? Cynics point to the flood of visuals as further evidence of our nation's growing illiteracy. People can't read, so show them pictures. If you strip away the cynicism, you will find some truth here. Continuing in its great tradition as a magnet for the world's immigrants, our society draws thousands of non-English speakers and readers every year. If we have to communicate with those who do not know the culture's dominant language well, we need methods other than prose sentences alone to convey information. To accommodate waves of travelers with limited English proficiency who rode New York City subways early in the century, transport planners marked train stops with tile drawings as well as English words all along the line.

Societies everywhere turn to visual aids in order to make information known quickly to a heterogeneous population. Think of the complex details conveyed by road signs through a variety of symbols and illustrations that can work independently of words. Along highways you can see signs without words that tell you of steep hills, no right turn, curving roads, no trucks allowed, throw trash here, no bicycles, cattle or deer crossings.

An interesting example of word and visual working in tandem almost to the point of redundancy is the stop sign. With the word for STOP in white letters superimposed on a red octagon, the stop sign is one symbol in which word and visual convey meaning together, and one in which the word is almost extraneous once you know what the red octagon stands for. If you don't understand the Spanish word PARE, for example, the familiar red and white eight-sided sign in Puerto Rico tells you what you must do. (Of course, you have to know what the sign means in your own culture in order to make the mental leap.)

In most airports, train stations, and public places throughout the world we can determine how to find lavatories, eating places, bars, water fountains, and newspapers from visual clues on signs containing familiar illustrations: a simply-drawn figure in a skirt represents a women's room, a figure in trousers represents a men's room, a knife and fork represent a restaurant, and so on.

So in one sense, familiar visual elements are like mathematical symbols and can convey information unbound to a particular society's written or spoken system of communication. When your child examines and comprehends the message of a visual communication, he's applying reading skills. One of our long range goals,

of course, is to move him to use those skills consistently in investigating pages of print.

Other than to convey meanings without heavy reliance on words, visuals have a variety of other uses as well. Sometimes we can understand a complicated written point more clearly if we see a picture or a drawing. Illustrations are especially helpful when we're trying to learn how to do or make or assemble something. If you've ever tried to put together a baby's crib or to make a model ship or to construct a headboard, you know how valuable an illustration can be. When you have to understand data, visual aids like charts, graphs, and tables can summarize complex material in a comprehensible format. Sentences to present information provided by visual data often can be interminable and tedious. Add to all these the society's conviction that pictures say more than words in much less time and space, and you can understand the ubiquity of visual aids in communication.

In early stages of language development your child relied very heavily on visual clues to learn reading. He discovered that golden arches mean McDonald's, that a white "Q" on a blue box means Q-Tips brand cotton swabs, that the white letters "M & Ms" on a brown cellophane package means yummy chocolate buttons in red and yellow and green. On the street corner he would look at the red and white octagon and at the age of two or three would read the word *stop*—that's the moment at which you knew you had a genius living with you!

The truth is (not to denigrate your little genius, of course) that your youngster was not reading words or letters as much as the total environmental context. In the early stages of reading development, the colors and shapes of the letters and the format of the message are just as important as the letters themselves. One 1980 study showed that children misread words placed in a familiar visual context; that is, the context ruled the way kids read the words. For example, if you wrote the word

McDonald's in the familiar logo for Coke—white scripted letters on a red background—your child would read *McDonald's* as *Coca-Cola*.

I'm telling you all this to remind you of how important visual elements are in reading. As your youngster advances through the early grades, and books become richer and richer with words, the words do not replace visual elements completely. Flip through your child's third-grade social studies book, fourth-grade reader, fifth-grade science text and you'll see a bounty of photographs, drawings, illustrations, charts, and tables. But despite this, and for reasons I haven't quite figured out, kids often neglect visual aids as they read. Perhaps it's the pressure placed on them to extract meaning from words and sentences, perhaps it's teacher's lack of attention in the classroom to the communicative power of visuals—in any case, children regularly ignore the visual accompaniments to prose. As a result, they block off pathways to understanding. One of the most important helps you can give your child is to get him to use visual aids whenever they appear in a reading selection.

This list of pointers will help you develop strategies you can use at home for your developing young reader. Talk with your child about them.

How to Use Visual Aids to Help You Understand What You Read

- *Do not ignore visual aids.* Many inexperienced readers think that pictures, charts, or other illustrations are merely decorative and, as a result, do not look at the visual aids carefully. But if you skip over an illustration, you might be skipping a piece of information that is important for understanding what you are reading.
- *Read carefully the captions, titles, or notes that*

help explain the illustrations. A caption is an explanation in words for a picture. Often a group of words or a sentence or two will tell why the illustration is important. In newspapers, photographs usually have captions that name the people in the picture and that often give other information as well. Captions and titles for charts, graphs, and tables often highlight the main point of a drawing. In addition, charts and graphs often include notes to explain what certain figures and symbols mean. Look at those notes carefully.

- *Try to connect the words that you are reading with the illustrations.* You may look at the picture before you read, or you may read and then study the picture. However, when an illustration appears with a writing selection, readers most often use the words and pictures together. You read a few paragraphs and then you examine the illustration to connect it to what you've read so far. Then you continue reading, returning now and then to the illustration. The point is to try to put together the picture with the sentences. Ask yourself questions. What is this picture showing me? What does the picture have to do with what I'm reading? Why has the writer included the picture? What does the picture tell that the words do not?

- *State visual information in your own words.* Illustrations do give information. Try to state that information in your own words. A graph or a chart, for example, puts information in visual terms. This makes it easier to look at lots of data quickly. From the information you should make comparisons and should state them in your own words. Otherwise, you can miss the point of the graph or chart.

Intersections: Words and Pictures

You've already seen in the last chapter how a picture or an illustration discussed prior to reading can help your child develop insights about the selection and can till her mental soil so that it's ready for sowing written ideas. But let's spend a moment or two exploring the interaction of words and pictures. First, we'll examine a magazine advertisement; and then we'll look at some of the formats that your child will face in his school reading.

Isn't this a delightful ad? Its primary target is not children—I don't think you'd find this in the "Kidsday" section of your local newspaper or in *Boy's Life*. It aims at the parents of kids (like mine) who adore dinosaurs. Nevertheless, from the whimsical cartoon and the level

Field Museum of Natural History

Caution: Dinosaurs on the Loose!

During Dinosaur Days

Every weekend in October is filled with dinosaur fun for all ages. See funny plays about silly dinosaurs. Make dinosaur hats and masks to wear. Enjoy dinosaur stories, films, crafts, and tons more.

It's all FREE with Museum admission. For details, call (312)322-8854.

Dinosaur Days - a prehistoric adventure the whole family will enjoy.

Field Museum of Natural History
Roosevelt Road at Lake Shore Drive
Chicago, IL 60605

Illustration by Tamar Rosenthal

of language, children are not excluded from the intended audience.

As a means of helping your child explore visuals and their relation to written language, this ad is a terrific starting point. What does your child think is the main point of the ad? What does she think the headline "Caution: Dinosaurs on the Loose!" means? You do have to consider the subtlety of the message. Children are very literal and the caption about dinosaurs on the loose can be puzzling unless you guide your child to see that the cartoon figures provide a humorous context. There are no real dinosaurs on the loose here. Ideas about dinosaurs are perhaps on the loose but not the extinct creatures themselves. Talk with your child about why the dinosaurs in the illustration are on a scooter. (Being on a scooter is being on the loose in a very contemporary sense.) Connect the headline and the drawing, along with the short paragraph. Spend time discussing vocabulary like *crafts* and *prehistoric*. See if your child can determine what *Dinosaur Days* refers to. As I've said many times, the world of advertising is very accessible to children, and we often miss opportunities for building reading skills because we pay too little attention to the ads that surround us.

Look now at this page (on page 121) from the first chapter of a sixth-grade science book.

This page helps me make a significant point. Ignoring the visual elements here robs a reader of essential information. In fact, many children would simply turn the page after they read the two prose paragraphs, giving perhaps only a cursory glance to the drawings. The one- or two-word labels above the illustrations shown in test tubes and beakers name categories of materials created through the wonders of chemistry. Yet even more than the paragraphs, the illustrations make those categories concrete with a wide range of products children can recognize easily. Without looking at the pictures and

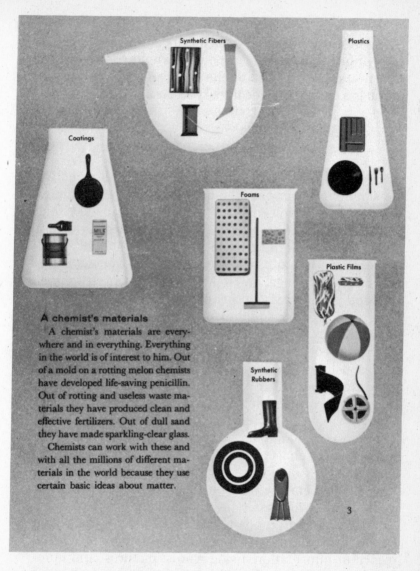

A chemist's materials

A chemist's materials are everywhere and in everything. Everything in the world is of interest to him. Out of a mold on a rotting melon chemists have developed life-saving penicillin. Out of rotting and useless waste materials they have produced clean and effective fertilizers. Out of dull sand they have made sparkling-clear glass.

Chemists can work with these and with all the millions of different materials in the world because they use certain basic ideas about matter.

integrating them mentally into the text discussion, a sixth-grader easily can miss the idea that as further evidence of their great contribution to humanity, chemists and chemistry bring us nylon stockings, beach balls, tires, records, synthetic sponge mops, and coated pans.

Further, examining the pictures helps us define terms in those labels. "Synthetic fibers," "plastic films," "coatings"—these are not familiar words to many eleven-year-olds, and using the illustrations to define the terms is a significant vocabulary-learning activity.

Being Graphic

The issue of visual aids is extremely important when we consider charts, graphs, and tables, key elements in presenting complex information in readable form. Key, that is, if the reader reads them! Think of your own reading habits: When was the last time you stopped to weigh the meanings in a graph, chart, or table that you saw in a newspaper or magazine? I'll bet that you pretty much ignored the attractive graphics some young artist labored to produce so that you could easily comprehend statistical data. I blame some of this graph- and table-phobia on poor school instruction. Teachers through the grades just don't take enough time to show children how to extract concepts from word and picture intersections. Once again, we see another area in which mom and dad can contribute to a child's critical reading skills. When your ten-year old is scratching his head over a social studies text, a chart or graph or table may not be too far away!

Let's concentrate here on those visually based print elements that youngsters face frequently in school readings. Charts and graphs reveal their meanings through direct word and picture interactions. A chart is a visual record of information, using words, pictures, and numbers. A graph, too, provides information visually, but with the explicit purpose of relating facts to each other. Bar graphs, line graphs, and circle graphs always make their points through visual comparison and contrast. Tables usually provide columns of information, words and numbers, using the visual layout of grouped lists without much further reliance on other pictorial aids.

Have a look now at a piece of what should be a familiar resource in many American homes, the newspaper *USA Today*. In a feature called "USA Snapshots: A look at statistics that shape the nation" the newspaper regularly provides unusual data in whimsical, cartoon-based charts and graphs, and those can help you influence your child's visual and verbal literacy. Look at the illustration below.

To determine the meanings in this bar graph, kids

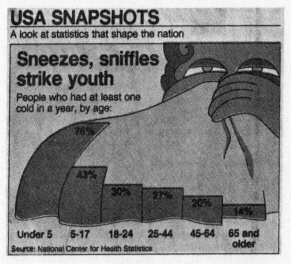

By Elys McLean-Ibrahim, USA TODAY

.must draw upon pictures, words, and symbols. Certainly the main idea of the graph is rooted in these combined elements. The graph is trying to compare the number of colds that people get in various age groups. Although the headline and the subhead make a good part of the point, journalistic style compresses the meaning dramatically, and readers must tease out the range of information provided. Only when we examine the stylized bar graphs do we see the scope of potential issues.

You can use the visual information to help your child explore vocabulary, too. How does your son or daughter define *sniffles?* The cartoon character offers clues. In a discussion on words used here, you might provide choices: are sniffles coughs? noisy breathing through the nose? young people's diseases? From the handkerchief, the covered nose, the fingers in a familiar position, youngsters can draw on the visual meanings to supplement what they know from the words and can guess reasonably at the definition. As another example, anyone unfamiliar with the word *statistics* would be wise to use the visual context clues here as well as the verbal.

As with most graphs, to understand meanings we must create linguistic equivalents of the illustrations, the symbolic language of numbers, and the words connected to them. When we read a paragraph, words on the page provide the linguistic basis for our understanding. For graphs and other kinds of visual-verbal entities, on the other hand, readers must formulate meanings through their own innate language and syntax. Certainly we draw upon any words and concepts that appear along with the visual. Yet, to solidify meaning in our minds (and to convey it to others) we must construct sentences on our own. In reading visual-verbal entities we make sentences in the manner of writers. Our own language must say what the piece seems to be saying.

Back to the graph we're examining: You need to help your child create sentences that state the meanings literally "illustrated" by the visual message and its interplay with the symbolic (mathematical) and linguistic notations. You need to help your child state the comparisons and contrasts that the various bars are projecting. As I said before, words clearly are not the primary mode of communication here. Yet readers must use words to indicate the various meanings offered in the graph.

Let's start easy, looking at data before we make comparisons. Can your child say, for example, that thirty percent of people more than eighteen years old but less than twenty-five years old had at least one cold in a year? (A quick math review may be in order. *Percent* means "out of a hundred." Thirty percent means thirty out of a hundred, which can be reduced to three out of ten.) If that statement, *thirty percent of those over eighteen but less than twenty-five had at least one cold in a year,* one of the relatively straightforward messages here, seems patently simple to construct from the information, consider the many props that beginning readers must use to develop it: the visual representation of the third bar from the left; the numbers in it and below it; the chart's headline and subhead—and, of course, your child's own linguistic and syntactic equipment.

To see the more sophisticated messages here, kids must learn to look at the sweep of information presented by the chart and not just at isolated elements. Higher-level meanings emerge when we consider the bars contrastively—what they mean individually and in relation to each other. With guidance, your son or daughter should be able to draw conclusions like these, for example:

- As people grow older, they get fewer colds in a year.
- Colds generally strike people at different rates, based on age.
- Between the ages of 18 and 44, people have about the same chance of getting a cold in a year.

There are others, of course. The point here is that with a minimum of apparent language in the graph, youngsters nonetheless must construct meanings with their own language and from a range of visual and verbal elements. By talking about the elements and helping your child see relations among them, you contribute markedly to your son or daughter's growth as a reader.

Here's a bar graph from a third-grade social studies book. Using very little language, the graph provides population data for five major American cities.

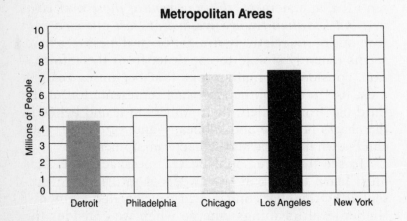

Metropolitan Areas

As you examine this graph with your child, here are some questions you should be able to answer together:

- What is this graph trying to show?
- What is a metropolitan area?
- What is the population in millions of people for each of the cities named here?
- Which area is the smallest? the largest?
- Which is larger, Chicago or Los Angeles?
- Which is smaller, Detroit or Philadelphia?
- Approximately how many people would Detroit have to add in order to be as large as Chicago? New York?

From the same book, I have reproduced below a chart that a nine- or ten-year-old is expected to use on his or her own and answer various questions. Here the information is not as visual as it is in the graphs we considered.

Businesses	Employees	Goods	Services
Telephone Company	786	Telephones	Phone calls; repairs
Power Company	1,009		Electricity and gas
Shoe Store	532	Shoes and boots	
Clothing Store	24	Clothing	
Supermarkets	1,112	Food	
Dairy Farms	342	Milk	
Construction Company	844	Housing	
Bus Company	203		Transportation

1. Which business has the greatest number of employees?
2. What services does the Power Company provide?
3. Which business repairs telephones?
4. Which business helps the people meet their need for shelter?
5. Which two businesses help the people meet their need for clothing?
6. Which two businesses help the people meet their need for food?
7. Which business helps the people go from one place to another?

In the graph on metropolitan areas, for instance, you didn't have to look at the actual numbers to draw conclusions. You could tell from the length of the bars just which cities had high population densities, which had low ones, and how they all compared to each other.

In the chart, however, although the information is visual, the visual elements do not provide comparisons.

You have to reach them on your own. Without your help, your child easily could flounder in interpreting the information and in using it to answer the questions. Assure that your child knows to read the information straight across the line; to use the column headings to give meaning to the words and numbers; to interpret the blank spaces; and, perhaps most intellectually challenging, to compare and contrast the information provided for the various businesses. You can tell from the questions that that particular skill is critical. Unlike a graph, no visual clues here relate the data. You need to assess the numbers and to determine, say, that the clothing store has the fewest workers, that two businesses offer no goods, that the power company employs about twice as many people as the shoe store.

In this table from a fourth-grade science book, all the information is numerical, other than the names of the planets, the column headings, and the words *days*

THE INNER PLANETS					
Planet	Average distance from sun (in millions of km)	Diameter (in km)	Length of year (in Earth time)	Length of day (in Earth Time)	Number of known Moons
Mercury	58	4,880	88 days	176 days	0
Venus	108	12,100	225 days	116.7 days	0
Earth	150	12,756	365 days	24 hours	1
Mars	228	6,784	687 days	24.6 hours	2

and *hours*. Instructions tell children to use the table to compare the inner planets. Several questions accompany the table: Which is the smallest planet? Which planet has the longest day? the shortest year? How much farther from the sun is Mars than Mercury? How much longer is a year on Earth than a year on Venus? Scale drawings at page bottom help children answer the first question; readers must use the table to frame responses for the others.

No easy task for a fourth-grader, wouldn't you agree? Graphs might have presented some of the information more clearly, but graphing all the comparative and contrastive data here might clutter and complicate the visual presentation. The table permits clustering of much information, but we have to make sense of it on our own.

Help your child understand the way tables work and remove some of the mystery provided by this compact box of information. Point out the column heads and explore their meanings. Help your youngster form the necessary sentences for several items straight across a line before setting her on her own. For example, for the second line down, your child should be able to say and understand that Venus is 108 million kilometers from the sun; that its diameter is 12,100 kilometers; that in the earth's time system, Venus' year length is only 225 days but that *one* of its days is as long as 116.7 days on the Earth; and that it has no moons. Your child may find some of these statements difficult to construct, and you'll need to work with her in constructing them.

After you read across the lines with your youngster, teasing out interpretive statements for the data, encourage her to make the comparisons that the questions demand. Raise other questions to lay information side by side. Don't shy away from making comparisons: it's one of the essential skills for critical reading and thinking. Investigating a table like this one will give your child insights for studying tables on her own.

Activities in which you help your child "read" both visual and combined visual and verbal entities from newspapers, magazines, and textbooks should be a regular feature of your home reading program. It's another phase in your effort to prepare your young readers for the demands of literate citizenry.

7

The Reading–Writing Connection

In 1940, the then-chairman of the editorial board of the *Encyclopaedia Britannica*, Mortimer J. Adler, wrote an article called "How to Mark a Book" for the *Saturday Review of Literature*. Adler asserted for his adult readers what must sound clearly like heresy to parents of young children. Owning a book fully, he said in absolutely timeless advice, "comes only when you have made it part of yourself, and the best way to make yourself a part of it is by writing in it."

I can see you cringing. Write in this expensive, lovely book I bought Leslie at birthday time? Nothing doing.

Adler pointed out that our worship of books on this level—physical objects to be revered and respected—is misguided. We love the thing, "the craft of the printer," as opposed to what it contains, "the genius of the author." Owning a book and simply placing it on the shelf means only that we have the book in our library. Truly owning a book means that we have it in our souls.

Now of course we don't write in books we don't own. Books we borrow from friends or from the library or from the school classroom must stay intact for others to use later on. But your child can learn that lesson at any age—a lesson I'm sure that you try to teach regularly. Yet, you must temper your proscription. "Don't write in this book" you want to reserve for books your child does not own. "Please write in this book!" should be your plea for any volume in your youngster's home library.

Why? As Adler wisely pointed out more than fifty years ago, reading a book should be a conversation between the reader and the writer. Good readers question what they find in books; they challenge what they read; and marking up a book is a way of recording the dialogue between the parties.

You really do know this, don't you, from your own days in school when you attacked review books or texts themselves or photocopies of magazine articles with much underlining, marginal comments, or highlighting. Let's start our youngsters off early in this wonderful conversational activity between the writer and the reader.

Yes, I Said Write in Your Books

I want you to encourage your child to read with a pencil in hand. You can suggest that your nine- or ten-year-old identify the words or sentences that he likes most, misunderstands, or disagrees with.

If you've made your child sensitive to the thrills of the magic kingdom of words (see Chapter 3)—imagery, sensory details, and figurative language—what better way to have your youngster connect with these essential concepts than by asking him to point out the word pictures from the story books and young readers' novels that register on his mind and emotions. Kids love the new highlighting pens, now in fluorescent pinks and blues, so much more dazzling than the old yellows I used years ago. Highlighting pens allow you to smear ink over sentences and still read the words beneath. Or try simple underlining strategies; a line or two drawn under a delightful image or interesting word or thoughtful sentence; a penciled circle around a key thought; vertical lines or asterisks or check marks or *X*'s in the left or right margins. Also, words and questions written in the margins—top, bottom, sides—serve as excellent talk points and memory prods when your child returns to examine the pages or chapters she loves or simply to talk with you about what she's read.

For informational texts—nonfiction books that provide facts and explanations—little is as useful for organizing details and identifying data than a child's markings on a page. I regret that our current system of using textbooks over and over in schools cuts a child off from so valuable a learning resource as writing notes and comments in the major books she uses daily. Nonetheless, we have to be good citizens and zealously guard the rights of future users by preventing our youngsters from marking up borrowed books. Yet home schooling parents often have to buy books to supplement the curriculum, and these are ripe territory for your child's handwritten words, markings, and comments. Those of you with children in school will often purchase from the bookstore biographies and autobiographies as well as nonfiction works—perhaps Brenda Walpole's delightful *175 Science Experiments to Amuse and Amaze Your Friends* or Russell Freedman's richly informative *Buffalo Hunt* or Franklyn N. Branley's vivid *Eclipse: Darkness in Daytime* (see Chapter 10 for publishing information and summaries)—and you want to encourage your sons and daughters to write in these books.

Let's look at a couple of paragraphs that open Chapter One of James Howe's *Morgan's Zoo*. Note how Sophie, a nine-year-old reader interacts with the text through a variety of pencil strategies.

ON SUNDAY AFTERNOONS the zoo was bustling. Fathers with their sleeves rolled up and jackets draped over their arms bought brightly colored balloons from the balloon man, <u>two for a nickel</u>, and presented them with the ?(admonition) to hold them tight to their wide-eyed children. Laughing mothers <u>pointed out the antics of monkeys who</u> ?(gamboled) and chattered and who, when they stopped to look out through the bars of their cages, screeched in a way that seemed to small ears to ?(fracture) and echo the sound of a mother's laugh. The children dashed ahead, leaving their parents calling out their names, anxious to see once again the Bengal tiger who had so resisted capture, the story was told, that he'd decorated more than one adventurer with stripes to match his own.

For many families, for most families living nearby, a summer without frequent visits to the Chelsea Park Zoo was as unthinkable as a summer without lemonade. It was just something families did together, like bowing their heads for grace before each meal and listening to the radio before they went to bed each night. Oh, it's true that sometimes on a Monday or a Wednesday or a Thursday, the children might put down their stickball bats and run off together to the zoo to

[margin annotations: "Two for a nickel? When was this", "Was he hurt? How do they catch tigers?", "We go to the zoo too."]

become jungle explorers hunting down lions or elephants or crocodiles. Or they might wander by alone on their way home from a piano lesson or a swim in the municipal pool to say hello to their favorite animal, the one who had become their special friend. But for the most part the zoo was a family place, and Sunday afternoon was the family time.

And for the animals . . . well, for the animals, the zoo was a family place, too. They saw themselves and all the people who worked there as one big family. And the people who came to. . . .

Do you see, first, how Sophie's questions reflect an interaction with the text, an interaction that otherwise might escape notice or, worse, might not even occur without a book-marking strategy? As children respond to the written word, many questions arise that, without outlet, can simply evaporate as reading proceeds. Writing questions and comments beside the words that stimulate reaction allow the two voices, the child reader's and the author's, to sing side by side.

Notice the first questions, an invitation to parent and child to discuss the setting of the book. When does your child think the story took place? What other hints in these early paragraphs suggest a possible time frame? (Consider the "listening to the radio" sentence in paragraph 3.)

Sophie's questions beside the first paragraph provide a good opportunity to talk also about *inference*, a reading strategy we'll explore in detail in the next chapter. Sophie is adept at using hints in the text to supply information not directly stated and has assumed, quite correctly, that the author, James Howe, is writing about a different time period from today's. The "two for a nickel" price tag on balloons that could cost forty or fifty times as much at a zoo in the late 1990s is a clue to the young reader about when events in the story may have taken place.

The questions Sophie raises about the tiger's capture provide excellent conversational touchstones and, perhaps, suggest a trip to the library to obtain more information from books or magazines (*Ranger Rick?*) or, perhaps, a National Geographics video. When she writes "We go to the zoo too," our children's home program of interaction with text through writing reaches its most significant point: Sophie has made the events in the story part of her own life by connecting them to her personal experience.

You should also note the checkmarks over words—Sophie liked the sound of those verbs—and the circled words with question marks next to them—Sophie's way of indicating she didn't know what these words mean exactly. But no rush to the dictionary here! Sophie can extract enough important information from the paragraphs without knowing the precise definitions of the words *admonition* and *gamboled* and the unexpected use of *fracture*. After you and your child talk about possible meanings to be derived directly from the text, you can look up the words later, if you wish, as a reinforcing activity that won't interrupt the reader's flow. (See "Context Leads the Way" in Chapter 2.)

How to Help Your Child Mark Up a Book

- Remember: We write only in books that belong to us. Putting pencil or pen to a school or library book or to a book borrowed from a friend is strictly forbidden. Explain to your child that marking up a book is highly personal and that our underlining or marginal comments can easily distract another reader.

- Help your child devise a flexible system by pointing out all the possible options named above: high-lighting, underlining, and putting asterisks, circles, brackets, checkmarks, vertical lines, *X*'s, and so on, in the margins.

- Support a conversation between child and author by encouraging your youngster to write comments in the margins. Questions and comments your child writes in the margins at the moment the author's ideas stimulate thought show a lively, engaged reader well on the road to critical thinking.

- Show your child how to mark up a book. Return to one of your old textbooks or another book you wrote all over to help you understand material. Perhaps a novel or biography or nonfiction work is holding your attention; if you're not a regular book marker, get started now and show your child how you're doing it. Your example is the best way to teach, as always. Or you might want to look together at the excerpt from *Morgan's Zoo* to illustrate what underlining, marginal symbols, and comments look like when produced by an aware reader.

Keeping a Reading Journal

If your youngster is getting appropriate instruction in writing, she already knows the value of making entries in a journal. An informal record of a child's musings about events or ideas that arise during the day, the journal is an excellent resource for topic ideas when a formal writing assignment rears up. A quick run through the journal reminds your youngster of thoughts that challenged her, and she can use these as springboards for drafting a paragraph or an essay for school. The journal provides an open territory for registering ideas, impressions, and insights.

A good source of inspiration for writing, the journal has other applications as well, particularly as an aid to critical thinking about books. A journal gives your child more space than the margins of a text in which to record thoughts, questions, and ideas, written in your youngster's hand and stimulated by the words and sentences on the page. The extra space for writing afforded by a journal allows your child to connect the words she reads with features of her life and inner world.

And that's the main point here. Critical thinking about books, at one of its most basic levels, is discovering personal meanings. The child who matures into an avid, discriminating reader learns to make the words he reads part of his life—what he thinks, what he feels, what he knows. Strong readers stop regularly throughout a book to ask, "What does this mean to me? How do my thoughts and experiences relate to what's on this page?" And successful readers know that the real dynamics in reading a book often lie in challenging the writer—in not accepting every word and idea as absolutely true simply because they appear in print. Many young people take all print as gospel, confusing ink and truth. Of course, many adults, too, accept uncritically what they read. The fool's gold of accepted assertions sparkles deceptively throughout human history. Remember Ptolemy? Holocaust denial literature? Linkages between intelligence and race? Critical thinkers have attacked many of these notions, but, teeth at the throat, they hang on, winning adherents who will not be confused by facts. You want your child to bring a healthy skepticism to what she reads and to get her to see that questioning, interpreting, and personalizing words in a book move us to higher and higher levels of understanding.

Toward that noble end you want to encourage your child to keep a notebook as a reading journal. Nothing fussy: one of those lined, black-and-white, marble-patterned composition books or simply some lined pages in a looseleaf. As your youngster reads novels, stories, biographies, nonfiction, newspaper articles, essays—anything of interest and challenge—suggest that she record her personal thoughts about what she's reading. Discourage any attention to grammar or spelling. As your youngster records impressions about the ideas she discovers, urge her to follow through on her thinking. Why does she feel the way she does about a statement or an event in the text? What emotions or experiences lie behind the impression she has recorded on her journal page?

A very effective reading journal activity is to ask your child to copy out on the left side of a blank journal page brief passages that stimulate him from the book he's reading; on the facing page, he should write his reactions, thoughts, and analyses of the passages. When he finishes the book—or several books—he'll have not only a ledger of his personal thoughts but also a collection of intellectually challenging statements drawn from the work. This activity generates a recorded conversation between reader and writer, a conversation that helps your budding reader explore ideas openly.

How can you stimulate creative, critical thinking about a book through journal entry activities? Help your child keep in mind these questions.

Questions to Address in a Reading Journal

- What does the book title or chapter or section title make you think about?
- How do you feel about the subject of the book?

What knowledge do you have about the topic or closely related topics?

- What do you think about the people portrayed in the reading? Do you like them? Do you understand their motives and actions? Would you like to meet these people? Why or why not?
- What events and experiences in your life are similar to or different from the incidents represented in the book?
- What scenes and places in the book remind you of what you yourself have seen at home, in school, in your neighborhood—anywhere, really?
- How do your own opinions on the topic match the writer's opinions? Where do you agree? disagree? How would other people you know feel about the writer's opinions or ideas?
- Where and how has the writer changed your mind about something, or at least made you acknowledge another reasonable point of view?
- If you could meet the writer face-to-face, what questions would you want to ask? What further information would you like to have?

Here are both a short selection from a history book and the reading journal entry it stimulated from a fifth-grader:

In the southwestern desert in the late 1840s, the U.S. Cavalry needed an animal capable of covering vast distances with little need for food or water. Major Henry Constantine Wayne, a cavalry officer, decided that the perfect solution was a camel. He proceeded to read everything he could on the subject of camels, what breeds there were, their habits and history. He also compared the climates of the American southwest and the Middle East, finding that they were very similar.

His studies finished, Major Wayne then wrote a formal proposal to the War Department in Washington. Eventually his plan was read by Senator Jefferson Davis who, as a student of history, was well acquainted with the role camels had played in the life of the Middle East. It took Davis and Wayne nearly five years to get Congress to see the wisdom of using camels in the west, and by the time they did, despite the fact that camels proved to be every bit as useful as Wayne said they would be, the transcontinental railway soon made camels obsolete.

—*Gerald Carson*

Its really amazing to think how america would be different if camels had become part of the old west. Imagine clint Eastwood or Kevin Kotsner bouncing around on a camel, showing what the West looked like in the movies it really makes you think that the people who lived back then really were building a new world that might have turned out different from what we see on television if one idea was excepted and not another. My uncle once told me that in the army they once tried to use zebras for awhile, but they were too wild to be usefull. I thought he was kidding but maybe he was right. I should ask my teacher or look it up somewhere. Where?

Why did it take five years for Congress to see the wisdom of using camels? How long does it take today to get someone in gov't to listen to a good idea?

You can see how this child interacts thoughtfully with the text by imagining, if only superficially at the moment, a different course of history based on the camel's presence in the American desert. Note how she links the author's ideas with information in her world—actors in movie westerns. Also note at the end of the entry the unintentionally innocent questions about government responsiveness! With these personal reactions to a book, parent and child will have much to talk about.

I also want you to acknowledge the various writing errors in this journal entry, none of which is consequential. Yes, we see run-on sentences, misspellings, incorrect capitalization, wrong word use. But the journal is a private document that is not meant to be shared publicly. And unless your child wants to use a journal entry as the basis of a formal writing activity, ultimately for public scrutiny, pay no attention to correctness! If your son or daughter asks about spelling, grammar, or punctuation, that's a different matter. Take time to explain. But otherwise, your main interest in helping motivate journal writing is to have your child release thoughts and feelings about a book, and nothing will impede the natural flow of ideas more than a hysteria about correctness.

Read On, Write On

I can't reinforce enough the interconnections between reading and writing. John Henry Martin, a brilliant if eccentric school administrator who died just a few years ago, developed a computer program for IBM called *Writing to Read*; the fundamental approach of the program is having very young children learn to read by composing sentences and stories on the computer without regard to orthography. Martin argued that *Writing to Read* kids, particularly urban minority youngsters, made dramatic strides in comprehension and language mastery. Accepted and used in a number of school districts over the country, the program has some serious flaws, and detractors question the validity of some of the research data on which it is based. Nevertheless, Martin made writing the linchpin of reading instruction, and if nothing else, his systematic use of writing as part of reading development is food for thought for all parents who want to help their youngsters succeed.

Sweeping through the instructional reading forest like brushfire these days is the concept of whole language, which, as you saw in Chapter 2, attacks basal readers as synthetic, condemns phonics as atomistic, and insists on real literature experiences for youngsters exclusively through reading real books. Critics have raised many questions about whether whole language should be a child's exclusive reading experience and whether whole language learning can adversely affect children's performance on conventional testing instruments. Nevertheless, the consensus among teachers is that whole language is a highly successful way of approaching reading instruction. Many schools and school districts across the country have declared themselves whole language institutions, and teachers everywhere are converting their instructional programs to suit whole language requirements.

A fundamental feature of the whole language program is the use of regular writing activities both before and after reading so that children can capture their thoughts and feelings in permanent form and can talk to themselves and book authors about ideas that emerge on the page. Largely rejecting short-answer, multiple-choice questioning techniques, whole language teachers see writing as a major ally in the reading development process.

In my book *Any Child Can Write* I lay out a comprehensive program for home writing instruction that can easily be managed at home by busy parents. Here, I want you to think of all the possible writing activities that might grow out of a book your child reads with your support at home:

> Write a letter to the author or publisher.
> Write a letter about the book to a friend or relative.
> Write a playlet from the book with speaking parts for Mom, Dad, and child.
> Draw a picture suggested by the book, and in a sentence or two identify the picture.
> Write a new ending for the book.
> Write a paragraph explaining what you liked or didn't like about the book.
> Design a new cover for the book and write a blurb for the back jacket flap or back cover.

As you can see, I'm not advocating those dreary "book report" ideas that have tortured generations of children with their prescriptive headings: plot, setting, characters, theme, etc., etc., etc. What better way to destroy a child's original thinking about a book and to reduce the author's story to a prosaic formula!

I'm recommending instead that through challenging activities at home you approach writing as a means of tapping into creative expression and, through self-reflection on a page about what a book means to your child, as a way to have him make a book his own.

Finding Secrets
INFERENCE

A colleague arrives at work one Monday morning at 9:30. She's usually there at 8:00 A.M., ahead of everyone else. She mumbles under her breath and shakes her head from side to side, biting her lip. She doesn't say "Hello" as she usually does, but instead, staring straight ahead, she storms past your desk. At her office she turns the knob roughly, throws open the door, and then slams it loudly behind her.

What's going on here? This is a classic bad mood scene, isn't it? No direct evidence, of course—your colleague doesn't *say* anything to you—but you can add up the pieces to figure out some important information for yourself. Clearly, she's angry or upset about something. To reach that judgment, you relied on what you saw and heard at the moment, but also on what you know about her usual behavior. No one had to tell you that she was furious. From her appearance, her actions, her body language, and her behavior, it was safe to *infer* that something irritated her. You were assessing the scene, and your natural ability to draw inferences fed you information that you needed in order to figure out her behavior.

Inference, Center Stage

What is *inference?* When we infer, we derive information by a complex process of reasoning that balances assumptions, induction and deduction, instinct, prior experience, perception, hunches—even, some believe, ESP. Many people define inference as reading between the lines. This definition, of course, is figurative. It says that being able to determine information in this way is like figuring out hidden meanings—beyond the apparent ideas expressed by words and sentences. More information resides on a page of text than what the lines of print say.

You can tell from this familiar metaphor—reading between the lines—that inference is usually intertwined with the reading process. In other words, we conceive of the act of inference as print-bound. Much of the essential meaning from a page does come to us as cues and clues in a writer's discourse. For example, we're constantly inferring information about scenes and characters as we dig into a novel or some other piece of fiction. We regularly plug in unwritten meanings that the book suggests to us. Similarly, as we read a nonfiction article in a newspaper or magazine, or as we read books about history, science, psychology—about any subject, really— we gather more from the text than the author states directly. I'll show some examples of this later on. Here, it's important to note that we make a transaction with print: Both what the writer says and what we *think* he says produce meaning. Using our own experiences as the springboard, we regularly dive into the uncharted sea of educated guesses.

Certainly inference is one of the essential skills that mark successful readers. A report recently published by the U.S. Department of Education's Office of Educational Research and Improvement insists that "Greater emphasis is needed on inductive reasoning and the power to generalize." The Educational Testing Service, who administers the Congressional study called the National Assessment of Educational Progress (NAEP), reports that children in grades four, seven and eleven at public and private schools "have particular difficulty with tasks that require them to elaborate upon and defend their evaluations and interpretations of what they have read." Without skill at reasoning inferentially from the printed page a child surrenders valued literacy skills.

But just as I asked you in the last chapter to think of reading in general as a broader, more encompassing skill than just deciphering meaning from page-bound words, I want you to see inference as more than a print-related skill.

I began this chapter with the familiar scene of Moody Molly to remind you how intimately you know and regularly engage inferential strategies. In adding up and assimilating details of the moment, in connecting it with prior experiences, you adduced information from your colleague's actions.

In making inferences, you've learned over the years how not to go too far beyond the information at hand. Otherwise your inferences might not be correct. For example, could you assume that the person I described was angry because she had had a fight with her son? Not at all. Nothing of what you saw or observed suggested that. On the other hand, you might have heard her mumble an angry remark to herself about her son as she passed. Or you might know for a fact that she fought with him often and that, when she did, her behavior resembled the behavior she displayed that morning. Then you might safely say to yourself, "Well, I guess she's been at it with Todd again!" The point, of course, is that you've learned that inferences must be based on both your own previous experiences and the moment's valid, available information, not simply on vague suspicions or wild guesses. Sometimes we're mistaken in inferring from a scene, but mostly we're on the mark.

Have you ever stopped to realize the countless inferential moments that fill our lives? We sense the signs of danger or safety as we cross a deserted city street late at night, we interpret the signals swiftly about remaining or fleeing when a strange character enters a confined public space, we adduce what we hope is an appropriate response to a questioner in a job interview—just to name a few. Most of these quick responses tap our abilities to infer.

Kids are just like us in relying regularly and instinctively upon inference to shape ideas about their surroundings. What child cannot use the skill to make meaning from the disjunctive sensory experiences of life? Infants, preschoolers, grade-school children—they are all well-tuned little inference machines, their gears grinding away regularly to unpuzzle a moment's experience. Your youngster knows how to "read" covert suggestions, to use whatever combination of logic, emotion, experience, instinct, and sentience is needed to illuminate meaning. Every time your child tries to figure out the best moment to ask a mercurial teacher when to go to the bathroom, or the appropriate context at home to beg you for Nintendo or some other costly toy, or the right language and behavior for asking neighbor Wallace for a big Girl Scout cookie order—in each of these cases inference underlies thought and action. Even a baby can pick up on your moods and respond to them. She uses your facial expressions, your sounds, your body language to infer your attitude and, quite unconsciously, reacts to it.

Of course, we don't know the origin of this priceless inference skill. Some people see inference as related exclusively to prior experiences. Certainly they contribute to our ability to use inferential reasoning. However, the process is much more complex than a one-to-one link with experience would allow.

The offbeat chemist-philosopher Michael Polanyi, who has proposed fascinating theories on how people achieve knowledge, insists on an incredible feature of human awareness that he calls *tacit knowing*. Certain knowledge inheres in us without our being able to tell how we reach it or what its parts are. "We can know more than we can tell," he says. For example, "we recognize the moods of the human face without being able to tell, except quite vaguely, by what signs we know it." For Polanyi, tacit thought "forms an indispensable part of all knowledge." We make discoveries, he continues, "by pursuing possibilities suggested by existing knowledge."

You probably have a hunch about what I'm getting at here. (You're operating in the tacit dimension now!) Your school-age child—your first-, third-, fifth-grader—has potent seeds of tacit knowing that you can nurture. Your youngster already knows how to use inference in everyday situations. As a parent, you want to highlight that skill, to celebrate it, and to help direct it at print situations. What I'm saying is that because your son or daughter already knows how to adduce information from the surrounding world, you can focus that skill on the words and sentences on a page. You're helping your child make discoveries by pursuing possibilities suggested in existing knowledge.

Thus, you're building on your child's strengths as an aware human being to empower him with literacy. Unfortunately, when teachers discover that kids of eight to eleven cannot use inferential skills in stories or essays, teachers perceive the instructional effort that ought to follow as *remedial*. It's the old pathological model of education again. Outmoded views of learning as an orderly accretion of skills through time and our rigid, institutional school systems brand such children as remedial, handicapped, disabled, or otherwise damaged. We're ministering to afflicted, as opposed to enabled, learners in such a model. Crazy, isn't it?

I'm directing you to see your youngster as an empowered learner. As a talented user of inference, he can, with your help, exercise the skill in the regular reading activities he faces in school and at home.

Looking at Inference with Your Child

Where do you begin? First, help your child articulate thoughts and ideas rooted in inference. What message does your youngster receive as he watches unfamiliar people at the movie house, in the library, at the supermarket? Observe a scene at MacDonald's—an altercation between a customer and one of the food servers, an obese man choosing carefully and deliberately at the salad bar, a four-year-old whining shrilly and pulling at his father's shirttails.

Talk about what you see. What information can your child adduce?

Who does she think started the argument? Why? What do you think led the customer to speak the way she did? How did the server answer her? Why do you think she answered that way instead of speaking more thoughtfully?

Why is that man eating salad, do you think? Why isn't he eating a double cheeseburger and fries? How do you think he feels watching what most other people are eating? Why doesn't he just forget his diet and enjoy himself?

Why is that child crying? Why doesn't he explain what he needs to his father? Why doesn't the father do what the child wants? How might you get the child to stop crying?

Focused moments in television shows also are rich sources of conversation that draws on inference. A vignette in a favorite half-hour situation comedy can stimulate dozens of questions and sustained interchange about people's motives and actions. Talking about familiar characters in children's shows similarly helps you stimulate inferential skills.

After focusing on these animated moments in real life or in media presentations, you want to highlight

more static representational forms as you move toward
considering inference in stories and text materials your
school-age child brings home each night. You saw in the
last chapter how important pictures and other visual
representations are in our print worlds. Using drawings,
paintings, or photographs, you can help your youngster
further tap her resources as a user of inference.

Look at this delightful picture of a school-age child
and see if you and your youngster can determine its central meaning. Inference plays an important part in our
understanding of the photograph.

Your son or daughter probably would cite the main
point here something like this: "A little boy in school is
counting on his fingers." How did your youngster know,
however, that the child was a boy? Certainly we don't
know for sure. Yet your child used tacit knowledge of
physiognomy as well as hair length and clothing ("*Spi-
derman*" on the T-shirt suggests—but does not guarantee—that the figure in the photograph is a boy) to make
a determination. How did he know that the child in the

photo was at school? Your son or daughter determined
the specifics of the scene through inference. Look at the
large institutional window and the chairs and desks set
up in the room. How did your child know that the figure
in the picture was counting instead of merely pointing
with his left hand and holding up his right hand, or simply looking at his fingers? Again, nothing captured with
certainty by the picture supplies the response. Your
child's use of tacit knowledge is a key to understanding
the photograph and its inferential meanings.

The immediate demands of real life scenes (like
those we considered at MacDonald's) stimulate needed
inferential skills for us to understand what we're observing. By raising questions with our children we're releas-
ing those inferential powers and stretching them as
much as we can. Unfortunately, with photographs and
other static visual images, it's easy to subdue our inferential powers. (You know how you yourself can flip past
a busy photo in the newspaper without digging in for
meanings.) Thus, you want to give your child lots of
practice in adducing information from a representational image. This practice will help in the reading of a
printed page later on.

I recommend that you explore photos, drawings, and
paintings in the books you read to and with your child. Ask
questions: What do you know about the person you see?
How can you tell? Why is the person doing what he's
doing? Where is the person? How do you know? When is
this happening? How do you know? We'll examine together
some concrete examples of how to do this later on.

A critical next step in highlighting the importance of
inference in determining meanings is to examine representational forms that combine both visual and verbal
elements on a page. Familiar items like cartoons and
advertisements build upon visual literacy and make the
leap into the symbolic entity of communication, written
language.

To understand what this cartoon means and to appreciate its humor, your child must rely on inference. He must use both visual and verbal cues. Here are some inference-based questions that you might pose.

Where does the scene take place? Well-dressed people sitting in a room and staring straight ahead, talk of prayer—these conditions imply a church setting as opposed to a movie house, say, or a classroom.

Why does the man make the comment to the child? We must infer his attitude about churchly behavior: People who pray should keep their eyes closed.

Why is he covering his mouth as he speaks? We infer that he wants no one but the child to hear him. From the implications of the scene, you see, we must reject other possible interpretations of his gesture that might suit other contexts—that the man has a cough or that he is merely stroking his face.

What does the child's question mean? We must infer that the man's eyes, too, were opened during the service, making him guilty of the same offence for which he criticizes the child. Determining that information from the child's comment accounts for the humor we respond to in "The Born Loser."

As you see, you can bring your youngster to a higher level of understanding through your questions and your linkages between the pictures and the words.

Putting the Plan in Action

Toward the goal of helping your youngsters apply inferential strategies at school, examine materials in popular
children's magazines, textbooks, and daily newspapers.

The next time you're in the dentist's or pediatrician's
office with your child, awaiting your turn with the doctor, reach for a copy of *Highlights for Children* and talk
about the always lively, always busy cover. To stimulate
inference skills, ask questions about motive and behavior. Try to determine why the children in the scene are
acting as they do. Define the setting, the time of year, the
time of day, if possible. In effect, you're asking your
youngsters to read between the lines—but here the lines
are people and features of the photo's visual landscape.
Here's one cover (page 154) from *Highlights* with some
questions that will engage inference.

- Where is this scene taking place? Is it a city scene
  or a country scene? How can you tell? What time
  of year is it? How do you know? Why are there so
  many children at the place? Which are the boy
  children? Which are the girls? How can you tell?
  For which ones can't you tell?
- Why is the hydrant (water pump) shooting out
  water?
- Why is the fire officer standing beside the pump?
  Why is he wearing boots? Why is he holding a
  wrench? Why is he smiling?
- Why is a boy sitting on the front steps? Why is he
  holding a basketball? Why is he holding a pair of
  sneakers? Why is there a child standing at the top
  of the steps? What does he have on his hand? in
  his hand? Why does he have those objects? Why
  isn't he outside with the other children? Why is
  one child who is wearing a bathing suit sitting at

the curb, holding a doll? Why isn't she doing what most of the other children are doing?

- Why are some children wearing bathing suits? Why are some children dressed in play clothes? Why are some children who are splashing about under the spray wearing play clothes instead of bathing suits? What do you think their parents may say when the children return home?

- Why is one woman standing at a window? What is she looking at? Who is next to her? Why aren't they outside in the water?
- One child is talking to the fire officer. Why? What do you think the child is saying?
- Why does the statement "Fun with a Purpose" appear on the cover? What does it mean? Who's having fun in the picture? What purpose does the fun serve? When have you ever had fun with a purpose?

Now look at this photograph from a fifth-grade geography book. The photo appears at the start of Chapter 27 called "Making the Most of Human Resources." Accompanying the picture is a caption "Skillful farming lets the Israelis raise crops in the midst of the desert." Your child might bring home such a textbook reading assignment, and you should be prepared to help him understand the chapter.

A first step toward that goal is helping your child

look at the photograph and use inference to flesh out meanings. You should know that in good textbooks, photos at chapter beginnings are more than just decorations. They are thought-teasers, and with careful examination they can open doors to critical thinking about the awaiting sentences and paragraphs. As I've already pointed out in Chapter 4, exploring ideas in a chapter or story *before reading it* will engage a child's thought and imagination, preparing her to deal with the information expressed in written language.

Use the photograph to stimulate your child to understand the chapter when she reads. Certainly the caption falls short in highlighting the scene's essential features, so there's not much there to go on. Ask your daughter what she thinks is happening in the photo. What does she think the point is? No doubt she'll see the sand and the rich patch of vegetation. Then ask these inference-rich questions.

- Why are these people growing food?
- What do you know about deserts?
- How is this an unusual scene?
- How do the farmers manage to grow the vegetables in the desert?
- What are the men at the boxes doing?
- What is the child doing? Is it a boy or a girl? How do you know? How do you think the child might be helping the farmers?
- What are the people in the fields doing? Why does one man have a white scarf about his head?
- What kinds of vegetables do you see? Why are the men placing the zucchini in the boxes? What will they do with the boxes?
- What does the title mean now that you've explored the photo? What does the caption mean?

Help your child derive answers to these questions. Fill in any blanks she may draw. The printed text material will expand the general notion of "making the most of human resources," but as you can see, the prose is rather skimpy.

Farmland from the Desert

Another country with few natural resources, but a rapidly growing economy, is the nation of Israel. The entire southern half of this small country is a desert, the Negev. Until about thirty years ago, very few people lived in this region. But the Israelis have built pipelines that carry water to the Negev, and each year more and more of the desert can be used for farming. Fruits and vegetables grown in the Negev supply much of Israel's food needs and are also sold in the produce markets of Europe and the United States. The exports help pay for the large amounts of equipment and raw materials that Israel imports for its growing industries. Like the Japanese, the Israelis have concentrated much of their effort on products that require technical skill. Important industries include food processing, cloth making, electronic equipment, and diamond cutting.

Nevertheless, your child will approach the concepts in the prose more securely because she has explored them visually, has connected them to her own thinking, and has used inferential reasoning to consider the issue's logical implications.

After you've examined visual, then visual and verbal materials, you should move next to print alone. Choose a simple prose paragraph like this one for which inference is critical to meaning.

After lunch Diane took her bike and sneaked quickly into the yard. She moved carefully to the plot of soil under the oak in back of the house as she checked to see that nobody watched her. She leaned her bicycle against the tree and bent down. All around dark clouds rumbled noisily in the sky; a streak of yellow zigzagged far away, and she trembled. Digging swiftly in the hot earth, she made a small hole and quickly took two crushed ten-dollar bills from her pocket. After she slipped the money into the ground and covered it, she breathed deeply and smiled. She was glad *that* was over! Now no one would find it or know how she got it. Certainly it would be there later when she wanted it.

This selection draws us into its web of meaning without any visual props like photographs or drawings. Here, a child must apply inferential skills in an exclusively verbal context. The simple passage about Diane is nonetheless rich in inferential meanings. How old is Diane? Nothing in the paragraph directly answers that question. Yet, we know from her actions (burying ten dollars in the ground) and thoughts that she's not a teenager, a young mother, or a three-year old, for example. We infer her age at about nine or ten. Also from her actions we can tell that Diane obtained the money suspiciously, although no sentences overtly state such information. To determine the setting (the scene occurs just before a summer rainstorm) and Diane's feelings after she hides the money (great relief), inferential reasoning plays a major role. Draw out these meanings with questions such as:

- How old is Diane?
- What time of day and year is this taking place? How do you know?
- How is Diane's behavior strange? Why do you think she hides the money?
- Where do you think she got the money?
- How does Diane feel after she hides the money?

If the questions here look similar to those I suggested that you ask for the nonrepresentational moments, the photographs and the cartoon, it's for good reason. But you've heard me connect visual and verbal reading before, in Chapter 6 and in other places in this book. My point here is that the way we make inferences from print alone is not unrelated to the way we make them from visual settings. Thus, we build from our children's visual powers to move them toward higher and higher levels of literacy.

Let me show you how inference leaps to the front in a typical passage from a textbook that your youngster will face at school.

This abbreviated selection (on pages 161 to 164) appears in a popular language arts text for sixth-grade children. It is an excerpt from a book called *The Blind Colt* by Glen Rounds. Excerpts, even self-contained ones as this seems to be, generally present many problems for young readers. Insufficient context plunges the child into an uncertain environment: When you examine the story later on, you'll see how jarring the opening sentence is. (You can tell that the passage is ripped out of a longer piece, can't you?)

The textbook editors who have used this narrative present it in a section on creative writing. Their objective is to highlight the issue of *conflict*, which they define as the problem faced by a character in a book or story. Two "Creative Activities," listed under that heading, follow the story. One activity asks children to think about another problem or conflict that the colt might have and then to write a story that tells about it. The other activity requires that children make a map to show the route that the blind colt took.

The two questions fall far short of helping children understand the selection's meaning. They make unwarranted assumptions, I feel, about what even very bright sixth-graders can do to engage text on their own. I am aware that the goal in the particular textbook is not to teach reading. Still, to provide so little guidance in how to extract meaning, to think critically about the material, is a terrible disservice to your kids, who have to make sense of the story. Even the notion of conflict, which the authors aim to explore, is poorly delineated here through the questions and comments. It's a blind colt against the elements making his way against great odds—certainly that is the issue in the story. Yet the subtle reaches of inference that a practiced reader should bring to the passage will enrich the meanings many times over. The questions keep a child from achieving, and offer no help to stretch his or her inferential skills. With good questioning strategies, a parent can help a child avoid the superficial and think more clearly.

What questions can we raise to help our children understand this story? How does inference operate here?

You know from previous chapters in *Any Child Can Read Better* how to focus attention on essential issues well before encouraging your youngster to read what's on the page.

Look at the pictures. What are they showing? How does your child imagine that a blind colt would feel? What problems would a blind colt have to face in his life? How does your child think the colt might have become blind? Has your child ever seen a blind animal—a horse, cat, or dog? or a blind person? How does a blind person manage to get around? How might getting around be particularly troublesome for an animal in the wild? If you have time, perhaps you might want to prepare a word map with your child (see Chapter 4). Using key words like *colt* or *blind*, you can help your youngster probe his tacit awareness of the concepts that Glen Rounds, the author, establishes in the story. Remember, I'm recommending all these steps as strategies for use before reading the selection.

A Story

People write stories for many reasons. Sometimes they merely want to entertain the readers. Other times they want to show how problems can be solved. The problem a character faces is called a *conflict*.

This story is part of a book called *The Blind Colt*. The book tells about many conflicts the blind colt has. In the story you will read, the colt faces a conflict caused by a snowstorm.

 # THE BLIND COLT

All day the horses drifted slowly ahead of the storm, always searching for some place sheltered from the wind, and always being driven out of such places as they found by the choking, swirling snow. Out in the wind the snow blew straight ahead and breathing was a little easier.

Sometime during the second night of the big blizzard the mustangs were picking their way along a narrow trail leading to the rimrock, when another horse stumbled against the blind colt and shoved him off the path. He squealed and lunged, trying to keep his footing, but the steep slope offered no foothold and he slithered downwards ten or fifteen feet before he struck the bottom.

When he picked himself up he was unhurt, for the deep snow had cushioned his fall. He had fallen into the head of a gulley, and on three sides of him were walls that were too steep for him to scramble up. He floundered around in the soft snow, whinnying frantically, but the rest of the horses were already out of sight in the storm and he was left alone.

He floundered around in the snow that was belly deep and getting deeper, trying to find a way back up to the trail. Before long he was exhausted and had to give it up. But he soon found he could not stay there. The snow eddied down

From *Macmillan English* © 1984 Thobunn, Arnold, Schlatterbeck, Terry story: Glen Rounds, "The Blind Colt" © 1941, 1960 by Holiday House Inc. © reserved 1969 by Glen Rounds.

into the pocket and piled up so fast that he'd soon have been buried in it. So he started moving in the only direction possible, following the bottom of the gulley downhill.

For what seemed like a long time he struggled ahead, slipping and sliding along the floor of the gulley as it wound steeply down hill, and lunging through deep drifts and patches of buck brush hidden under the snow.

The wind whined and made strange crying noises as it curled over the edges of the banks above him. The weight of the snow in the air presed down on him. He was soon drenched with sweat from his exertion and his terror. Luckily he was too frightened to stop; if he had he'd have soon frozen.

The gully he'd fallen into finally opened into another larger one. Here there was more open space and the snow was not drifted so deep, but still he could not climb the sides. All he could do was keep on drifting.

It must have been near morning, and he was weak and shaking with weariness, and his steamy breath had frozen, forming icicles in his nostrils until his breath was nearly cut off, when he sensed an obstacle barring the way. Moving cautiously up to it, he found a wire fence cutting across the

canyon here. For a while he stood still against it, undecided. But soon the force of the storm drove him on and he turned in the direction that led quarteringly away from the force of the wind.

He went on cautiously, feeling a trace of a well-worn path beneath the snow beside the fence. A little farther on the fence ran uphill, but the canyon being wider here, the wind had flattened the drifts out somewhat and the blind colt was able to flounder through without much trouble. After climbing out of the canyon it wasn't long before he found that he'd drifted into a fence corner. The other fence joined the one he was following at right angles and to go in either of the directions that were open now he had to face directly into the wind, against the full force of the storm. He couldn't do that and it looked like he would be trapped there in the corner until he froze to death as so many other horses would be in this storm.

But as he moved restlessly, leaning against one of the fences, it suddenly fell away from him. He moved forward carefully and felt the cold touch of barbed wire around his feet. But he didn't get tangled in it and was soon safely across. The wire gate there had not been fastened securely and had fallen down as he rubbed against it.

So now he was once more in the open and could drift directly ahead of the storm. The ground here was more level and traveling much easier.

He had stumbled on for some time when a sudden lessening of the wind startled him. He stopped short and threw up his head and shook it to free his ears and nose of snow. He knew that something near by was breaking the force of the wind. And when he cleared his nostrils enough to sniff, he smelled horses somewhere up wind. Maybe it was the bunch he'd lost, and his mother. He whinnied and followed the smell as fast as he could and soon came to an open-fronted shed banked up and roofed with musty hay. Inside were horses, warm and safe out of the storm.

When he came close he learned that they were strange, and he was suspicious of the unfamiliar smells of the shed. But he was tired and cold and lonely, so after a time he moved carefully into the warm darkness. But a sudden squeal and a pair of heels on his ribs drove him out.

For a time he was driven out whenever he started in among the other horses. But after a while he found himself between the wall and the side of a pot-bellied old horse that took only a half-hearted interest in driving him out, and let him alone after a few nips.

The heat from the bodies of the closely packed horses made it mighty warm and comfortable in there and it was only a little time until the blind colt was sound asleep beside old Spot.

Glen Rounds

Creative Activities

1. **Creative Writing**   Think about another problem, or *conflict*, that the blind colt might have. For example, it might encounter an unfriendly animal. Write a story that tells about the problem. Describe how the colt manages to solve the conflict.
2. Draw a map showing the route that the blind colt traveled. Use the details in the story to help you. Your map may include the rimrock, trail, gulley, walls, fence, and shed.

Once you've set the stage through relaxed living room or kitchen-table conversation, you can guide the actual reading. Drawing on the strategies I explained earlier, you can frame questions and directives that lead your son or daughter to find the main point here. Also, you can guide your child to extract important facts from the story and to attend to vital vocabulary like *mustang, rimrock, lunge, floundered, gulley, obstacle,* and so on.

But my main objective in this chapter is helping you build inference skills with your youngster. After your child reads the selection, use the sample questions in italics. Comments after the questions point to possible responses and avenues for exploring inference with your child.

- **Why was the blind colt out in the snow?** You should lead your child to infer that the colt is part of a pack of wild horses seeking shelter from the blizzard. It's obvious that the storm is whipping the animals, but nothing states why the animals are there instead of in a barn, say.
- **Why was the colt thrown into the gulley?** We must infer that the dangers on the trail forced the small animal to lose footing. There was no evil on the part of the stumbling horse who pushed him down.
- **Why doesn't he rejoin his mother and the other horses he was traveling with?** Why does he follow the bottom of the gulley downhill? The colt's exhaustion indicated the terrible dangers he faces alone against the elements of nature. Deep snow piles force him to drift aimlessly along.
- **Why does the colt stand against the wire fence, undecided?** Help your child infer that in the midst of dangers all decisions seem agonizing, although we sometimes have to make quick choices. If your daughter were in the same predicament, why might she hesitate? Maybe the wire is so unfamil-

iar as to shock the colt? Maybe he recalls its association with humans and hence is leery. Nothing in the text supplies the answer, and your child will be drawing upon her own experience and imagination to try to understand the colt's motivation.

- *Why do the other horses try to drive him out when he finally reaches shelter?* Animals instinctively grow uneasy at unfamiliar creatures, even those who are part of their own biological families. Perhaps the quarters are too crowded. Perhaps the horses sense that the new colt will drain their food supply or place other burdens on the sheltered community.
- *What do you think it felt like to be blind in the situation that the colt finds himself in?* From her experience and imagination, encourage your child to adduce the stresses and strains that sightlessness would provoke for the animal.

In discussing inference, I have tried to move you and your child into advanced reading strategies. Not only will classroom teachers expect skilled inferential reasoning from your son or daughter but also most reading assessment tests, with their endless multiple choice questions, will attempt to probe your child's inference skills straight through the grades. Work on them at home and you'll be helping your youngster progress.

The Crystal Ball

PREDICTING OUTCOMES AND
DRAWING CONCLUSIONS

■━━━━━━━━━━■

Mature readers always reach beyond the text they are reading. They know unconsciously how to interact with print, regularly uncovering new meanings and making inferential leaps that connect with other thoughts, ideas, or experiences. As you saw in the last chapter's discussion of inference, a piece of writing almost always means more than it says, and the awake reader constantly fleshes out suggestions, nuances, and implications to enrich the reading experience.

In this and the next chapter, I want to talk with you about some high-order inference skills: *predicting outcomes*, *drawing conclusions*, and *generalizing*. These three skills work together because they involve the reader's ability to follow a trail begun but not completed by the words on the page. The three skills all relate to inferential reasoning in that they require readers to evolve meanings derived from the prose.

Remember our definition of inference? When we infer, we uncover information that is unstated—hidden, if you will. The information expands upon the writer's words. Using what the writer tells us, we plug into the complex circuitry of ideas by adducing what's not exactly stated in what we're reading. We dig out meanings, shaping and expanding the writer's ideas. Predicting, concluding, and generalizing move us toward wider and deeper meanings in what we read. Let's take them up one at a time.

Looking Ahead

An engaged reader regularly looks ahead to what will happen next—what will be the next event in a chronological sequence, what will be the next point in a logical progression, what will be the next thread in the analytic fabric the writer is weaving. We base our predictions on prior events or issues in the narrative or analytical sequence. Making correct predictions involves our ability to see causes and effects, stimuli and results, actions and consequences.

Your child already knows how to predict outcomes. Right from her earliest days in the crib, she has used important analytical skills instinctively. Come near a hungry infant with a bottle of milk and watch the agitation. Take a book from the shelf beside your toddler and she assumes her "story" pose—in bed, under the covers, blanket at her nose as she awaits a familiar outcome.

As your child grows older, she continues to recognize familiar actions and their almost certain effects, especially if you've established guidelines for behavior at home and in the neighborhood. (Whether or not she uses this information to her and your advantage is another matter!) For example, your little girl knows very well what will happen if she messes up her room. She knows that you'll be angry and probably lecture her, that she'll have to clean up before she can do anything else she likes, that she may be punished, and so on. Similarly, she knows the consequences of watching more television than she's allowed, of eating too many chocolate kisses, of wearing only a light coat in a winter chill. With reasonable accuracy, she can predict the outcome of putting her hand out to a snarling dog, touching a flame, giving Grandpa an unsolicited kiss, submitting homework neatly and on time, pleading gently for ice cream on a hot summer afternoon.

Of course, none of the supposed outcomes follows immutable law and occurs exactly as anticipated. People and events are never absolutely predictable, fate and human nature forbidding thoroughly accurate advanced calculations each time around. Yet we have learned through experience that certain events are foreseeable, in the sense that we can guess that they will happen, or that instances very similar to what we expect will happen.

Because the ability to predict outcomes is so valued a skill from the early grades onward, help your child read better by practicing the skill whenever you can in your child's nonprint world. Observing the world around you, at the supermarket or on a walk in the park, for instance, you and your child can try to predict what will happen from what you see and hear.

Look at this list of suggestions, ticklers really, to stimulate your own conversations with your youngster.

Making Predictions: Possible Points of Discussion

- Look at the sky and the trees. What will the weather be like today? How can you tell?
- Watch children waiting at the corner for the school bus. What will happen when the bus pulls up?
- Throw pieces of bread out in the backyard? What outcome can you expect from that action?
- The letter carrier rings the doorbell. What do you expect to happen after that?

- You bring home an excellent report card from school. What happens next?

Of course, you can pretty much predict what your youngster's responses will be in each case. Yet, you want to accent your child's reasoning over any categorically "correct" answer. In fact, even though experience suggests one clear answer in each case, multiple responses surely are possible here. Everybody knows how unpredictable the weather is; in spite of our guess that a crisp, clear morning bodes well for the whole day, you wouldn't want to bet a day's wages against the possibility that a sudden cloud could dampen your picnic plans.

Have some fun with your youngster as you consider the many possibilities here. Test the validity of the outcomes your child suggests by asking her to explain why she thinks as she does. Which results seem likeliest? Why? Kids love to get silly here, and you want them to enjoy their own minds working on the questions. Still, personal experience is the proving ground for most of our projections, and you always should anchor your child's point in reality and logic. Not every anticipated outcome can be valid, no matter how much fun we have sailing on the wings of fancy and imagination.

Efforts at predictions connected to personal experience will help your child practice an important skill before she applies it to print. You can explore making predictions in other nonprint arenas as well, always relying on insights from your child's immediate sensory world. Here again, I'm talking about the many visual representations that surround us.

Look with your child at photographs and drawings in magazines, newspapers, and picture books and examine what you see with an eye towards figuring out what will happen next. Use that crystal ball! Let's look again at Eileen Christelow's cover drawing for *Mystery Cat and the Monkey Business* by Susan Saunders for a terrific

illustration to encourage thinking about predictions. How will things turn out here?

These questions will stimulate lively conversation about the illustration:

- Why is the monkey frightened? What do you think the cat wants to do to the monkey?
- Why are the girls running? What do you think they will do once they reach the pole?

- What will the monkey do next?
- Suppose the girls weren't there? What do you think would happen?
- Suppose the girls succeed in pulling the cat away from the monkey? What will they do next?

A conversation rooted in these questions will stimulate skills at predicting outcomes. You could construct questions like these for any visual experience you share with your youngster, especially the covers of new books added to your child's library. Study the cover illustrations before you read the book or even look at the pictures inside. What does your child think will happen based on what the cover tells him? You know by now that talking about the cover of a book in advance of reading it is a good way to stimulate your child's interest, especially if you have a reluctant reader living in your house.

Draw on other available representational images. Go through the family photograph album and talk about what the subjects might have done just after the camera froze them on film. Newspaper photographs, alive with action, provide excellent points of discussion regarding possible outcomes. Uncomplicated snapshots of ordinary people on the street, formal pictures of governmental leaders or dignitaries in somber poses, candid shots of well-known movie stars waving over their shoulders—all these will help you talk with your youngster about what might occur next. If your child could stand at the scene with a camera, what does she think she might capture in a photograph taken five minutes later? ten? thirty?

Another excellent resource for predicting outcomes before turning to written words is to look at advertisements and cartoons. As I've explained before, these combine both visual and verbal elements, and even inexperienced readers can draw on familiar visual contexts for practice. For a surefire activity with kids of all ages, I like to show the first two or three frames in a comic strip and withhold the final frame, asking a child to suggest what he or she thinks might appear there. The key here is not in being "right" but in providing a logical outcome consistent with the characters and events portrayed in the earlier frames.

Look at these two sections of a popular comic strip. What does your child think will happen next?

I asked my ten-year-old Saul to draw the next frame for this comic strip. His drawing appears on page 174.

Our conversation helped draw Saul's thinking to the surface. His picture shows Archie disguising his nose in a sock in order to hide his pimple. Why did Saul think the events he drew in his picture would occur? What features of the earlier frames led him to make those predictions? Well, he felt, Archie was so upset about that pimple that he'd have to hide it in some way, no matter how ridiculous he looked and no matter how hard it might be to breathe.

Then we looked at the final frame produced by the artist, Dan Da Carlo (on page 175), and compared the two.

It was remarkable, you might think, how close Saul came to Da Carlo's version. But I think not. Most kids can weigh events and project them onto the future. Go

through the Sunday funny pages and play the "What's the last frame?" game.

Once we show our youngsters how well they can project outcomes in visual and visual-verbal situations, we need to connect this skill with prose experiences that do not rely on visual support.

When you're ready to consider predicting outcomes in print alone, start with single sentences. Use sentences that are clearly causal in nature and from which you have removed the final clause. Ask your youngster to supply an appropriate ending. What does your child suggest to complete this sentence, for example:

If you read books with very small print in poor light. . . .

Your youngster will see (perhaps without being able to explain it) that the word *if* here sets up conditions that affect the sentence's outcome. From the words, the syntax, and your child's own experience, he may know that in such a situation eyestrain is bound to follow. We cannot predict with absolute certainty that small print and poor lighting produce eyestrain, but if your child produces a sentence like this, he was using available clues to predict outcomes accurately:

> If you read books with very small print in poor light, *you may strain your eyes.*

Now try out these other alternative sentence endings to see if your child thinks that they too may be possible outcomes:

> If you often read books with very small print in poor light,

1. *you will not pass your test Friday.*
2. *you will have to take aspirin.*
3. *you may not learn the meanings of impor-tant new words.*
4. *you'll never enjoy reading.*
5. *you should play soft music on the radio.*

None of the predictions here is as valid as the one in the sentence regarding eyestrain. Why? Item 1 is off the mark because many people who read small print in poor light could pass an exam with no trouble at all. Item 2 makes an absolute statement that in many cases would be inaccurate: Some people, yes, but not everyone who reads under such conditions would develop a headache bad enough to require aspirin. In 3, the light and print size might not interfere with a determined reader's ability to learn new words. Item 4 does not indicate an appropriate outcome for the conditions established in the first part of the sentence: Some people might enjoy reading very much under the conditions described. Similarly, although soft music can accompany dim lights, playing the radio is not a logical outcome of the sentence, and item 5 is not cor-rect. The issue of small print becomes irrelevant here and poses a further challenge to the proposed end of the sen-tence.

As you talk about sentences like these with your child, listen to the way he reasons. Help him weigh the logic of his thoughts as they develop from the stated issues. Also, encourage him to think ahead to events that might result from the information given. Explain that even though he might not know an outcome for sure, he can use evidence from the sentence to make reasonably accurate forecasts.

Here are some other sentences and possible out-comes. Which are valid? Which are not? Why?

People who do not smoke or drink, who exer-cise regularly, and who eat foods that are good for them . . .

never have to go to the doctor.

generally are in better physical shape than
people who don't take good care of their bodies.

are part of a growing number of Americans
who watch their health carefully.

worry too much about their health.

try to convince others to change their ways.

After losing all their games last season, the
Holden School baseball team felt . . .

guilty that they didn't try any harder.

angry at the other teams for cheating.

disappointed at not being able to play well
enough to win.

happy to have participated in a special season.

that they should play only basketball next
season if they wanted to win.

After you've practiced with these unfinished sentences and the possible choices for endings, and after
you and your child have talked about the valid and
invalid outcomes, you're ready to consider a full paragraph and some follow-up questions. Here goes:

Sound is made when the particles that make
up a gas (such as air), a liquid (such as water), or
a solid (such as iron or wood) move rapidly back
and forth. This back-and-forth motion is called
vibration. When an object vibrates in air, the
object pushes air outward from itself in a series
of air-waves. When these waves strike our ears,
we hear a sound. For example, when a gong is
struck, the gong vibrates. The metal shell of the
gong moves first in one direction, then in the

opposite direction. When any portion of the shell moves in one direction, it squeezes together air particles in its path as it shoves them outward. As the same portion of the shell moves in the opposite direction, the air particles behind it are spaced out. (Of course, when the air on one side of the vibrating portion is being squeezed together, the air on the other side is being spaced out.) The alternate squeezing and thinning out of air particles produces sound waves.

If you stop the gong from vibrating, you can predict that the

1. air will stop touching the gong shell.

2. sound will get louder.

3. sound will remain the same.

4. sound will stop.

Based on the selection, if you cause a stick held in the air to move back and forth rapidly, the

1. stick will keep pushing the air one way.

2. air will not be affected by the stick.

3. stick will create sound waves in the air.

4. air particles will become disorganized.

If you are on a planet with no air and a gong vibrates next to you,

1. you will not be able to hear the gong sound.

2. you will be able to hear the gong very loudly.

3. the gong will stop vibrating very soon.

4. the gong will squeeze its own air.

You can safely predict here that because vibrations

produce sound, stopping them will cause sound to cease. Only item 4 is correct in the first case.

In the second example, your child should be able to predict that a rapidly moving stick (see the clue in the second line about iron or wood?) in air will create sound waves. Here, your youngster had to use her own experience to know that a stick is made of wood and that if, as the passage says, rapidly moving particles that make up wood produce sound, then a stick, being a wooden object, can produce sound under the stated conditions. Only item 3 is appropriate here. The other choices don't make much sense. At first glance, you might think that the particles would become disorganized, but that assumes they were organized in the first place. Nothing in the passage suggests that item 4 is correct.

For the last question, your child should be able to predict that the absence of air means the absence of sound. Item 1 is the only valid outcome to predict from the passage.

The ability to draw conclusions is very much related to predicting outcomes, and is the subject of the next section. Once we examine that skill, I'll provide some guidelines for helping your children sharpen their abilities with these important critical reading elements.

Drawing Valid Conclusions

The courtroom falls silent as the jurors solemnly step to the oak box. A faint stir sweeps through the crowd as the court official booms, "Ladies and gentlemen of the jury, have you reached your verdict?" All eyes leap to the head juror. She rises slowly and clears her throat. "The jury has concluded," she announces, "that the defendant is not guilty."

On television or in the courthouses of America it is the verdict in this scenario that would rivet your attention. But here I am interested in the jury chief's verb, *concluded*.

How many times in a day do we use that word and apply its meanings? The intricate process of thought and analysis, of weighing evidence to form an opinion and reaching a decision from careful observation, surely is not reserved to courtrooms alone. The process drives our reasoning as we go about our daily business. Regularly we reach conclusions about people, events, and ideas. As careful thinkers, we try to look at the "case" in the way that a good jury looks at its case, considering what we see and hear and think, looking for patterns, fitting all the information together to determine current or future action.

Examples?

- You watch a red Corvette weaving in and out of lanes, taking absurd risks, endangering pedestrians and other vehicles, and you conclude that you're seeing a drunk driver.
- You hear regular reports of scandals at city hall and you conclude that the mayor and his appointees, whom you supported in the past, are crooks.
- You watch your boss' eyes glaze when you reveal the persistent family problems that cut your job productivity, and you conclude that you'd better not discuss these issues with her again.
- You gain three pounds every time you pig out on jelly doughnuts and chocolate milk, and you conclude that you'd better say no tonight or you won't fit into the black lace cocktail dress you're wearing to your brother's Saturday night wedding.
- Mrs. Allen chases your son from her front lawn each time he runs after a bouncing ball, and you conclude that Mrs. Allen just doesn't like children on her property.

Reflecting on typical events like the ones I've described above, you can stimulate a level of critical thinking that invites your child to draw accurate conclusions. When you carry on conversations with your youngster about daily events, asking questions like *Why?* and *Why do you think so?* and *How?* and *How come?* you stimulate him to make judgments. As you probe for causes, ask for opinions, encourage thinking about courses of action, you are tapping a skill in everyday life that your child can apply to print.

Here are some other familiar events and a few conclusion-generating questions that you might like to try with your youngsters:

- A woman is closing up her hardware store for the night. She puts different keys into three separate door locks. She sets the buttons on an alarm security system. She pulls down a large steel curtain to cover completely all the windows and doors of her shop, and she uses a padlock to secure the curtain at the pavement.

Why do you think she does what she does? What makes her perform these actions? Under what conditions would she not have to fasten so many locks and carry out the other steps to secure her shop? You can tap the skill of predicting outcomes here. Do you see how closely it is related to the skill of drawing conclusions? Ask your child: What do you think might happen if the woman forgot to carry out her safety routine one evening? How do you know? Can you know for sure?

- A robin flies back and forth from the ground into

the midst of a hedge. Each time, the bird is carrying a piece of twine, a twig, a shred of yellow cloth.

What is she doing? Why? How do you know? Predict outcomes here too: What might you find if you looked carefully in the bush later this afternoon? tomorrow? three weeks from now? two months from now?

- Dozens of cars are lined up along the high school street, and they pull slowly into the school yard. Local teenagers, dressed in shabby work clothes, are soaping the cars and rinsing them clean. Each driver pays two dollars, and all the money goes into a large box.

What's going on here? Why are the teenagers washing cars in the school yard? Why are they collecting money? Predict outcomes: What do you think they will do with the money?

Another way to practice drawing conclusions with your youngsters is—you probably guessed it—to look together at newspaper and magazine photographs and to try to reach some judgments about what you see. Look at this snapshot of a person and a manatee, a large sea mammal sometimes called an "underwater elephant." The picture on page 183 is from *Ranger Rick*, a very popular magazine around our house.

What is going on here? What conclusion can you draw about the scene? Who is the person, do you think? What is she doing? Why does she have writing tools? What is the manatee doing?

Just as in daily occasions or when we examine nonprint representations like photos or illustrations, we similarly can engage our minds in drawing conclusions when we read. We note patterns of thought and action

and use those patterns to make judgments about characters and events. We put together facts and details logically in our minds in order to draw valid conclusions.
Like the other efforts I've tried to explain, the skill of
drawing conclusions builds upon your child's awareness
of a selection's main point and the various details that
support it.

Look at this short selection from a simple essay
by Camus. (Yes, your child can read and understand a paragraph written by Camus.) Follow-up
questions stimulate your youngster's ability to draw
conclusions.

Ever since our departure, the seagulls have
been following our ship, apparently without

effort, almost without moving their wings. Their fine, straight navigation scarcely leans upon the breeze. Suddenly, a loud plop at the level of the kitchens stirs up a greedy alarm among the birds, throwing their fine flight into confusion and sending up a fire of white wings. The seagulls whirl madly in every direction and then with no loss of speed drop from the flight one by one and dive toward the sea. A few seconds later they are together again on the water, a quarrelsome farmyard that we leave behind, nesting in the hollow of the wave, slowly picking through the manna of the scraps.

Here are some questions about the passage. To answer them, you'll have to build on your youngster's abilities to draw conclusions.

The seagulls are following the ship because

1. the men are playing with them.
2. they are angry at the noises from the ship.
3. they are hungry.
4. they are confused.

The "loud plop at the level of the kitchens" is probably

1. the sound of a dead bird falling from the sky.
2. the drop of the engine or anchor to slow the ship down.
3. a man falling forward.
4. the sound of leftover food hitting the waves.

The men probably throw scraps overboard because

1. they have to get rid of unwanted garbage and left-overs.
2. they like the seagulls.
3. the seagulls are hungry.
4. the seagulls annoy them.

How did you manage with these questions? Let's take them up in turn. From the behavior of the birds at the end of the paragraph, we know that they are hungry. The phrase "picking through the scraps," among other clues, allows us to draw that conclusion.

Even if your child doesn't know the meaning of *manna* (here it means the sudden, unexpected source of material pleasure or gain), he can conclude that item 3 is correct. True, the writer tells us that the seagulls whirled in confusion, but that's not the reason they were following the ship. We have to rule out item 4. And nothing in the selection suggests that either 1 or 2 is correct.

What conclusion do you draw about the loud plop beside the kitchen level? Certainly that action and the alarm and the birds' subsequent seaward diving make us conclude that the noise is scraps of food hitting the waves. Only item 1 works here.

In the third question we reach our conclusion by reflecting on the men's behavior. Nothing in the selection tells how they feel about the birds: we don't know whether the men like the gulls or are annoyed by them. We also don't know if the men think the seagulls are hungry or even if the men care that the seagulls may be hungry, for that matter. We have to reject all the choices but item 1. The men are dumping unwanted garbage and leftovers into the sea.

Drawing Conclusions and Predicting Outcomes

I promised to provide some practical hints for helping children predict outcomes and draw conclusions. Remember that before turning to print, we practice these skills by exploring our child's world, talking about shared moments, familiar scenes, photographs, illustrations, television programs, and so on. This practice sets the right conversational tone about the books we read later on with our youngsters and the various selections they bring us from their own reading.

How to Predict Outcomes and Draw Valid Conclusions

Predicting means guessing at what happens next based on what happened before.

Concluding means determining some logical outgrowth or forming some opinion or decision.

To predict accurately and to form appropriate conclusions, draw on your own experience. Use clues in the passage; test your conclusions and proposed outcomes against what you know from experience and what you have already read.

- Be aware of the main idea of the selection. Think about the action being described. What events have occurred? What events logically should follow the events you've read about? Do you see a pattern or sequence? Does the sequence suggest any results that may not be stated by the writer?
- Pay attention to the vocabulary. Use sentence clues to figure out meanings, but don't get hung up on words whose meanings you don't know exactly. As I pointed out before, you could get by nicely without knowing what the word manna

meant in the paragraph about the gulls. With a little time, however, a child could use clues in the passage to figure out that manna has something to do with food, although he might have missed the nuance of miracle.

- Think about the people described in the selection. What do their character and previous actions suggest about what they might do next? Often characters in children's books are predictable in that the authors show them acting again and again from the same character trait or inclination. Help your child identify the thoughts, feelings, and actions of characters in order to figure out what the characters might do next.

- Think about what you would do, or what would happen to you, if you were in the circumstances being described.

- Ask yourself after you read: What will happen as a result of these actions or events?

- Consider the overall picture suggested in the reading. Does it point you in one direction or the other? Which details back up your ideas?

- Before you make a final judgment—whether you are drawing a conclusion or predicting an outcome—be sure that the reading supplies enough evidence to support your judgment. Do not build your conclusions and predictions exclusively on your own opinions, likes, and dislikes. Of course, use those experiences as the starting point for your thinking. But always test your conclusions and predictions against evidence in the selection you're reading. If you feel that the evidence is not sufficient, what kind of information would you need to reach an accurate conclusion or to guess at what might happen next? It's always all right to say that you're just not sure of the outcome.

Let's try to put these concluding and predicting talents to work together. Examine these passages and use
the succeeding questions to guide conversation about
the skills we've looked at in this chapter. Both pieces,
incidentally, are related to science—a tough area for
many elementary school kids and, unfortunately, the
one their teachers are most likely to set youngsters
learning on their own.

The second selection that follows, the piece on
dinosaurs, is more difficult than the first. Nevertheless,
because the content is so compelling for most kids, you
should try it with your youngster. Look first at the
vocabulary question (question 1) so that you can help
your child explore some difficult words through context
clues (see Chapter 2) or through any other available
means.

> The resolving power of an optical instrument,
> such as a telescope or a microscope, is the mea-
> surement of its ability to distinguish clearly
> between two different things. Anton van
> Leeuwenhoek (1632–1723) is listed in the Bio-
> graphical Dictionary of Outstanding Men
> because he was the first to arrange simple lenses
> as a primitive microscope and call the attention
> of the Royal Society of London to living forms in
> a drop of water. Up to that moment, his useful-
> ness to society had been as a family man and
> custodian. Leeuwenhoek's invention helped the
> human eye to distinguish clearly among living
> protozoa, very small single cell animals. This was
> a simple beginning that led to more sophisticated
> generations of instruments and incredible
> advances in science and medicine.

1. The main point of this selection is

   a. to define resolving power
   b. to discuss Leeuwenhoek's contribution to
      improving the resolving power of optical instru-
      ments.
   c. to explain the ability of the human eye to see
      one-celled animals.
   d. to call attention to the Royal Society of London
      to living forms in a drop of water.

2. We may conclude from this selection that the better the resolving power of a microscope or tele-
   scope,
   a. the more sophisticated the instrument.
   b. the more important Leeuwenhoek's family life.
   c. the less we need to rely upon the human eye in
      scientific observations.
   c. the more protozoa in a drop of water.

3. It is correct to assume that a direct outcome of
   Leeuwenhoek's primitive microscope was
   a. the growth of the Royal Society of London.
   b. his increased usefulness as a family man and
      custodian.
   c. his improved ability to arrange simple lenses.
   d. high-powered microscopes and telescopes in
      use today.

Correct answers here are: 1. b; 2. a; 3. d.

   It is interesting to compare the brain of a very
large dinosaur with the brain of an equally large
modern mammal like the whale. The largest
dinosaurs weighed as much as 100 tons. Whales
also weigh as much as 100 tons and are, as the
dinosaurs were in their time, the largest animals
alive today. The brain of a large whale is a huge
mass of grey matter, nearly a foot and a half

across, that weighs about 20 pounds. The possessor of this mammoth brain is an intelligent animal. Some whales have a remarkable memory capacity; they can memorize a complex whalesong that goes on for hours, and repeat it note for note a year later. The brains of the largest dinosaurs, on the other hand, such as Supersaurus, were only the size of an orange, and weighed about half a pound. Yet that small amount of grey matter had to exercise control over the same 100-ton bulk that is commanded by the 20-pound brain of the largest whales.

Scientists who specialize in the study of brains and intelligence have plotted charts of brain weight against body weight for many kinds of animals. They find that when the ratio of brain weight to body weight is as small as it was in Supersaurus, the behavior of the animal is stereotyped, automatic, and unintelligent. The reason is clear: A large body has many large muscles and needs many nerve fibers for its coordination. When the large body is controlled by a small brain, every neuron in this brain must be used to move the body through its basic survival routines: find food! flee from the predator! and so on.

Supersaurus was not an unusually stupid dinosaur, and dinosaurs were not unusually stupid reptiles. In fact, dinosaurs had normal intelligence for reptiles. Of course, there was a spread in braininess among the dinosaurs. But the same is true among modern mammals; plant-eaters like the cow are among the least intelligent mammals, while alert carnivores like the wolf are among the most intelligent. However, the dinosaurs as a group were generally less intelligent than the early mammals as a group. This held then, and still holds today, all the way up and down the scale of sizes. A little lizard, for example, has a considerably smaller brain than a chipmunk of the same size and displays a far less flexible repertoire.

1. Without using a dictionary, determine definitions of the following words. Reread the sentences in which each word appears for clues to their correct meanings.
   a. possessor _____
   b. capacity _____
   c. stereotyped _____
   d. neuron _____
   e. predator _____
   f. carnivores _____
   g. repertoire _____

2. The main idea of the passage is that
   a. dinosaurs were much smarter than most people think.
   b. whales have brains that weigh twenty pounds.
   c. dinosaurs were about as smart as other reptiles.
   d. dinosaurs and other reptiles are not as smart as mammals.

3. A Supersaurus and a modern whale
   a. have about the same live weight.
   b. have about equal intelligence.
   c. have brains the size of oranges.
   d. live underwater.

4. We may conclude that carnivores
   a. do not eat reptiles.
   b. are smarter than plant eaters.
   c. are stronger, but not smarter, than their prey.
   d. display stereotyped behavior.

5. Animals with small brains in relation to their body
   sizes
   a. cannot remember much.
   b. cannot survive well.
   c. are almost always reptiles.
   d. display flexible behavior.

6. From the information presented in the selection
   you can predict that lizards probably
   a. have better memories than chipmunks.
   b. adapt quickly to changes in their environment.
   c. have a less complex signal system than chip-
      munks.
   d. will outsmart a wolf.

7. We may predict that, if a whale finds an obstacle
   in its way, it will
   a. search for several ways to get around it.
   b. not remember the obstacle for long.
   c. flee.
   d. keep trying to swim directly through the obsta-
      cle.

8. We may conclude that a living Supersaurus
   a. used many different methods to defeat its ene-
      mies.
   b. could not control its muscles.
   c. could not adapt easily to changes in its environ-
      ment.
   d. evolved a complicated signal system.

9. We may conclude from the article that
   a. turkeys would be smarter than eagles.
   b. eagles would be smarter than turkeys.
   c. a big dog will always be smarter than a small
      dog.
   d. large lizards would be smarter than turkeys.

10. We may also conclude that

a. animals with bigger brains are always smarter.
b. dinosaurs were the stupidest animals to walk the earth.
c. all mammals are carnivores.
d. animals range in intelligence.

Answers? Here are definitions for the highlighted vocabulary:

A possessor is someone who has or owns something.

Capacity is the amount something can hold.

Stereotyped means made to fit an overly simple idea or belief.

A neuron is a nerve fiber.

A predator is an animal that hunts other animals.

Carnivores are meat eaters.

A repertoire is a choice of behaviors.

Here are correct choices for the remaining questions:
2. d; 3. a; 4. b; 5. a; 6. c; 7. a; 8. c; 9. b; 10. d.

How did you do? Being aware of outcomes and conclusions will help your child interact thoughtfully with print. Use your crystal ball to peek beyond what you've read.

10

Faraway Views
GENERALIZING

It's been a rough Tuesday, especially in your dealings with teenagers. A mother of two young kids yourself, you expect a modicum of respect from kids ten, fifteen, or twenty years younger than you are. But today, no such luck. In Stop 'n Shop a nineteen year old stock boy packing apple sauce jars nearly knocks you over as he hoists a huge carton from a dolly to the floor. Of course, he gives you no apology.

At Burger King, the order taker sneers at you when you present a fifty dollar bill; she mumbles a snide remark under her breath about your confusing a fast food store with a bank.

The gas jockey at a new Exxon station gives you fifteen dollars' worth of premium when you ordered ten dollars' worth of regular and zealously begins a shouting match, demanding that you pay up because you should have been sure that he heard what you wanted.

A few other similar experiences have set your teeth on edge. Kids, you grumble. Deteriorating in manners. No good, today's generation. No respect for their elders. Self-centered. Care only about their own needs and feelings.

Seeing the Large Picture

If you can remember formulating principles like these or others like them, congratulate yourself as a high-order thinker. Even though the thoughts themselves might result from unhappy experiences, you've used your good brain power to establish a broader context for your experiences. Go ahead and pat yourself on the back!

What you've done is to exercise another major strategy that marks mature thought: *generalizing*. The ability to generalize helps you interpret your surroundings and helps you probe deeper meanings from it. It allows you to see relations between specific circumstances and more abstract conditions. Psychologists say that the process of generalizing is a process of discovery; when you see similar elements in diverse circumstances you take a conceptual leap forward in your thinking.

To some, one of the primary goals of education is to create thinkers who know how to generalize. As he advances through the grades in school, or in a home education program, print material will challenge your youngster more and more to generalize from what he reads.

Let's look at the issue in a little more detail. When you generalize, you extend meanings beyond the specific conditions at hand. Generalizing allows you to apply what you've experienced to an expanded context. You use facts, details, information, and ideas; from particular information you generate broad concepts and principles.

As I've said before, the skills we're looking at in this chapter and the two before it are connected quite directly.

Generalizing is related to making inferences; making inferences relates to predicting outcomes and drawing conclusions; and all four connect with each other, corners in a square of higher order thinking. True, not everyone defines these skills in the way I do. Many teachers prefer to see the skills all as variations of inference and not worth distinguishing. Nevertheless, I believe that it is very useful to examine the concepts separately.

Let's try to do just that by returning to your miserable day as an invader in a teenage world. You might *infer* ("read between the lines") on a case by case basis, some particular details that help you understand the actions of each offender. Isn't that the Jones boy with those lethal apple sauce jars? In a home with divorce and illness and barely enough money to go around—and just last week the boy's sister taken to the hospital—well, maybe that explains the youngster's actions. How could a kid with such problems concentrate on anything, you might wonder. Your reasons don't *justify* the boy's action in the aisle, of course, but perhaps they do explain it. Remember, inference is often guesswork: You're exploring currents beneath the surface to satisfy your understanding. And, depending on how angry you are (and how fair you want to be intellectually), you try not to go beyond the available information.

When you *conclude*, on the other hand, you add up impressions and engage in thought that helps you see consequences, causes, and effects. What can you conclude about Terrible Tuesday on the mean streets? One valid conclusion is, "I got no respect from any of the kids I dealt with today." (So you sound a bit like Rodney Dangerfield. Nobody's listening.) Or, you might draw this conclusion, depending on how paranoid you felt: "The teens I had to deal with today hated me." You wouldn't conclude—though you might like to in order to justify your anger—"All the teens I dealt with today were brain dead!" In your mind you've summed up the experiences that you had and you drew conclusions based on those experiences. Apparently some conclusions are more valid than others.

When you *generalize*, you up the ante one more chip in the critical thinking game. You use your experiences to derive broad rules or principles that might apply in other related contexts. From particulars you develop propositions: "Kids today don't show adults any respect"; "Teenagers don't like anyone over thirty-five"; "The younger generation doesn't think the way our generation thinks." Notice the sweep of these statements, rooted in the inferences you made and the conclusions you drew. Each statement proposes a kind of axiom or tenet.

These tenets that you created from your experiences are not all equally appropriate, mind you. Some are too broad, some too unyielding in stating their conditions. You know that, of course. If you really had to think carefully about your "rules" here, you'd probably make modifications, add disclaimers, perhaps soften some of the absolutes.

The chart below categorizes the statements we've examined:

INFERENCE	CONCLUSION	GENERALIZATION
Something is bothering the Jones boy today.	I got no respect from the teens I dealt with today.	Kids don't show adults any respect these days.

Laid side by side, these statements are clearly interrelated and look similar in some respects. Again, I'm not suggesting any rigid definitions for the three thinking strategies, just that you keep in mind the different qualities of thought that each one implies.

Let's have some fun by looking at a few outcomes and conclusions that we used to illustrate concepts in the last chapter and lay them alongside a series of generalizations. Based on your knowledge and experience, which generalizations do you think are valid? Which are not valid? Why? Your ten- or eleven-year-old can investigate these with you; talk about the statements and see if the two of you agree or disagree.

Conclusion: You hear regular reports of scandals at city hall and you conclude that the major and his appointees, whom you supported in the past, are crooks.

   Generalizations (Which Are Valid?):

   1. All politicians are dishonest.

   2. Politicians can have trouble resisting graft and corruption.

   3. City politics everywhere is basically crooked.

   4. Scandals can force people to withdraw support from strong and popular governments.

   5. Scandals always defeat politicians in the end.

   6. Some dishonest people ruin the good name of parties and politics.

   7. Withdraw all support from politicians at the first hint of scandal.

   8. People revise their opinions of politicians based on performance.

Conclusion: You watch your boss' eyes glaze when you reveal the persistent family problems that cut your job productivity, and you conclude that you'd better not discuss these issues with her again.

Generalizations (Which Are Valid?):

1. Bosses never like to hear about employees' personal problems.

2. Some employers see explanations of behavior as excuses.

3. Never talk to an employer about personal issues that may be affecting your job performance.

4. If you must discuss personal problems with your employer, don't do it too often and choose your opportunities carefully.

5. No one can tolerate a person's complaints about problems.

6. Sometimes it's hard to show appropriate sympathy for someone's personal problems.

Conclusion: You gain three pounds every time you pig out on jelly doughnuts and chocolate milk, and you conclude that you'd better say no tonight or you won't fit into the black lace cocktail dress you're wearing to your brother's Saturday night wedding.

Generalizations (Which Are Valid?):

1. Doughnuts and chocolate milk make everyone fat.

2. People who gain weight may have trouble fitting into their clothing.

3. Being thin is a highly desirable goal, especially if you are planning to attend a formal party.

4. Showing restraint in eating may help you avoid problems in wearing clothes later on.

5. Avoid carbohydrate-high sugar treats at all costs.

6. It's hard staying thin when so many delicious foods regularly tempt us.

Each numbered instance under the three conclusions above is a generalization. But not all the generalizations are valid, given the stated conclusion. Some generalizations go too far beyond the information given. Others build on partial truth but allow no exceptions and hence become absolutes. The valid generalizations above are all the even-numbered statements. Odd-numbered statements are not viable: they go too far.

When we read, generalizing allows us to transcend the immediate print details to larger issues in new settings. We have to construct generalizations carefully, based on material in the reading. We have to watch out for the pitfalls when we try to generalize about features of our nonprint worlds.

As I've already said, of all the high-order reading skills, teachers acknowledge generalizing as one of the most important and one of the most difficult. Not only does a child have to know and identify the main idea, understand vocabulary and key details, make inferences, and draw conclusions, but she also must use all the information she gathers in those processes to formulate principles—valid principles—based on what she has read. It's a tall order, so don't underestimate the effort.

I don't want to pass over the reference to main ideas here, even though we spent quite a bit of time examining the concept in Chapter 5. When a main idea is not clearly stated in a selection—that is, it is only implied— the reader has to formulate the main idea herself. This process often relies on generalizing. When you reflect on all the key points in a selection and try to generate one main idea that covers them all, you are generalizing. You can't be too broad, you can't be too specific, and you must use available information to state the generalization appropriately. You want to help your child practice at home so that he doesn't stumble in formal classroom situations.

Home Practice in Generalizing

One of the best ways I know for giving your child practice in the critical reading and thought skill of generalizing is through the mental process of classification. When you *classify*, you group things together according to some organizing principle. When you *generalize*, you create a principle based on things you've observed. You use related data to develop a concept.

Do you see the connection? Classifying is the same process as generalizing, but on a different level. James Moffett, a leading researcher in language arts and reading skills, sees inseparable connections among classifying, generalizing, and thinking itself. He says "thought consists only of relating. Concepts result from sorting things into classes and sorting is relating different things according to a common trait."

Let me explain classification by relating it to a lesson I observed a number of years back. An imaginative writing instructor was teaching the concept to beginning college writers in an effort to get them to use classification as an essay-organizing scheme. As soon as class started, she opened her large leather pocketbook and dumped its contents on the desk. "I'm sick of being such a slob!" she said. "All this junk is mixed together in this bag and I want to organize the stuff in some reasonable order. Help me!"

Students examined the mess on the desk and, engaging in lively conversation, talked about how to group the diverse contents—lipstick, lifesavers, paper clips, pencils, earrings, coins, gum, everything you could imagine and then some. Several schemes were suggested. One student proposed organizing the contents by function: cosmetics, writing-related materials, edibles, jewelry, and so on. Another student suggested organizing the contents by size: big things here, smaller things there, tiny things somewhere else. Yet another suggested an arrangement by color: reds, blues, browns, and so forth. One clever young man suggested making groups according to value: expensive, moderately priced, cheap, utter junk.

As a volunteer lifted the objects and asked where to put them, the class directed one student to make the groupings on the teacher's desk. Some groupings were not inclusive enough and hence served no useful purpose. Some categories overlapped too much, causing confusion about where to place an object. In addition, when many objects still remained in an unclassified pile, students again knew they had to return to the drawing boards.

After students had discussed the relative merits of each plan, and after they had arrived at a satisfactory definition of *classification*, the teacher reinforced the concept by turning over a box of fancy chocolates on the desktop. "How would you classify these?" she asked. Again, a lively discussion followed. The students compared their proposed groupings with those that the manufacturer had listed on the box cover. Satisfied with the first part of the day's work, students ate the bon bons as they read paragraphs and essays based on classification principles.

This demonstration lesson helps me make some important points. The first is that classification involves generalizing at its most basic level. How did the young men and women determine which groups to propose? The students observed particular phenomena and then generalized from them. The categories they created were the "rules," the generalizations, drawn from observations. Just as you developed a concept about your experiences with local teenagers—they don't have any respect, remember?—students in this writing class developed concepts about what they saw on the desk. Each created category is a generalization. Being able to classify means being able to see lots of particulars and being able to relate a certain number of them to each other, that relation determined by some broad principle. When you look at chocolates and says, "These are creams, these are fruits, these are nuts" you've made three categories and produced three generalizations.

The second point I want to make here is that the teacher drew on everyday, non-book experiences to help students see that they already knew how to generalize. It's a point you've heard me make many times before: Build from existing strengths, from your child's storehouse of tacit knowledge (our friend Michael Polanyi again!), and you build self-confidence to ease the skills transfer when you focus on printed words.

I'm not pretending that all the generalizing skills we're talking about are *exactly* alike. Certainly, it's easier to generalize about concrete, observable objects that stand motionless on a desk and that we can move about physically—gum in this pile, a pocket comb in that one—than it is to group abstract thoughts and ideas. Nevertheless, the general statements that a teacher will expect your child to make from his reading and thinking relate in kind to those he can produce for conditions in his environment.

And you must keep in mind that your child already knows how to classify, although she may not be able to state the organizing principle easily each time without assistance. When she puts look-alike toys together in the closet, when she organizes M & M's in piles by color, when she separates coins into different groups by size, color, or value, she's establishing categories. This is a very important point. Think of your youngster as a child endowed with the ability to classify, not as a child who needs remedial work!

Take another tip from the college teacher I told you about. Make your practice sessions active. That is, encourage your child actually to cluster the related objects in separate piles. The physical action is significant because it reinforces the abstract notion of the "group." Not only did the writing teacher's students create discrete concepts, but they also used the concepts to push things together. The students observed; they classified objects (that is, they produced generalizations); and then they moved the objects into the proposed categories. I've learned from many years' experience that any time you can connect action and thought, as the teacher did here, you can create fertile conditions for learning.

Stimulate your child's practice with generalizing, then, by asking him to look at desultory information, to create some order for it, to state the reasons for the categories he produced (here's where your thoughtful, probing questions will produce good results), and then to do something active that demonstrates the integrity of the groupings.

Where to begin? The possibilities are limited only by your imagination. I've listed a number of suggestions for easy conversation with your child:

Making Categories at Home

Help your child classify:

1. toys in the closet or toy chest

2. clothing in the dresser drawers

3. food in the cupboard or refrigerator

4. special toys—dolls, trucks, hats

5. books on the bedroom shelf

6. food items on the shopping list

7. items in the medicine chest

8. tools and other objects in the basement or garage

9. baseball or movie star cards

10. photos in the photo album or photo box

11. photos in magazines and newspapers

12. advertisements in magazines and newspapers

13. favorite television programs or films

14. favorite foods

15. favorite games

For any of the suggestions above, use your child's age and current abilities to gauge how much to expect. Ideally, you hope that your youngster can look at a set of apparently disparate materials, can propose different categories, and can fit items appropriately into those categories. In addition, you'd like your youngster to look again at that same collection of items and propose a different set of groups based on alternate organizing concepts. Yet, you have to help build up your child's skills to reach this point.

With young children and other beginners at classification, you may have to establish categories in advance, either on your own or with your child. For example, if you're grouping home photos or pictures and illustrations in a magazine, propose some categories prior to the activity. "Let's try to group the photos in this magazine. Let's put all the pictures of babies together, all the pictures of teenagers, grown-ups, senior citizens, and so on." Or, you might say, "Let's go through this book and find all the pictures of red things." Or, "Let's look for dogs, cats, and birds in this book." If your youngster understands and applies the directions, your next step is to encourage her to suggest the groups. "How else might we arrange these pictures? Yes, that's a good idea—by alphabet, all the *a*'s in one group, the *b*'s in another, and so on. That would take a long time, wouldn't it, if we had to classify all the pictures? Let's just do some of them.

"Any other kinds of groups you can think of? Sure, we can group the pictures according to the places around the house that the people are in. Bedroom people here, kitchen people here, and so on."

What's essential, no matter who proposes the categories, is that the items included fit the groups and that your child understands and can state the general principle that rules the individual categories *and* that connects them. When he says, "These are in the same group because they are all yellow" and "We're grouping these pictures by color"; or "These belong together because all the people are happy" and "We're grouping these pictures according to the emotions the people express" your youngster is learning how to generalize.

Don't forget the importance of active learning. Once you agree on the categories, wherever possible, start putting the objects in groups. (Many items on the above list lend themselves easily to direct actions. Other items are more abstract and require think-aloud categories or, if you wish, paper and pencil.) When your child develops a plan for organizing toys in the closet, help him shift the toys to places he recommends—stuffed animals beside the shoes, toy trucks on the back shelf, matchbox cars opposite the shoes, baseball cards in a cigar box. When your child helps you classify items on your supermarket shopping list, let him take his own cart and select the appropriate foods in two categories, say, as you do the rest.

It's easy and fun to do these classification projects with your child in informal sessions at home. No pressure now: You're building generalizing skills by tapping competences that your child already has, so rejoice in her energies and talents.

If your youngster likes to write, you can continue to sharpen category-making skills by encouraging your child to use a Sense Chart, a strategy I recommend in *Any Child Can Write*. With a sense chart, your child classifies sensory impressions that she receives at a given, defined moment. She records sights (including colors and actions), sounds, smells, tastes, and sensations of touch. This paper and pencil exercise is more abstract than the others we examined: Your child has to identify the sensory impressions and record them in appropriate columns. Also, some of the images recorded rely on more than one sense impression. Still, the categories are named in advance, making the effort not beyond your eight- or nine-year-old's abilities.

Topic: Gino's Pizza Parlor

Sight	Sound	Smell
fingers kneading white dough	ring of a cash register	tangy smell of garlic and pepper
bubbling mozzarella cheese	quarters and dimes clinking on the blue counter	cigarette smoke
red tomato paste	cries of "One slice and a coke"	hot dough
crisp brown crust	rumble of the juke box	sweet orange drink

Touch	Taste
wave of heat from the oven	spicy sauce
hot olive oil on my fingers	fiery sausage
cool ceramic counter	hot, bland cheese
icy cup of Coke	
greasy dollar	

Making Generalizations from Reading

I pointed out before that teachers consider generalizing a critical thinking and reading skill. When children read, they must be able to extend meanings beyond the ideas developed in the passage at hand. Here's a brief passage typical of selections your youngster might find in a social studies book. I've provided some multiple choice questions clearly focused on generalizing; once again, these help you see how study questions or commercial tests probe your child's critical thinking.

> One rainy morning in 1955, Harry Van Sinderen left his home in Washington, Connecticut, to drive to his office in New York, about a hundred miles away. The rain turned into a downpour—the heaviest he could remember. Switching on the car radio, he learned that he was in the midst of a tropical storm that had swung inland from the coast, and that streams were flooding all through northern Connecticut. A few minutes later he got worse news: A dam on the Shepaug River above Washington had broken, and the resulting flood had wiped out the center of the town, with considerable loss of life and property.
>
> Harry drove on to New York, walked into his office, and wrote out his resignation as chairman of the board of the export-import company he had managed for many years. He then drove back to Washington, through the still-pouring rain, and appointed himself Chief Rebuilder of the town. He was sixty-six years old at the time.

Harry Van Sinderen would probably be part of which larger group of people:

1. men and women interested in town and city planning

2. those meteorologists (weather experts) who are interested in tropical storms

3. those who are slightly insane

4. those dissatisfied with their jobs because they are not making enough money

Mr. Van Sinderen's actions suggest

1. that people should not go outdoors in tropical rainstorms

2. that a manager's job is often dull

3. that driving a car to and from work each day is a great drain of energy

4. that people late in life can change careers for meaningful work

Harry Van Sinderen would agree

1. that personal success in business and finance is a person's key aim

2. that service to the community in a time of crisis is more important than personal goals

3. that people should carry heavy insurance in case of disasters like flooding

4. that unexpected storms in Connecticut are violent

The first question asks your youngster to make a simple generalization that's very closely connected to the classification skills I've encouraged you to practice. Here, your child has to say to herself, "What do I know about this guy Harry Van Sinderen that allows me to put him into a group?" The group is the generalization. Your child must determine the qualities that Harry van Sinderen has, qualities that make him similar to other people for whom a category exists. See how we're going beyond the information given in the passage? Let's analyze the responses here and come up with the appropriate answer.

Based upon Van Sinderen's concern for damage to the city from the rainstorm, and based upon the statement that he made himself Chief Rebuilder of the town, the idea that he has interest in town planning is clear. Even though he may have acted strangely in giving up his company job, and even though people often leave jobs for higher-paying employment, we have no evidence that Van Sinderen is either slightly insane or underpaid for the work he does now. And just because he found himself in the midst of a heavy downpour we cannot conclude that, like some meteorologists, he has a special interest in tropical storms. Only answer 1 is a fair conclusion for the first question.

The second question requires your child to go even further beyond the paragraph specifics. Mr. Van Sinderen, a man of sixty-six years, suddenly resigned one job to take on another he thought more important. We can generalize and say that his actions suggest that age does not have to stop a person from making major changes in his or her life's work. Using Van Sinderen's decision, we've developed a general rule, more or less: People late in life can change their careers for meaningful work. This is not a general statement that everyone would agree with, but information in the paragraph supports the generalization. For the second question only 4 is correct.

All the other statements in question 2 are generalizations too, but nothing in the selection supports them. It's a general rule that people should not go out in tropical storms. But Van Sinderen really benefited from his ride in the heavy rains—they helped him make an important decision. And although it's often generally true that driving each day drains energy, nothing in the paragraph substantiates that idea. Further, even though Van Sinderen quit his job, and even though we suspect, in general, that a manager's job often has dull moments, we cannot validate the idea from paragraph information. For question 2, then, we would have to reject choices 1, 2, and 3.

Question 3 also requires you to make some rules based on the paragraph. Though we know generally that for many people financial and business success is a key aim, we do not know that Van Sinderen would agree. (In fact by quitting a high-level job his actions imply that those forms of success may not be essential to him.) Choice 1 then is not correct. Choice 3 is also a generalization, and a very reasonable one at that. Many people would agree that heavy insurance can help in times of disaster. But there's nothing in the passage you have read to show that Van Sinderen agrees with that idea. We have to rule out choice 3, therefore. Choice 4 is not correct either. It is much too broad. It suggests that any unexpected storm in Connecticut is violent. How can we make that generalization from this paragraph, which talks about only one storm?

For the third question, then, only 3 is correct. Van Sinderen did make a personal sacrifice by giving up his secure job as chairman of the board; he made that sacrifice in order to help in rebuilding his town after a very serious storm. His actions suggest that he would agree that people in times of crisis should give up their own personal goals to serve their communities. That is a fair generalization from this piece.

Want to try another selection and some questions about generalizing? Here goes.

Soon after the Drake family moved to Tahiti, they found a lovely site for their new home. It was on a hill where many tropical plants were growing. A small stream rushed down the hillside.

The Drakes wanted their new home to be the kind of house that the Tahitians built before Europeans came to the island. It was to have wide porches and a thatched roof. Of course, they planned to include a few modern conveniences—like running water and electricity.

The newcomers were sure they would have no trouble finding someone who could build such a house. They also thought that it would not cost very much. In fact they had a difficult time finding a Tahitian who was interested in their project. The builders they spoke to could not understand why the Drakes did not want a modern house.

The Drakes finally convinced a builder that they really wanted an old-fashioned Tahitian house. They explained that such a house was cooler and more practical than a European-style house would be.

After all, the Tahitians of long ago found out through experience what kind of house best suited their environment. European homes were meant for a different land and climate.

In a short time, the floors were laid on cement blocks, and the walls were put up. The roof caused some real problems for the Drakes. They had trouble finding someone who knew how to make the thatching.

There were only a few Tahitians who still knew the art of thatching. They were mainly elderly people who lived in the country. Most homes on the island had composition or metal roofs.

Finally, the builder located some men on Little Tahiti, where many pandanus trees still grow.

They still knew how to make the pandanus into thatch.

The Drakes had to do a great deal of talking before the men agreed to do the work. The new house was quite large and would need a lot of thatch. The men took the job only after one of them was promised a sewing machine.

The Drakes were now ready to order bathroom and kitchen fixtures and appliances. These had to be shipped from New Zealand. Electricity was brought to their new house on lines from Papeete. Water was piped into the house from the stream that flowed through their property.

At last the house was finished. The Drakes were delighted with it. All the windows opened outward—like awnings. When the windows were all opened, the couple felt as if they were living in a tent.

The kitchen was in a separate building that was connected to the main house by a breezeway. That meant that the heat and smells of cooking were far from the parts of the house where the Drakes spent most of their time.

Native Tahitians are most likely to

1. keep to traditional ways.

2. prefer a modern way of life.

3. not do business with Americans.

Traditional craft skills (such as roof thatching)

1. are getting lost in the modern world.

2. require more training than skills for modern jobs.

3. can be profitable in today's world.

Traditional cultures

1. survive over modern cultures.

2. are out of date for today's world.

3. may have good ideas that we can apply to the modern world.

The generalization that you can make safely among the first set of possibilities is that Tahitians prefer a modern way of life (answer 2). You can see this from their surprise that anyone would want to build an old-fashioned house and from the fact that almost no Tahitians cared to learn how to make traditional roofs, even though the leaves were free. The other two answers counter the story details.

The second generalization that you can make is that traditional skills are being lost (answer 1). You can see this from the difficulty that the Drakes had in finding workers. The story, however, gives you no evidence to judge whether the traditional skills are harder or easier to learn than modern ones. You know only that people are not learning the old ones. And even though the Drakes are willing to barter a sewing machine for a traditional craftsman's work, few other people seem interested in hiring such workers.

Finally, the last generalization you can make is that traditional cultures may have good ideas that we can apply to modern life (answer 3). The house is an example of just that. Some traditional ideas were combined with modern conveniences to make a house that fits the environment. This example in fact shows that traditional cultures are not totally out of date, therefore ruling out answer 2. Yet we cannot say that such cultures survive over modern ones; the way that the house was constructed really challenges the Tahitian pattern as shown in the selection. Answer 1 is wrong here too.

I think that you'll find these pointers useful.

Tips for Making Valid Generalizations

As you look at passages with your child, guide him or her to make valid generalizations. Remember, when you generalize you generate a rule, concept, or principle that goes beyond the specific information in the reading. To make accurate generalizations:

1. *Be sure that you understand the main idea and key details in the reading.* (Sometimes, you have to generalize as one of your first efforts at understanding what you read. In order to state the main idea when it is implied, you often have to generalize from the available details in the selection. See Chapter 5.)

2. *Pay particular attention to predicting outcomes and drawing appropriate conclusions from your reading.* Often, generalizing is the next step after drawing conclusions, the second skill building on the first and going beyond it. Once you've stated a conclusion, think about whether it could apply to other related situations or conditions. If you produce a generalization from a valid conclusion, weigh carefully whether it really does apply to the new context.

3. *Do not go too far beyond the information given.* Zealous generalizers often make statements that are too sweeping (you've heard the phrase "sweeping generalization," right?) and much too broad in their scope, despite the fact that the generalization might have a degree of truth to it or might be anchored in a valid conclusion from another, more limited context.

4. *Do not prohibit exceptions.* Often, a generalization works against itself by including excluders, words that prevent exceptions and that prevent reasonable people from accepting the premise on which your generalization is built. The culprits: words like *absolutely, never, always, must,* and *certainly.* You can avoid generalizations that are too rigid by using words like *sometimes, often, occasionally, probably, usually, might,* and *often.*

The High-Order Skills Together: A Review

Let's look now at a textbook selection that your son or
daughter is apt to tote home on the school bus. You'll
also be interested in seeing some typical questions provided in a home reading assignment, a class practice
exercise, or a commercial assessment measure. These
questions deal with the high order skills we've been talking about in this chapter and the ones directly before
it—inferring, predicting outcomes, drawing conclusions,
and generalizing. I've taken the selection from an upper-
grade elementary school social studies book. Here you
see a glimpse of the Bedouins, nomads who live in the
deserts of North Africa, and the values that these people
instill in their children.

The Bedouin people think most highly of people who show loyalty. To them loyalty does not
mean that one is devoted to a country, a place, or
a leader. Loyalty means being faithful to one's
family and tribe.

The Bedouin take pride in their ancestors.
They do not admire a hero from an ordinary or
poor family as much as one who comes from an
honored family. They particularly respect those
who have inherited a good name and then have
passed it on to their children.

A man's position among the black-tent people
depends upon his ancestors, relatives, and fellow
tribesmen. If they are honored, he is also honored. If they are disgraced, he too is disgraced.
Therefore one carefully guards the honor of his
family, his lineage, and his tribe.

A man can protect his family's honor by being
brave and generous and by giving protection to
those who ask for it. He also guards it by carefully watching the women of his family.

A Bedouin woman cannot bring honor to her family, but she can bring disgrace. Even if a woman only looks as if she has done wrong, she may be killed. The honor of her family depends upon her virtue.

1. Based on this passage, you can predict that a Bedouin man will feel disgraced if he
   a. does not succeed at business.
   b. needs to ask for help from his brothers.
   c. does nothing when a member of his family is insulted.
   d. does not help a stranger who asks for assistance.

2. From this passage you can predict that if a Bedouin woman betrays her husband with another man, the
   a. woman will be punished.
   b. other man will be punished.
   c. husband will ask for a divorce.
   d. woman will be forgiven.

3. From this passage you can conclude that the Bedouin people
   a. respect people who leave their families to seek success on their own.
   b. respect people who value their families above all else.
   c. blame government officials who use their power to get special favors for their families.
   d. are self-centered.

4. You can conclude that Bedouin women are
   a. treated as the equals of men.
   b. always listened to carefully when they tell their side of a story.
   c. respected for the many things they do.
   d. not respected as much as men.

5. You can generalize about this passage that the Bedouin people
   a. are a peaceful people.
   b. center their lives around their families.
   c. are not concerned with status and honor.
   d. are quick to recognize individual excellence.

How did you both do? Check your responses and talk about them with your child: 1. c., 2. a., 3. b., 4. d., 5. b.

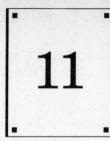

11

Moms and Dads as Reading Helpers
GOOD BOOKS THROUGH THE GRADES

Read some chilling statistics, reported in an accurate Roper Organization survey a short time ago. Pollsters telephoned a nationally representative cross section of 1,000 families with kids from three to fourteen years old.

Over ninety percent of moms and dads said reading was essential to their boy or girl's success. But of those with a child who could read, only 66 percent were happy with how their youngster was reading.

According to age group, these are the numbers regarding parents who thought their child was interested in reading:

SCHOOL LEVEL	PERCENTAGE
Preschool	56%
Kindergarten–second grade	59%
Third grade–fifth grade	53%
Beyond fifth grade	39%

At best, therefore, according to parents, six out of ten youngsters in any of the four groups found books stimulating.

Of all the families surveyed only forty-four percent said their children read for pleasure each day.

The implications are astounding. Personal happiness, future education, good jobs, enlightened citizenry, the society's continued advance: these all are at stake. Looking beyond the elementary and junior high school years, a Carnegie Foundation survey of 5500 college professors revealed that 75% think undergraduates at their institutions are seriously underprepared in basic skills; 66% think their colleges are paying too much money and spending too much time teaching what students should have learned prior to college admission.

The failure of our schools to develop essential skills, the pervasive indifference to books among our children, the minimal achievement level at which so many youngsters hover throughout their educational lives—these are grim barriers to knowledge, happiness, and success. We read about this new study, that commission's report, those irrefutable data. We worry for awhile and then shrug with resignation. I'm not hopeful that the depressing statistics we hear about so regularly will improve any time soon, no matter what changes we make in our country's formal educational system. But in the informal realm—the home, the supermarket, the playground, the various child-parent intersections—fertile, untilled soil stretches out around us.

At the core of how society measures educational growth and achievement, of course, at the heart of learning and knowledge, are books and the skills needed to use them profitably. True, the media explosion in the last fifty years has supplemented books as the sole repositories of knowledge, adding simple visual, action video, and auditory means of conveying information.

The computer with its almost illimitable retrieval system and its potential for integrating many media as instructional tools has challenged our methods of acquiring knowledge. This challenge burst upon us in a manner unparalleled since Guttenberg's printing press, in another age, revolutionized learning.

It's important to realize, however, that the computer in many ways has increased what we have to read and not decreased it. Churning out information, computers deluge us with more data requiring interpretation than anyone ever dreamed of. Many people moan and groan about how technology is doing away with the need to read, but I see it instead as increasing that need beyond measure.

In the 1990s there is more to know than at any other moment in past history. In fact, for example, scholars estimate that 90% of all scientists who ever lived are living today. Think about that fact for a moment. Think about all the scientific discoveries reported in the last fifty years. Think about the incredible strain that new information so rapidly garnered places on a lethargic educational system. Think about the endless spectrum of options curriculum planners, school administrators, and teachers have as they try to lay out a learning program for your child. Think about how crowded an elementary school teacher's day is, especially with our current hysteria about content—facts, data, information bits. What does a teacher include? exclude? After teaching the minimum essentials, teachers may sacrifice the painstaking practice needed to perfect reading skills.

Whether or not you agree with this approach is not the point. The point is that we have a swiftly flowing river of information, which is becoming a stronger torrent each day. Even in the best of all worlds, formal educational structures alone—schools, classrooms, libraries—are not enough support to create a nation of successful learners. There's too much to do, too little time, and too many distractions.

Your child needs you to help him learn.

For many years the education establishment insisted on sole guardianship of curricula. Parents were unwelcome invaders in the land of intellectual and academic growth. Teach your child moral and religious values; make him or her a "good" boy or girl; and leave the rest to the teachers and administrators. That's the message my parents took away from their encounters with educators in the fifties and sixties.

Such a position was untenable then, and it's even more untenable now. Given the complex world we inhabit and the growing need to learn more and more about it, parents are essential contributors to their children's education. If you don't play a role in your child's push toward knowledge, your youngster will face many disadvantages throughout his educational career.

I'm not recommending that you become your child's teacher. I've taken great pains to point out regularly in this book my opposition to defining your household role as formal learning master—unless, of course, you're a "home schooling" parent and can manage the serious emotional and intellectual demands on your family and time that a rigorous teaching program at home will bring. Moms and dads have a much more important job to do: establish positive learning conditions at home; be loving, knowledgeable learning facilitators; and help your child be a better reader.

In this book I have aimed to invite you, the parent, into the scheme of teaching and learning and to give you the information you need to help advance your child's reading through the grades. You have a rare opportunity to stimulate critical thinking, to integrate your child's surrounding world into print-based learning, and to guide and shape the educational excellence of someone you love deeply. I want you to avoid the frustrations of the Baltimore parents I mentioned in the first chapter who didn't know where to begin in helping their children improve as readers at school. With what you've read in *Any Child Can Read Better* you can deal thoughtfully with the various history, geography, English, science, health, and computer activities and assignments that your son or daughter will bring home for your advice and support. You'll help your child answer his or her own questions and, by asking several of your own, you'll be stimulating active and critical thought within a variety of school subjects.

I believe without reservation that any child can read better—better than he or she is reading now, better than he or she has learned in school, better than teachers expect your child to read on his or her own. Let me end my comments by telling you what awaits you on the remaining pages of *Any Child Can Read Better*. With your interests in your child's reading development, you should carve out some time to guide your youngster's choice of books for independent reading. From the earliest years onward what your child reads on his own affects quite dramatically the observable measures of school success, such as course grades, achievement tests, SATs and ACTs. Parallel to the required reading your child does in textbooks at school should be a home program in reading for enjoyment and knowledge.

Here again, don't count on the schools to guide appropriate choices based on your child's individual interests and talents. Other than a broad assignment category—"Read a biography"; "Read a book of nonfiction"; "Read a work of fiction about animals"—your child will not get much guidance in tailoring the activity to her interests. Yet choosing those independent readings are very important because they help establish your youngster's long-range commitment to reading. A couple of wrong turns here and you risk losing a lifetime reader. You don't want your child counted among the almost 50% of kids from third to fifth grade who aren't interested in reading. You don't want your child counted among the 61% of kids beyond fifth grade who aren't interested in reading.

To counter that bleak prospect in part, I've devised this list of recommended books with titles that will interest your child from first grade through sixth grade. It's an extensive list, I admit; it includes books I like and books I've found that kids like. It covers a range of selections and interests—fact and fancy, fiction and nonfiction, science, biography, poetry, fairy tales—in short a range of options for growing children's diverse interests.

But this is not just a book list. I've also provided a rather full summary of each selection so that you can talk intelligently about the book with your son or daughter and can provide some enticing details. Ideally, of course, you should read the book too, preferably with and, when you can, aloud to your child. (No matter how old your child is she'll love for you to read to her.) However, in case time slips away from you and you can't read the book you've recommended, I've given you enough of a summary to carry on a useful conversation. But remember: If you can, read the book.

Most important in this list, however, is the instruction you'll find book by book in tackling the critical thought skills so necessary for reading success. I've tried to give you conversational prompts, questions designed to engage your child with vocabulary, fact-finding, inference, drawing conclusions, making generalizations— with all those cognitive processes that sharpen reading abilities and heighten pleasure and understanding.

Here they are in alphabetical order, with grade levels indicated for each book. Read. Talk. Enjoy.

175 Science Experiments to Amuse and Amaze Your Friends.
Brenda Walpole. New York: Random House, 1988. (Gr. 3–7).
This attractive collection of science experiments gives your child
practice with a style of writing common in textbooks but less
frequently found in recreational reading. Short explanations
coupled with colorful illustrations lead kids to solve problems
independently. Yet your youngster will use the same skills of
inference, of drawing conclusions, and of forming generalizations.

The experiments are organized in four major sections dealing
with water, air, movement, and light. Each section begins with
an intriguing question such as "Why does a hot air balloon rise?"
or "If you spin this multi-colored disk, what color would you
see?" To explain how you and your child can use this book, we'll
use the activities on "Light and Shadows" in the section on light.

Notice the box titled "Light and Shadows" on page 132. The
highlighted paragraph explains the scientific principle behind
the activities, the principle that light travels in straight lines.
Give your youngster a chance to become comfortable with this
concept. Talk about the picture of the sunlight shining through
the trees. Has your child ever seen light shining through trees
like that? Talk about how those beautiful sunbeams are separated rays of light that cannot curve around trees. Has she ever
seen sunbeams shining through clouds? What might separate
light rays in clouds?

The activities are sequenced from simple homespun shadow
tricks through sun clocks and measurement of sun shadows to
studying eclipses or shadows in space, but your child can pick
any activity that is suitable and interesting. Read the questions
next to the illustrations to focus your child's thoughts on the
topic. For example, ask what will happen when a shape is held
different distances from a light. What happens to the size of the
shadow? Your child can predict the outcome, then try it out and
finally read the short explanation on the next page to compare
her explanation with the author's. Talk about what happened to
the shadow. What generalization or rule did you learn from the
shadow's changes? If your child makes a shadow clock, ask her
to predict when the shadow will be closest to the pencil. Why
should it be closer at that time? Relate this concept to her own
experience by talking about other shadows your child sees
changing during the day: shadows of trees, buildings, people.
When does a house's shadow stay close to the walls? When does
its shadow reach far away?

Enjoy this chance to make reading part of your child's active exploration of her world.

A *Dolphin Goes to School.* Elizabeth Simpson Smith. New York: Morrow, 1986. (Gr. 2–5). Squirt the dolphin got his name from his love of teasing: He squirted his trainer out in the Atlantic Ocean at their first meeting! Playful, teasing dolphins become good performers, trying hard to please human audiences. But playfulness meshes with hard work at the dolphin school Squirt attended. This book follows Squirt's school days from his capture in the ocean to his graduation to become a performer.

Your child may think it strange that the word "behavior" is used frequently in the book. Talk about its special meaning here. Compare that meaning to the meaning we usually have for "behavior." Consider why the author talks about behaviors instead of "tricks." Do you have a different feeling for an animal that does "behaviors" rather than "tricks"? How do the connotations of the words compare and contrast?

Squirt's sensitivity and ability to communicate, both with people and with other dolphins, are the most compelling aspects of this book. To share this appreciation with your child and to encourage a broader view of the issues involved in dolphin training, ask about the feelings the dolphins and trainer have for each other. What can we infer about the attraction between dolphins and people? Remember how Squirt came up to his trainer voluntarily out in the ocean and began to play with him. What do you enjoy about watching dolphins? What details or episodes about communication between dolphins show that they regularly "talk" with each other and give each other emotional support. From *A Dolphin Goes to School*, what generalizations can you draw about the relations between humans and wild animals?

With your child consider how Squirt's capture revealed the bond between people and dolphins. Compare the capture and training of wild dolphins to the capture and training of wild horses or other wild animals. Would the dolphins ever be trained using straps and harnesses? Would the trainers ever speak of "breaking" a wild dolphin as trainers talk about other animals? Consider the concern for the dolphin's health and comfort. How is the dolphin treated? What generalizations can you make about the training of a dolphin?

During the training, notice the attention the trainer gives to the happiness of the dolphin. Think about the training the day that Squirt's friend had her baby. Also consider the effect of the glass tank on Squirt's performance. What conclusions can you draw about the influence of a dolphin's feelings on his ability to learn and perform?

Have your child watch for details that indicate how much the trainers know about dolphins. The description of Squirt's capture and his trip to the school offer an opportunity to infer much regarding the trainer's knowledge and duties. Use that information to draw conclusions about the kind of training and character a trainer should have. Ask your child to evaluate the rewards of the job, at least the satisfaction of working with the animals. Would your child want to work as an animal trainer?

The Amazing Bone. William Steig. New York: Farrar, Straus & Giroux, 1975. (Gr. 1–3). *The Amazing Bone* is an excellent story for building reading skills. A read aloud can offer more intellectual stimulation than the typical learn-to-read book. Its rich vocabulary evokes the lushness of spring or the cold, threatening sound of a knife being sharpened. Words like "ravenous crocodile" or "odiferous wretch" will expand word storehouses. Use context clues to determine meanings wherever you can. I recommend focusing a conversation on new words to make them a part of your child's active vocabulary with questions like "Do you think the fox is as ravenous as the crocodile?" or "Do you think that odiferous wretch really is a smelly rascal?" Include practice with predicting outcomes: "What will the fox say when the bone calls him an odiferous wretch?"

This tale of Pearl and her amazing bone draws on a young child's already established literary background. Even a very young reader will recognize elements borrowed from "Little Red Riding Hood." Zero in on comparison-contrast skills with questions such as "What were Pearl and Little Red Riding Hood doing?" "Where were they?" "What do the wolf and the fox want?" "What characters do you find in one story but not in the other?" "Which villain, the fox or the wolf, is more wicked?" "Which one feels a little sorry for his victim?" "Which one wants his meal to be tasty and delicious?" "Which ending do you like better?"

Enjoy more of guessing what will happen next, that is, predicting outcomes. Patterns within the story may be repeated—but are not necessarily repeated. Before you turn the page ask whether the fox will run away. Will the fox be like the robbers? What can you conclude about the fox when he doesn't fall for the bone's trick? Do you think Pearl will escape from the fox? Why? Why do you guess that the fox will be dangerous as soon as he meets Pearl?

Unusual things happen with the bone—things that could never happen in real life. But can anything and everything happen? What general rules govern the bone? What statement in the story tells you that the bone is limited in what it can do? Do you like the world that Pearl and the bone live in? Why or why not?

Amos Fortune, Free Man. Elizabeth Yates. New York: Dutton, 1950. (Gr. 4–8). Amos Fortune, born the son of an African chief, came to Boston on a slave ship in 1725. At fifteen he entered Caleb and Celia Copeland's Quaker household, legally a slave, but living more as a member of the family. Amos freely gave Caleb his loyalty, substituting Caleb for the father he had lost in Africa and postponing offers of freedom until Caleb's untimely death sent Amos to a new household. After years of service Amos earned his own freedom and the freedom of several other slaves. His character and craftsmanship earned him the respect of the white as well as the black community.

Elizabeth Yates based her book on original documents, but added details to create a lively and readable story. With your child look at the list of original documents in the introductory pages and discuss which details of the story are most likely additions supplied by the author. Can you be certain which elements are from original documents? Do you think the story of the reading lesson at the Copeland's is taken from Amos' papers or created by Yates? Are all details of the story authentic? For example, is there icy water, or are there seasons as we know them in tropical Africa?

The reader learns a great deal about Amos in the first pages of the story. What qualities remain a part of him through his life? Discuss how Amos proves his commitment to peace during his capture and in later years. Talk about his vision of himself as a protector of his people and his belief that his noble birth made him a servant of his people. How does the scripture reading in the Copeland's Bible bring together his early vision of himself and his role in his new life in America? Can you infer that Amos' vision for himself gave his life direction and meaning? Talk about the special place Amos kept for his sister. Compare his sister with the women he later freed. What were some characteristics his sister shared with the first ones Amos freed?

Have your child compare Celia's and Caleb's attitude toward Amos when he arrived at their house. Why do you think Amos did not speak? Do you think it strange that he remained silent? When Celia states, "I will teach him as I teach the other children," what can you infer about her estimation of Amos' intelli-

gence? What can you infer about Amos' intelligence and capabilities as he bargains in the market and carries on his trade as a
tanner?

A conversation about this book should evaluate Amos' views
of freedom. Why did Amos try hard to procure freedom for several others in the last months of their lives? Why was it important at that time? On page 162 Amos argues that "it does a man
no good to be free until he knows how to live." Discuss together
what Amos means by knowing how to live. Does Amos mean
that some people will not deserve freedom? How should people
become ready for freedom? Would some people today judge that
Amos was too submissive?

Help your child evaluate the respect Amos received from both
blacks and whites. How does the letter from the father of Amos'
apprentice indicate that Amos was considered a good role model
and teacher for a white youth? Do you think Amos would be a
good role model today?

Buffalo Hunt. Russell Freedman. New York: Holiday House, 1988.
(Gr. 3–7). Introduce this book by looking at the illustrations,
which are reproductions of paintings by nineteenth century
artists. Talk about the historic value of these paintings. How are
these paintings like photographs? How does the sequence of the
paintings show you the history of the buffalo's dramatic disap-
pearance. You will probably want to provide some historical
context for the importance of these artists. How many white
men then had witnessed a buffalo hunt or even visited the
plains? Imagine the awe and excitement of the painters when
they saw the buffalo. What courage would it take to get close
enough to paint a buffalo hunt? What other dangers did the
painters face during their wanderings among the various tribes?

Why does the author begin the book with Indian legends
about the origin of the buffalo that show that the buffalo was a
special animal? Help your child evaluate the buffalo in Indian
society. Consider how much food one buffalo provided and the
number of buffalo that hunters could kill in one hunt. Weigh the
dangers, strategies, successes, and failures of the hunt. Would
you agree with the Indians' conclusion that the buffalo hunt was
worth the danger?

Several events greatly affected the buffalo hunt. Help your
child select these important developments and evaluate their relative importance: the arrival of the horse, the coming of settlers
on the wagon trains, the sale of buffalo hides and tongues back
East, and finally the development of a new tanning process for

buffalo hides. (Did you expect the gun to be a more important influence on buffalo hunting?) How did horses affect the hunt? When would you have preferred to hunt without horses? Why did settlers in wagon trains kill buffalo? Why did other white hunters kill buffalo? Were they the only ones to hunt for profit? Which development contributed most to the loss of the buffalo? What was the influence of people back East who had never seen a live buffalo? If each person in the East bought one buffalo hide, how many buffalo would have been killed? Do you think those purchasers of buffalo hides ever realized they were changing the West? How did those purchasers of hides change the lives of the Indians?

What was the result of killing off the buffalo? What do you know about the use of the buffalo for Indians? What happened to the Indians after the buffalo disappeared? Who, in your judgment, was responsible?

The Carp in the Bathtub. Barbara Cohen. New York: Lothrop, Lee & Shepard, 1972. (Gr. 1–5). Imagine eating a friend for dinner! Twice a year Mama keeps a carp in the bathtub for a week so that she will have a good fresh fish for her famous gefilte fish at holiday time. But during the carp's stay in the tub, Leah and Harry, the children in the family, feed it; the carp becomes their friend. Especially the year that Leah is nine, they have a particularly happy and intelligent fish whom they name Joe. How can they let Mama kill him with the club and serve him for dinner on Passover?

You and your child can enter a lively conversation about eating animals. Do you picture your hamburger as having once been an animal? Do you worry about how it gets to your plate? How do you feel about hunting or fishing? Does the hunter know the animal being hunted? Talk about the difference between eating an animal raised on a huge cattle ranch and eating an animal raised as a pet. What is special about the pet? How do you think the rancher thinks about the animals?

In the story Papa explains that certain animals are meant to be eaten while others are not. Consider Leah's response that she does not want to eat a friend. Are Papa and Leah really talking about the same thing? What is the difference between eating a certain kind of animal and eating one particular animal? What has happened when that animal became singled out from the others and brought to live with people? What worries Papa most during the carp crisis? How will Mama feel if her family doesn't like the meal she prepares for them?

As Papa talks about the carp, your young reader can also learn how he feels about his family. Have your child look at the illustrations. How do the children and Papa reach for each other? Are the children happy to see Papa in the crowd? How does conversation among family members indicate that they love each other? What details in the story indicate that the family cares for each other? How do they know—that is, what details allow the inference? Why does Papa bring home the cat? Why couldn't Mama understand the children's choice of the name Joe for the cat?

Let your child know how much he has inferred about the family's life. How expensive is their apartment compared to others around it? What kind of neighborhood do they live in? Are the neighbors rich or poor? Does the family have enough money to live comfortably? Do they have much extra money? Mama goes to extra trouble for her fresh carp. Is Mama a smart shopper? Why do you think so?

Talk about the secret the family keeps from Mama. Are they being kind or unkind when they hide their feelings about the gefilte fish? Is such a secret dishonest? What would you do if you were Leah or Harry?

The Children of Green Knowe. Lucy M. Boston. Orlando, FL: Harcourt, 1977. (Gr. 4–7). Tolly is alone as usual as he watches flooded fields from the window of the train. His journey to his great-grandmother's house ends with a boat ride from the watery road to the doorstep of Green Knowe. The boat takes him to a different world.

Lucy Boston has painted the scene at Green Knowe with the subtle techniques of an impressionist. Many details, individual points in themselves, blend together to form a richly imagined setting. Talk with your child about how the floods, the reference to Noah's ark, and the name Green Noah make you think of an isolated spot where animals come for food and safety. From Tolly's first moment in the house, boundaries between real and unreal, large and small, past and present grow indistinct. Discuss the moment that Tolly slips into the house, when big, old mirrors reflect images of each other so that Tolly does not know which door is real, nor which reflection is really himself.

At times details act as heralds of the future. Why is Tolly afraid when he hears a peacock scream? Sometimes the clues are conflicting. Talk about the uncertainty of facts, especially on Christmas Eve. That night two people saw St. Christopher moving, but in the morning icicles hang from the motionless statue.

The world remains mysterious and uncertain without solid evidence. This is a book that deserves a second reading just to appreciate the layers of detail that create a believable world from an unbelievable story.

Green Knowe gives Tolly what he needed most—a family. Granny, who has a significant name, Mrs. Oldknow, tells Tolly stories of three children who lived at Greene Knowe in the seventeenth century. Have your child compare Tolly with Granny. How are their names linked to the names of the previous children? How are their childhoods similar? Consider the loneliness they both feel. How did Granny's games with the children parallel Tolly's experiences? Have you ever felt that a character in a book was almost as real as someone you knew?

After Tolly has come to feel close to the children, after they are like brothers and sisters, Granny leads Tolly back to a comfortable acceptance of the real world. Sharpen critical thinking skills by contrasting Tolly's very down to earth Christmas guest with Toby, Alex and Linnet. How do the earlier and contemporary children play with Tolly?

Much of the magic of this book rides the wings of poetic language. Take turns pointing out your favorite figurative expressions. You might mention, "He tossed his notes up, like a juggler tossing balls." Talk about how a voice singing could be like a ball tossed by a juggler. Think of other similes or metaphors that could describe singing. Discuss how metaphor, a new way of looking at a scene, makes the scene seem more real.

How real does the book become for you? Lucy Boston wrote the book about her own house in the English countryside. How real do you think the story is for her?

Come Sing, Jimmy Jo. Katherine Paterson. New York: Avon, 1985. (Gr. 5+). Let the cover open your discussion. Ask why there are two pictures of the same boy and then compare the two pictures. What do you see in both pictures? Do you predict the guitar will be important? Who or what is with the boy in the pictures? Describe the people. Where might you see people like them? Talk about the expression on the boy's face? Is it the same in both pictures. Is he happy or sad?

Katherine Paterson quietly carries her reader into James Johnson's suddenly turbulent world. After spending his first eleven years in his grandma's peaceful, remote house, James' becomes Jimmy Jo, a country music star. Singing in public, James is haunted by a fear of failure, and he simultaneously feels cut off from his family as his relationships break apart. His stage fright, his fear of leaving home and his loneliness are part of the burden that comes with his gift. Your discussion can relate James' burden to your child's own experience and understanding. Has he ever been afraid of going to a new school, playing in a recital, or joining a new soccer team? Does everyone sometimes experience fear of the unknown and fear of failure? What obligation do we have to ourselves, our family and others to challenge our abilities? What can James offer the world? What might your son or daughter contribute to make the world better? Talk about contributions. Do gifts need to be unusual talents like James' to be worthwhile? How would the world be worse if we let fear of trying stifle our abilities?

Help your child appreciate James' difficulty in his new life in the city. Talk about how the other kids at school are different from James. How does the school secretary make James feel out of place? Discuss the undercurrents among the adult members of the family. How can you tell that Olive and Earl are jealous of James' success? What details in the story tell you that something is wrong that James does not understand? After finishing the story, think back to clues regarding the family secrets. Talk about James' loneliness. What prevents him from feeling close to his family or to friends his own age?

As you and your child explore James' search for his identity, consider the effect of Olive's and James' new names. How does Olive change when she becomes Keri Su? Why does James feel uncomfortable with the name Jimmy Jo? Does he feel he is the same person? Help your child search for an explanation for the name change besides the appeal "Keri Su" and "Jimmy Jo" are supposed to hold for the audience?

The worst threat to James' identity is the stranger who claims to be his father. How do James and the family try to ignore the stranger and why is the stranger frightening? Discuss Eleazor's response that it's not so bad to have multiple daddies. Talk about Eleazor and James' boat ride. How does the day in the boat give James peace and strength?

The climax of the story occurs when James confronts the stranger. Talk about the distinction James makes between being a father and a daddy. How does James sort out his own identity by facing the stranger? How does James' meeting with his father enable James to respond to Jerry Lee and Grandma's request that he sing with the family? Talk with your child about James' acceptance of their love and how he shares that love with the audience. Review the sequence of Jerry's use of his glasses.

Remember when Olive first took his glasses off? How did James feel? How did the first audience appear to James? Talk about how "James" wears classes, but "Jimmy Jo" doesn't. Notice that James wears his glasses during the last performance. Discuss how he no longer seems torn between being James and Jimmy Jo. Compare his vision of the audience with his earlier impressions of audiences. Compare his love for the audience to his emotions during past performances. Evaluate the effect that James' new love and security in his own family have on his feelings for the audience.

Country Fair. Gail Gibbons. Boston: Little, Brown, 1994. (Gr. 1–4). With colorfully detailed illustrations somewhat reminiscent of Grandma Moses, Gail Gibbons, winner of the *Washington Post* Children's Book Guild Award for nonfiction, moves us through a country fair—from the carpenters nailing stands together before it opens to the explosion of fireworks to light up the darkness, "a perfect way to end a perfect day." We see the high school band leading the way from the gate for ticket purchase; we see the tents and stands—a ring-toss booth, a bingo tent, face painting. And the refreshment stands: popcorn, fries, pizza, chicken and hamburgers, homemade ice cream. Children will love the illustrations of the ferris wheel, the carousel, the Mad Mouse ride racing along the track to the delighted screams of the passengers. Look for the Haunted House and the clowns as well as the celebrations of fall harvest, prized fruits and vegetables awaiting the judges who will award blue ribbons to the growers of the best entry in each category. And don't miss the canned fruits and vegetables, the flower arrangements, and the arts and crafts displays. You'll see farm equipment, calf judging, goats, pigs, chickens, riders showing their horses—all competing for prizes. A horse-and-buggy race fills a two-page illustration. Right before the fireworks, a band plays country music as everyone sways to the rhythms.

The illustrations here can be a rich source of conversation because of their lively details and rich characterizations. You can see how the various people feel about the events they're participating in. And the illustrations help you tease out useful facts from the text. For example, you can see a blacksmith at his anvil as he hammers a hook into shape. Talk about the role of the blacksmith, how the anvil works, how hot coals play a part in his work.

You'll certainly want to talk about fairs in general. Why do people hold fairs? Even if you're an urban dweller and have never seen a country fair, perhaps you and your child have visited one of the street fairs in your city. What common elements can you and your youngster find between a street fair and a country fair? What parts of this country fair would your son or daughter like to visit? Why? What entry could your child bring to any of the contests?

One of the elements I like most about this book is the last few pages, "Planning a Country Fair" and "A History of Fairs." In other words, after she tells her story, itself rooted in realistic details, Gibbons further explores the facts behind the fair. In the first exposition, she shows with words and pictures how much time and how many people it takes to put a country fair together. We learn about committee meetings months ahead of the event; we learn about the entertainment schedule, the choosing of the judges, the promotional campaign. From the history of fairs we learn the link to the Latin *feria*, meaning festival; we read about the country fair's connections to ancient festivals of worship; we explore the Middle Ages fairs for the Christian saints, for example, St. Bartholomew's Fair in England; we learn that the first country fair in America was held in New Haven, Connecticut, in 1644. I love these factual details because they provide solid background to the imagined story of the book.

Talk about the facts with your youngster. Use the page on planning a country fair as the starting point for a more general discussion about planning and scheduling. What events in your child's life require sustained planning? Why do people plan? What advantages accrue to the thoughtful planner?

Crow Boy. Taro Yashima. New York: Viking Press, 1952. (Gr. 1–4). *Crow Boy* is usually shelved with books for young children but it is a story full of meaning for all ages. The simple language offers depth of feeling, compassion, and a thoughtful look at human values.

The brief story evokes the entire school career of a young boy, from his first day until his graduation six years later. We never know the boy's real name. At first he is Chibi, or "tiny boy," a timid, lonely child, unable to do his lessons or to make a friend at school. Once you establish that fact, ask your child to predict what may happen.

Year after year Chibi remains an outcast until, in his last year, a friendly new teacher discovers how much Chibi knows about the garden outside the classroom. What does your child infer about the new teacher? Compare him to the old teacher and to Chibi's classmates. Why might this teacher be interested in

Chibi? In all those years the whole school had noticed Chibi only to give him a derisive name. No one was prepared to see "stupid" Chibi on stage at the talent show. But Chibi's performance awoke a new feeling in all his classmates. Through imitation of the crows' sounds Chibi had heard on his long walk to and from school each day, everyone saw him afresh and suddenly appreciated his arduous daily trek to school.

Talk about how this book makes you feel. Do you like Chibi? Have you known anyone who didn't seem smart and was left out at school? Do your feelings change as you read the story? What do you think Chibi is like in the beginning? Do you feel sorry for him? What do you think about him when he becomes Crow Boy? Does Chibi change? Help your child articulate the emotions experienced in the story. Talk about feelings of failure and loneliness, of wrongdoing and sadness. Describe Crow Boy's pride and self satisfaction as he does his family's work. How would you describe the feelings of the talent show audience as they learn that Chibi was the only member of the class with perfect attendance? What generalizations can you draw from *Crow Boy?*

Taro Yashima's illustrations of a Japanese village create a scene distant from an American child's neighborhood, yet the text could describe an American school. Look at the pictures before reading the book with your youngster. Talk about how the same problems can arise in two very different cultures. Are kindergartners ever afraid on the first day at your school? Why? Is there anyone in your school who can't do the regular lessons? How does such a child feel about being in school? Has anyone in your class ever spent the day looking at the ceiling or out the window? What would happen to Chibi at your school? What might have happened if Chibi had had his last teacher all his years at school?

The Cry of the Crow. Jean Craighead George. New York: Harper-Collins, 1980. (Gr. 3–7). Mandy understands why her father and brothers kill the crafty and hungry crows that threaten their precious strawberry crop. Yet she hates the sound of their guns and secretly adopts a baby crow whom she names Nina Torrence.

Children will get caught up in the excitement of learning the meaning of the crows' cries—sounds of warning, the signal to search for food, the call to join the group. While Mandy learns to distinguish to sounds of the crows, Nina Torrence perfectly mimics several phrases in English. Talk about what your child can infer about Mandy's and Nina Torrence's learning. Especially mysterious is a phrase uttered by Nina's parents' killer, a phrase that the young crow learned during the fearful attack on the nest. Discovering the speaker of the phrase—and hence the killer of the crows—is an important clue in predicting the outcome of the book. As your child progresses through the book, ask who might have said, "I've got you."

Here is an excellent opportunity to discuss with your child what real human language is. How do the crows learn to communicate with each other? How do crows learn human language? How do crows use human language?

Fearing that growing independence will entice her away, Mandy separates Nina Torrence from the wild crows despite her mother's warning that later Nina will be too old to join the wild crows and will have to live with people. Discuss with your child how Mandy tries to keep Nina Torrence a baby. Compare Mandy's treatment of Nina with the way Mandy's mother, Barbara, treats her. Does Barbara encourage Mandy to be independent? How does Mandy have to make adult decisions in dealing with the crow? Discuss why Mandy ignores the ominous warning that a once-injured crow like Nina might seriously endanger her attacker. How might Nina become dangerous?

Relations among family members are crucial to the outcome of the novel. In what way does Mandy's opinion of her father change? Is her father understanding? How are the women of the family different from the men? What generalizations can you draw about them? How do the nurturing women contrast with the hunter males? How does this contrast reflect men's and women's behavior in your surroundings? Discuss why Mandy's younger brother, Drummer, wants so desperately to be like his father and older brothers.

Learning about a facet of the natural world is another advantage of this book. Few of us have felt much curiosity about ugly, raucous crows. Yet here their feathers are a soft, beautiful black. Their noise is intriguing, full of meaning. Their abilities extend far past our expectations for a mere bird. What does the author want us to realize about the discoveries we can make if we look carefully enough at the animal world?

Eclipse; Darkness in Daytime. Franklyn M. Branley. New York: Thomas Y. Crowell, 1973, 1988. (Gr. 1–3). What could be more exciting than watching the sun disappear! Branley's book is a colorful and artistic study of what an eclipse is and what eclipses have meant to people through the ages. Its illustrations rival those of good picture books. In addition to teaching physical science, *Eclipse* also shows how people have reacted to eclipses through the ages. Using the book as a springboard, a young reader can imagine how ancient people looked at the world and why people were afraid when the sun disappeared. Why did ancient people who believed the eclipse was caused by a dragon eating the sun have reason to think their theory was correct? Why did their actions seem effective?

Eclipse brings real scientific information within the reach of a beginning reader. The vocabulary is limited; the text is not too long. However, such condensed information makes greater demands on your child's skills. Because the author wants to avoid difficult words or long paragraphs for beginning readers, many of these transitional expressions that guide us through our reading are missing. Help your child mark the beginning of new topics. When does the author tell you what an eclipse is? When does the section on animals' reactions to an eclipse begin? Where does the story of the ancient theory of the dragon begin?

In keeping with the needs of beginning readers, Branley explains new vocabulary carefully, but the short text provides no opportunity to reuse a new word frequently and in varied contexts. I would suggest providing extra practice with such words. For instance, in the text the word "solar" is defined as "of the sun." Have your child guess at definitions for expressions containing the word "solar." Use words like "solar energy," "solar heat," or the "solar system." What do those expressions mean? Play with the words. What would a "solar burn" be or a "solar dial"?

Finally, bring the eclipse into your child's own life. Read the times and places future eclipses will occur. Talk about how old your child will be when future eclipses take place and where on the globe she would have to be to see it. Can she predict what things will be like in her immediate surroundings if she should experience an eclipse?

Everyone Knows What a Dragon Looks Like. Jay Williams. New York: Macmillan, 1976. (Gr. K–3). Mercer Mayer's beautiful illustrations add an exotic air to Jay Williams tale set in China. When you and your child pick up the book, talk about the scene on the cover. Does it look like any place you have been before? Do you see a dragon in the picture? Does it look like dragons you have pictured before? Talk about the bald, old, fat man sitting in the foreground. Is he rich or poor? How can you tell? Would you like to know him? Why?

Wild horsemen threaten the city of Wu on the northern border of China. With an army that can look brave, but cannot fight well, the Mandarin and the councilors decide their best hope is to pray to the Cloud Dragon. The next day Han, a poor road sweeper, sees a little, bald man who declares that he is the dragon. But the Mandarin and his cohorts rudely laugh at the old man's offer to save the city provided they treat him with courtesy. Only poor Han extends hospitality to the stranger. In thanks to Han alone, the man, who is indeed a dragon, saves the city.

Direct your child's attention to the attitude of the city's rulers toward the dragon. How does their reaction contrast to Han's? Think about what each person expects a dragon to look like. How are all the councilors similar to their expectations of what a dragon will look like? What conclusions can your child draw about the Mandarin and his advisers? How does their image of a dragon reflect their own place in life? What generalization can you make about the Mandarin and his councilors?

Lead your child to discover why the dragon chose to appear as an old man. Would the dragon know what the councilors were really like if he had appeared as they expected him to be? What keeps the important people from recognizing the dragon? Suggest that your child contrast Han and the councilors. Why is Han the one who can learn about the dragon? What can your child conclude about the Mandarin when he says, "But best of all . . . now we know what a dragon looks like. He looks like a small, fat, bald old man"?

Have your son or daughter compare this story to other stories such as "The Emperor's New Clothes." What kind of person sees the truth in both stories? Do you know any other stories in which an important figure comes disguised as a stranger in order to test a person's real character?

Han receives two rewards—one from the dragon and one from the city. Talk about the differences between the two rewards. Compare the beautiful vision of the dragon in the sky with the gold pieces and the important sounding new title, "The Honorable Defender of the City." How does each gift reflect the character of the giver? Ask your child what she thinks is the value of each gift.

Ferret in the Bedroom, Lizards in the Fridge. Bill Wallace. New York: Holiday House, 1986. Bill Wallace's opening pages carry the reader into the sixth-graders' world during a school election. Liz Robbins, a candidate for sixth grade class president, tells the story. Help your child appreciate how Liz's language creates a grade school atmosphere. Find expressions like "I felt like a real snot" or "the microphone was real skinny." How would the book be changed if the narrator said, "I felt extremely disappointed in myself" or "the microphone was cylindrical, about one inch in diameter"? Here, attention to denotation and connotation really pays off.

Despite the enthusiastic campaign plans of her friend Sally, Liz guesses that her chances of beating sleek and gorgeous Jo Donna Hunt are slim. Mishaps with the exotic menagerie that Liz's zoologist father keeps at their house plague Liz's campaign. As Liz's popularity plummets, even the cute new boy at school calls her by her hated old nickname, Lizard, proof that her dad's animals spoil her image at school.

You and your child can discuss whether having exotic animals indicates that the family is as unusual as Liz complains. Discuss how Liz' parents act, judging how much they are like typical parents. To what extent does Liz's concern with being different come from the opinions of Sally and the girls at the campaign meetings?

Are the girls fair when they get upset over the mishaps with the animals? These situations are fun to discuss not only because the incidents are wild and comic, but also because you can lead your young reader beyond a simple yes or no answer. Certainly her friends would be distressed, but is their complete rejection of Liz justified? Have your child evaluate the situation and predict how her own classmates would react in the same situation.

As you discuss Liz's final campaign speech, you can focus on the main themes of the novel. Explore the differences between desire for popularity and loyalty to friends (including relatives). How has Liz's need to be popular changed? Compare Sally's betrayal of Liz when threatened by Jo Donna's "Miss Piggy" posters to Liz's loyalty to her father and their animals.

Finally, discuss what Liz learns about Shane Garrison in the last chapter in light of the sequence of events: Shane's initial friendliness, Liz's response, the speech, the election and their friendship. How would the conclusion have been less satisfying if Liz had learned earlier of Shane's animals?

Five Finger Discount. Barthe de Clements. New York: Delacorte Press, 1989. (Gr. 4+). In a small town next to the reformatory Jerry keeps his identity secret. He is a PK, a prisoner's kid. Only two other kids know his secret, but one, Edward Troller, uses it for blackmail. Keeping slippery, mean, little Troller from going public is difficult for Jerry, who wants to make friends and avoid trouble in school.

Jerry can trust his secret with Grace, the girl next door. Grace introduced herself as a PK, but her family doesn't seem like Jerry's. Ask your son or daughter to look for clues for what PK means in Grace's family. What can your child infer from the use of initials "PK" to identify the children instead of the words they refer to? After discovering what kind of PK Grace is, consider each family's effect on its children.

What can you generalize about children growing to be like their parents? Where do you see the mistakes of the parents reflected in the book's children? Do children in general reflect their parents? Talk about theft in Jerry's family, meanness in Troller's, and manipulation in Grace's.

Explore together the author's attitude toward theft. What character seems to reflect the author's own ideas? Also look for the author's opinions as you see Jerry's understanding develop. First investigate Jerry's lack of concern for anyone owning or losing the lumber for the tree fort. Discuss how his awareness of theft changes during the story. What is his main worry when he takes the sandals? How does the theft of his jacket teach him about the results of theft? Study the influence of Grace's comments. Is it good for Jerry to feel miserable and embarrassed? Does Jerry reach greater understanding after he worries about others thinking of him as a thief? What generalizations can you draw here?

Ask your youngster to discuss his prediction of the future for Jerry and his dad. Will they keep the promise they made looking at the North Star? What has Jerry seen in his father's face when it looked like a Halloween pumpkin caved in with age? Encourage your young reader to work toward a judgment of Jerry's dad and to support that judgment with concrete details. Weigh the comment of Jerry's gradmother, his dad's last mistake with the shoes, and his dad's concern for Jerry's future.

De Clements' portrayal of Grace's morality makes a good back-drop to the questions of theft in Jerry's family. Discuss Grace's proficiency at manipulating her mother. What can you conclude about Grace's honesty? What do you think of the way Grace won the pumpkin contest? Did she cheat? Talk about the different circumstances of Grace's life, especially the gifts of her rich grandmother. What does Jerry mean when he says, "Life is simple when you're in the middle of your family eating roast chicken"?

When Grace's father suggests that each face reflects its owner's personal history, Jerry begins to look closely at faces, the Trollers' mean, pinched faces, Grace's family's full, innocent faces, and finally his father's broken face. Talk about faces as windows to drawing conclusions about people's character.

The Friendship. Mildred Taylor. New York: Dial Press, 1987. (Gr. 2–6). A good way to start talking about this book after your youngster reads it is to question whose friendship is referred to in the title. The story centers on a confrontation between a white store keeper and an old black man. It is told by Cassie, a nine year old black girl, who witnessed the incident with her brothers. Is the friendship between Tom Bee and storekeeper John Wallace? If so, is it a real friendship? What is the denotation of the word friendship? The connotation?

Talk about how Cassie lends her point of view to the story. Cassie and her brothers have an unpleasant encounter in the store before Tom Bee arrives. What does their experience tell you about the Wallaces? What might Dewberry Wallace leave out if he were telling the story? How would the story be different again if Jeremy Simms, the white boy, had told it? Could Tom Bee add other pieces to the story? How might John Wallace tell the story?

Details in the descriptions allow the reader to infer a great deal about the lives of the characters. Notice the date on the new catalog in the store. When does the incident take place? What conclusions can you and your child draw about the economy in 1933? Talk about the size of the store and its sparsely-covered shelves. What do you conclude on the basis of these details? Notice how everyone is dressed, both black and white. Does anyone in the book wear expensive clothes? Does anyone have any extra money? Do any of the kids get much candy? Talk about the speech of the characters. What can you conclude about their styles of life from their way of talking? Are there any differences in the way they speak?

Discuss the significance of the names blacks and whites use for each other. Talk about the status that "Mister" carries and why that status is important to the white people in that area. After talking about the area's customs, think about why John Wallace says he must "save face." Explain this metaphor to your child. Think about what other people are saying. Notice, however, whom the children respect. Which person in the book actually is called "mister"? Discuss what conclusions you can draw regarding John Wallace's motives for insisting on the "mister" with his name. What do you know about the thoughts of the other whites in the store? Do you predict that John Wallace will be prosecuted for using his gun?

Ask why Tom decided to call John Wallace by his first name after so many years. Do you think Tom always wanted to call him John? Why does Tom yell "John" over and over almost like a challenge in the last lines of the book?

Consider what Tom's emotions might be because his friendship was not acknowledged for so long. What friendship exists between Tom Bee and John Wallace now? Why, would you conclude, has John Wallace not acknowledged Tom Bee for many years? Finally, what generalizations can you make about friendship from this book?

Grandfather's Journey. Allen Say. Boston: Houghton Mifflin, 1993. (Gr. 1–4). In this Caldecott Medal winner, Allen Say combines a moving tale of love of two countries with breathtakingly beautiful illustrations that have the crisp fidelity of photographs. Grandfather's journey starts when as a young man he leaves Japan to see the New World. He is amazed by the beauty he finds there—rock sculptures, endless farm fields like the sea, factories, buildings, mountains, and rivers. After he returns home and marries, he and his bride move to San Francisco, where they have a baby girl. Unable to forget his homeland, Grandfather travels back to Japan when his daughter is nearly grown, and rejoices in his friends and the familiar landscape. He buys a house in a large city nearby; his daughter marries; and the author is born to the new couple. Grandfather talks often of California and plans a trip—but war interrupts everyone's life, and he never gets to see his beloved California again. The author does get to California, but like his grandfather, he longs for Japan. "The funny thing is," he says poignantly, "the moment I am in one country, I am homesick for the other." Say concludes that he now understands his grandfather and misses him very much.

Pay attention to the vocabulary here, particularly words like *sculpture*, *bewildered*, and *towering*, all of which your child should be able to define using both the context and the excellent illustrations. Build on inferential skills by asking why Grandfather surrounded himself with songbirds and why the Japanese village "was not a place for a daughter from San Francisco." What does Say mean when he says that the falling of bombs during the war "scattered our lives like leaves in a storm"?

See if you and your youngster can test some of the generalizations that can emerge from this book. Why do people get lonely for places where they no longer live? When people leave their homelands for adventure or other reasons, do they find what they expect? What are some of the advantages in moving to a new country? some of the difficulties? Would your child like to move to another part of the world, even for a short time?

The Great School Lunch Rebellion. David Greenberg. New York: Bantam, 1989. (Gr. 1–5). *The Great School Lunch Rebellion* is perfect for the child who is moving beyond easy readers, but its humor also can appeal to children through fifth grade. The out-of-hand food fight, in the tradition of Tom Sawyer and Huck Finn, brings out the enjoyment we have all had in celebrating rebellion in children's literature. Looking at the cover of the book before reading it, your child can infer where the scene takes place. Ask what the food looks like on the trays. Do the kids object to having food in their hair? How can you tell? Ask your child to describe the teacher. What might she be shouting? Compare the expressions on the children's faces with the teacher's expression. When your child begins reading, he will immediately notice how the author exaggerates the awful qualities of school lunches. Your child may exclaim that the description, although fun to read, is obviously overstated. Talk about the emotions the author evokes. Although your school lunch doesn't literally "hop away on grimy little feet" and it doesn't actually make squirrels fall over dead, does this description make you feel what it's like to look at a bad lunch? This description is an example of metaphorical language. Look for other examples of exaggerated metaphors or other figures. What does the author mean when he says that Jay once ate a tray? See if your child thinks that Jay's teeth could bite through plastic, or is the author using a metaphor to imply that Jay was willing to eat just about anything served to him? What is the author intending when he describes "soup made from monkey spit/Chunks of chewed-up bubble gum/And sweaty catcher's mitt"?

The boy narrator of the story uses wonderful techniques in his arguments justifying the rebellion. What does your child predict as the rebellion's outcome? How does his prediction match the story? After finishing the story, your child might enjoy creating alternate endings for the story—really another form of predicting outcomes. Be sure the endings result logically from the preceding events.

Children will laugh over the ironic humor of the conclusion. Depending on the maturity of your child, you may want simply to discuss the humor here, or you may want to introduce the concept of irony. "As a mark of our deep gratitude/It's camel liver stew!" proclaims the principal to perfect Teddy who alone gets to eat that lunch. What does the author really mean? Is camel liver stew a special treat?

Enjoy the flow of language and the rhyme. Ask your child what the story would be like if it didn't have rhyme. Would it be as funny? Would it sound as good?

Throughout, enjoy the fantasy and freedom of a desire never to be fulfilled in real life!

How to Eat Fried Worms. Thomas Rockwell. New York: Dell-Year-ling Books, 1973. (Gr. 3–6). Thomas Rockwell has created a perennial favorite in his saga of worm eating. Alan challenges his friend Billy to eat fifteen worms in fifteen days. The resulting fifty dollar bet pits Alan and his partner Joe against Billy and his helper Tom. The vivid personalities of the boys and their imaginative trickery make ideal entertainment for middle graders. What do you infer about Alan's personality from the challenge he proposes? And about Billy's from his accepting it?

Talk about how the boys differ from each other. Who is the most determined? the most persuasive? the most cunning? How does Joe exploit Billy's weaknesses? Which kind of trick is Billy good at figuring out? Would anyone you know take a bet like Billy's? Would any of your friends enjoy daring you to do something you wouldn't like to do?

What would the boys be like in other situations? Develop greater understanding of the characters by encouraging your youngster to predict how the boys would act in various situations. Imagine them at the zoo with monkeys escaping from their cage. Would anyone try to scare the monkeys back into the cage? Would any of the boys try to find someone else to take the blame? Might one of them have been responsible for the monkeys' escape in the first place?

Is the author more sympathetic to one side or the other? Help your child evaluate the author's sympathies. Do chapter titles indicate a preference for one side? (Parents may have to provide some historical background for the chapter titles derived from World War II events.) What other clues suggest the author's sympathies?

Talk about the struggle in the book and your child's own reaction to it. When does the competition get more intense? When does the author make the bet look like a full-fledged war? Do you want Billy to win? Would you feel bad if he lost after eating all but one worm?

Help your son or daughter evaluate the fairness of the bet. Is eating fifteen worms worth fifty dollars? What would be the worst thing you would do to win fifty dollars? Do you think Billy earned his money?

In the Year of the Boar and Jackie Robinson. Bettie Bao Lord. New York: Harper, 1984. (Gr 3–7). Shirley Temple Wong, a character based largely on the author's own life, leaves her clan's large home in China for an apartment in Brooklyn in 1947, the year of the boar, and also the year that Jackie Robinson was the rookie hero of the Brooklyn Dodgers. Life in Brooklyn is hard and lonely until Shirley learns to play baseball. Through baseball she at last makes friends in her new country, and with them she cheers Jackie Robinson and the Dodgers to the pennant and the World Series against the New York Yankees. Baseball and Jackie Robinson become symbols for life in the United States, symbols of the success possible for every person.

The old optimism of faith in individual capabilities blends with recent recognition of cultural diversity. Shirley enters P.S. 08 understanding nothing of the language or customs of her classmates. Her strong spirit and quick mind help her through her adjustment to American society. Do prereading warmups: Do you know anyone who has come from a foreign country? What were their experiences like? After reading the book, talk about how Shirley's situation helps other students see the way international students feel when they enter American schools? Might some of them have more trouble than Shirley? Why or why not? Are any of Shirley's problems experienced by all students?

One day Shirley's teacher used the game of baseball to illustrate how each person fits into American society. Talk about how each team member plays for himself and for the team. Compare how baseball teams work together with how football, soccer, or basketball teams work together. Where do you see each person play as an individual, while still having his or her achievements help the team as a whole? Which sports subordinate individual play to team play where an assist to a teammate is as good as a score?

Why does Shirley identify with Jackie Robinson? How does Jackie Robinson stand for minorities in general? How do minorities get along with each other in Shirley's school? How does your school compare to Shirley's?

Compare the enthusiasm Shirley eventually comes to feel for America with her love for her old home and family in China. If you have ever moved from one place to another, did you eventually wish that you could live in both places? Retell the story of the Chinese girl who became two people to live two separate lives which eventually merged back into one life. Discuss what this story means to Shirley.

Talk about how Shirley will be a big sister to her baby brother. What will she teach him? How will her teaching bring together her American life and her Chinese life?

Joyful Noise. Paul Fleischman. New York: Harper, Collins, 1988. (Gr. 3+). *Joyful Noise* is poetry to be read aloud by two voices, which echo and blend with each other, creating an impressionistic image of the seasons as lived by insects. In these poems you will find humor, play, and new perspectives.

Help your child read it through for vocabulary and meaning before you "perform" it together. (Holding a 3×5 card or bookmark under the line can help you both come in on cue.) Take turns choosing your favorite passage.

Enjoy the musical rhythm. Talk about how the words make you feel as you consider both connotation and denotation. Vocabulary and assumed knowledge may be challenging for younger readers, yet children meet that challenge. Some words like "vaulting" in "Grasshoppers" become clear from context. Before reading "Mayflies" discuss the life cycle of this insect who lives its full life in one day. The echoing voices then will reflect the poignant contrast of our time and a mayfly's time. Talk about still another perspective of time in the "redwood centuries" later in the poem for another vision of time and a contrasting form of life.

As you read, notice how you see the world through different eyes. Sometimes it is humorous as in the moth's serenade to the porch light, "I drink your light like nectar." Sometimes it is wondrous like the chrysalis' description of snow. Enter and enjoy this world created by words.

At some point you may want to separate what is hard fact and what is a human vision imprinted on an insect's state in life. For example, in "Honeybees," discuss what the poem tells about a bee's daily life. Yet what can we know about the mind of a bee? What part of the poem is really a human thought? Let such discussions arise naturally, perhaps after you have incorporated the emotional impact of the poem into your literary life. Personification characterizes much of the poetry here.

Jumanji. Chris Van Allsburg. Boston: Houghton Mifflin, 1981. (Gr. 3+). As usual, author Chris Van Allsburg takes the reader out of every day reality. In the almost surrealistic events here, you will find numerous openings for discussion. Imagine two typical children, bored with their toys, finding under a tree a board game labeled "especially designed for the bored and restless." Ask your child to pick out details in the game's instructions that are important clues to the outcome of the plot. Does it seem strange that the game will not end until one player reaches the last square and yells "Jumanji"? Appreciate Peter's ironic comment on the excitement of the game when he lands on the square with the inscription, "Lion attacks, move back two spaces." What has happened to our normal sense of reality when a lion appears at that moment? Talk about the children's personalities. Are they cowardly or are they brave? What can your child infer about these kids when Peter and Judy realize they must face the dangers of the jungle—lions, monkey, hippos, a volcano, and snakes—in order to finish the game and get rid of the lion?

Your child can draw much information through inference both from the text and from the illustrations. Looking at the stark neatness of the house, what can you conclude about the lifestyle of the family? Why would you conclude that the monkeys and hippopotamuses are especially out of place in this particular house? Why would Mother be more upset with the monkeys' mess than the lion's roar?

Your child also has probably inferred knowledge about the childrens' age and their relations with their parents. How old do the children appear in the illustrations? What games do they play? (The toys that the children are playing with in the pictures seem to be for younger children. This discrepancy might be confusing.) How well do they read? The parents trust the children home alone. Do the children worry about keeping the house neat for their parents?

Enjoy the scene of the adults' return. Does Mother expect them to have had an exciting afternoon? What reaction tells you that the adults don't believe the children's adventures occurred? Talk about the language the parents use with the children. What can you infer about the parents' real interest in the children's afternoon? You and your child can share your explanations of why the adults' heads are not shown in the illustrations.

I love the impact of the final page. Talk about what Judy and Peter know about the game as they watch Daniel and Walter carry it home. In your conversation encourage your child to pull together the knowledge that she has of the game and her knowledge of Daniel and Walter. What does she conclude when she puts that knowledge together? What prediction can be made for Daniel's and Walter's day?

Last One Home Is a Green Pig. Edith Thatcher Hurd. New York: Harper Collins, 1959. (Gr. K–3). When Duck invites him to race home, Monkey replies, "Last one home is a green pig." Finding himself behind, Duck soon hitches a ride on a girl's bicycle only to be left behind when Monkey finds a horse to ride. The race's speed escalates until both Duck and Monkey are flying home, the winner uncertain until the last second. Beginning readers will love the action and quick change of pace delineated with just a few words.

Compare each new vehicle with the one before. What happens each time Duck or Monkey gets something new to ride on? What happens each time you hear "up the hill" and "down the hill"? Help your child generalize about the increased speed of new modes of travel.

You may need to talk about why Duck didn't fly home in the first place. Did he think it might be unfair? Does it make a better story this way? Would monkey have raced a flying duck? What other reasons can you think of?

Develop your child's ability to predict the outcome of a story by discussing who has the advantage at the beginning of the race? Who can run faster? Who is ahead? Were you surprised at the end of the story?

In reading the story through you can infer a great deal about Monkey's and Duck's feelings for each other. Pose questions about Duck's and Monkey's friendship. Do you like Monkey's words to Duck after the race? What do you think they did the next day? What else might Monkey have said? How would that comment make Duck feel?

Help your child evaluate the race by relating it to his own experience. Would you like to give a racer a ride on your bike? Do you like races yourself? How is Monkey and Duck's race different from races you have been in? What is the difference between being tricky and cheating in a race?

The Living Earth. Eleonore Schmid. New York: North-South Books, 1994. (Gr. 3–6). Lavishly illustrated by the author in vibrant earth tones of green and brown, *The Living Earth* is a paean to the earth's cycle of life. I love the way the illustrations fill the pages completely over a two-page spread, with the words of the story printed on the bottom of each page.

Schmid talks about the changes we see and those we don't— water seeping into mountains, only to freeze and crack the rock, for example. She describes the earth's layers and the filtration effect of topsoil, as well as the growth of seeds by means of mineral release from humus. Detailed illustrations of plants and roots enhance the prose. We learn about and see the living organisms in soil and the constantly renewing nature of the earth. We also see the larger animals that live in the earth, from worms and snails to mice, moles, and foxes. Schmid sees the removal of forests to make new fields for farms as part of the earth's cycle, and she follows the farmer through tilling, planting, and harvesting crops. Yet she reminds us of the problems caused by the use of chemicals to destroy insects and plant diseases. She also points out the sacrifices we make in harvesting natural resources: "What has taken nature millions of years to create," she writes, "is being used up by humans in a very short time."

As you read this book to or with your child, use the wonderful illustrations to explore the themes. On the next to the last page, for example, ask your youngster to identify as many objects as she can. You'll see radishes, dandelions, onions, and petunias. Look closely and you'll see lady bugs, a snail, and a butterfly. Schmid recommends that the reader grab a handful of earth, sift it through the fingers, and smell it. You and your child do these activities together, talking about your impressions as you go along. Be sure to talk about the "city pages," where Schmid points out that even amid asphalt and concrete "the smallest patch of city soil can support the cycle of life."

What is your son or daughter's view of the cutting down of forests? of the use of pesticides? Talk about the advantages and harm that these acts cause. How can we use science and nature to everyone's advantage without destroying the planet?

Maia; A Dinosaur Grows Up. John R. Horner and James Gorman. Courage Books, 1987; [First published by Museum of the Rockies, Bozeman MT, 1985]. (Gr. 2–5). *Maia* gives a picture of one dinosaur, a maiasaura, from the day she hatches until she cares for her own young. Maia, who is quick and lucky, escapes the perils that plague baby dinosaurs, especially raids by meat eating Troodons who snatch baby maiasaurs from nests. John Horner, a noted authority on dinosaurs, paints the life of one type of dinosaur as researchers now think it was lived. Maia's mother feeds Maia and her siblings when they are too small to leave the nest and later teaches them where to find their own food.

Here is an excellent opportunity to distinguish fact from fiction. Although fictional, the dinosaur Maia was created to be typical of maiasaura. Ask if Maia herself really lived. Could the things that happened to Maia have happened to real maiasaurs? Could they have hatched like Maia? Do you think Troodon snatched the babies as they do in the story?

Have your child think about Maia in the egg and about how she hatched. Do we know whether baby dinosaurs squeaked inside the eggs? Could we find out? What would make us think that they might squeak? (Have you ever witnessed eggs hatching?) Could we find out what noises dinosaurs made?

Using the story of Maia, lead your child to make generalizations about maiasaurs. What would they eat? How fast would they grow? How would they learn where to find berries to eat? Help your child draw conclusions about the size and ferocity of the Troodon? Were adult maiasaurs afraid of Troodon? Were the babies afraid of them? What protected the babies from Troodon? When could the Troodon snatch the babies?

Talk about how new discoveries—for dinosaurs the discovery of new fossils—change scientific theories or guesses. Why was the old theory that all dinosaurs closely resembled modern lizards very plausible and reasonable until recent fossil discoveries showed dinosaur families nesting together as birds do? Talk about how our new ideas will probably be changed in the future.

Matilda. Roald Dahl. New York: Viking, 1988. (Gr. 3–7). In this recent book Roald Dahl uses the same elements that created the success of *James and the Giant Peach*. Again you will find a sweet, sympathetic child in the care of the worst possible guardians. In addition to having evil parents, Matilda is also up against a school principal named Trunchbull whose goal is to squash and terrify as many children as possible. Matilda, however, does not accept injustice without fighting back, and her brilliant mind more than makes up for the disadvantage of being young and small.

Dahl's humorous use of language is a delight to children. Some adults may hesitate to expose youngsters to his vivid descriptions, but children love them in the same way they love the monsters in *Where the Wild Things Are* and the giants "Fe, fi, fo, fum" in "Jack and the Beanstalk." Share your feelings about Miss Honey's warning that Trunchbull "can liquidise you like a carrot in a kitchen blender." Talk about how Dahl used metaphor in comparing Matilda to a scab that her parents must put up with until they can cast her off.

Perhaps your child will notice the difference between British and American English. He will certainly notice the word "telly" for "TV," and will easily guess its meaning. Other British expressions will take more thought to understand. What does it mean for Matilda's dad to "diddle a customer"? Help your child learn to infer other meanings from illustrations or from context. Look at the picture on page 35 and talk about Mr. Wormwood "skulking" around the room with his hat glued on. Ask how he is moving. Does he want to be seen? You might also figure out what brogues are. (Since they are on Miss Trunchbull's feet, they must be shoes.) Knowing Trunchbull's physique and personality, you can guess that they are heavy, sturdy shoes, not delicate sandals or high heels.

Dahl's characters are either good or bad, and they are fun to describe and draw conclusions about: the dishonest used car salesman, the dumb blond with heavy make-up who watches soap operas and plays bingo, the huge tyrant who is out to get everyone. What generalizations can you make about the villains? What do they think about children? Are they as smart as the children? What happens to the villains in the end—do they get their reward?

Discuss the punishments of the villains. Did justice prevail? Did the just get rewarded? Can you make a judgment about justice when both the crime and the retribution are so exaggerated as to be unreal?

Nate the Great and the Sticky Case. Marjorie Weinman Sharmat. New York: Dell, 1978. (Gr. K–3). Nate the Great, hero of a series of detective stories for beginning readers, here attacks the sticky case of the missing dinosaur stamp. I like this book for the humor and creative problem solving it provides within the limits of a simplified reading format. Before your child starts reading, look at the picture at the front of the book. Ask what Nate is doing. What does he have in his hand, and what is its purpose? What is Nate looking at through the magnifying glass? Talk about how Nate is dressed. What makes him look like a detective?

Invite your child to enjoy the play with words as Nate gets stuck on the sticky case, as he realizes that there are "two sides to every stamp," and as he searches for "something big that is small." Friend Claude loses things often, but doesn't "lose his way." Laugh together at this humor and talk about the varied meanings of the words.

In this case, detective Nate helps his friend Claude find his missing stegosaurus stamp. One rainy afternoon after Claude has shown three friends his dinosaur stamps, his favorite, the stegosaurus stamp, turns up missing. Questioning witnesses in true detective fashion, Nate learns that the stamp had been on the edge of the table, but that it has disappeared from the room. Nate's first great idea, to check out the dinosaur museum for clues, is a dud that leads nowhere. Help your child appreciate Nate's rethinking of the problem when his first hypothesis doesn't pan out. Talk about how Nate approaches the question in a new way. Ask about what other information Nate considers as he rethinks his problem. Which details become clues? Think about the rain and the activities of the various children. Remember the sequences of events. Who arrived at the house before the rain. Who arrived after the rain? How did Sludge help discover the most important clue?

Several passages demand that the reader infer meaning. For instance, Annie thinks that the stegosaurus is pretty while Nate finds it ugly. To understand this contrast the reader must understand how Annie's and Nate's feelings for her dog, Fang, are reflected in their attitudes towards the dinosaur which Fang resembles. Annie, of course, loves Fang and finds his smile adorable. Nate, on the other hand, is actually afraid of Fang. Talk about how the reader realizes Nate fears Fang when Nate decides it is time to go home after seeing Fang smile. Again Nate's fear can be inferred when he is glad that the stegosaurus in the museum is not capable of doing anything. Finally the active reader can infer why Rosamond was selling tuna cans and cat hairs at the yard sale. A few "why" questions on these incidents can help your child practice her skill in drawing inferences or can illuminate her already developed abilities.

Obadiah the Bold. Brinton Turkle. New York: Viking Press, 1965 (Gr. 3–6). Obadiah admires bravery and hopes someday to become a bold pirate. He builds a dream and sees it destroyed, but rebuilds his original dream to form a new and better vision of the future.

Prepare your son or daughter by discussing the book's cover. Talk about the boy with the spyglass. Do you think the boy is Obadiah? Look at the sailing ship and talk about where the boy is. Can you infer from the way he is dressed when the story takes place? What might he be looking at with his spyglass? Talk about what adventures Obadiah might be dreaming about.

Obadiah's dream of becoming a pirate is destroyed during a game in which Obadiah and his brothers play pirate. Help your child see that this is a pivotal point in the story. Compare what actually happened to Obadiah as a pirate during the game to the image of a pirate's life that Obadiah had pictured. What had Obadiah admired about pirates? Could Obadiah see the pirate as admirable while he was jailed and made to walk the plank? What does Obadiah's ignoring his spyglass indicate about what has happened to his desire to become a pirate?

After losing his dream of becoming a pirate, Obadiah seeks advice from his father. Discuss with your son or daughter what we know about Father and how Father helps Obadiah regain his dream for the future. What can your child infer about Father's willingness to stop his work to talk to Obadiah? Does Obadiah expect Father to be sympathetic, and does he fulfill Obadiah's expectations? Talk about the return of the spyglass as a sign that Obadiah again has a vision of a brave and exciting life at sea.

Obadiah the Bold can expand your youngster's vocabulary with exciting words evoking the sea. See if your child understands the significance of Mother's reference to a "friendly pirate"? Encourage your son or daughter to work towards an understanding of old nautical vocabulary such as "keelhaul," "yardarm," and "Davey Jones." What is happening in the story when these words are used? Ask your youngster if he would like to live in Obadiah's world, a strict, orderly world but a world offering the exciting adventures of the sea to explore.

Ordinary Jack. Helen Cresswell. New York: Macmillan, 1977. (Gr. 3–6). Helen Cresswell has created a wonderful book about an ordinary boy born into a family of geniuses. Unnerved when his eight year old sister beats him in swimming laps, Jack, who is eleven, desperately needs to improve his status in his family. Under the tutelage of his Uncle Parker, Jack sets out to become—or at least to appear to become—a Prophet. Your child will laugh at Jack and Uncle Parker's plots to display Jack's supernatural powers by having Jack's family witness his visions and prophecies: Jack's acquired skill in looking just past someone's ear to create a Vision, his mysterious prediction of the man in the purple suit, and his grand finale in which the family gathers to watch the Giant Bubble and the Great Brown Bear.

Have a conversation about the difference between appearance and reality. Ask your child how many of the Bagthorpes worry as much about appearance as about what they actually achieve. Talk about how William dramatizes his ham radio hobby through his anonymous radio informant. Is Rosie's painting as exceptional as you might at first expect? Discuss the irony of Uncle Parker working hard on his image as a relaxed man of leisure. What can you conclude when only Jack admits reading comics, but Jack's father is discovered reading the whole pile of comics? What generalizations can you make regarding the family's urge to create an image. Although Jack feels that he is different because his "genius" is an act, isn't he much like the rest of his family?

Although Jack shares some qualities with the rest of his family, your child will be sure to find the contrasts far more obvious than the similarities. Talk about Jack's concern for his dog, Zero. Bring up the family's reading material, and Jack's choices for birthday presents (remember Uncle Parker's comment), as well as the way each spends free time.

Early one morning, away from the normal Bagthorpe turmoil, Jack meets Grandpa listening to the birds sing in the garden. You might even want to read again the passage on page 143 in which Jack suddenly realizes that he, William, Tess and Rosie might someday grow as old as Grandpa is now and that they might wear a hearing aid and wake up at dawn. Consider how Jack reevaluates the importance of being a genius. How does his view of being a prophet change? Why does he now feel happier and more free? Take time to share fully and honestly your own values on achieving success and on projecting the image of success. Let your child appreciate the costs and rewards each of the Bagthorpes has reaped.

Owls in the Family. Farley Mowat. 1962. New York: Bantam, (Gr. 2–6). Before reading *Owls in the Family*, many people picture owls as fierce nocturnal hunters, who by day disappear to sleep. Wol and Weeps, orphaned owls adopted into Billy's family, quickly alter that image. It's hard to imagine an owl following a boy to school, hitching a ride on the handlebars of his bicycle. Wol and Weeps are based on Mowat's memories of owls he had in his childhood. He teaches about animals here just as in his well-known book, *Never Cry Wolf*.

The owls appear full of emotion, Wol feeling amused from his teasing or pouting when laughed at, Weeps cuddling up to Mutt for security. Encourage your child to look carefully at the emotions attributed to the owls. Do owls really have such emotions? Perhaps they do. How does the author describe their emotions? Does he see them with human-like feelings? What emotions have you seen in animals? What habit of Wol's tells us that he is careful and gentle with people?

Wol and Weeps, living in a human environment, yield rich information on the instinctive and learned behaviors of owls. Help your child distinguish between the habits acquired from humans and their instinctive behaviors. Think about the story of Wol climbing the tree with his beak and claws. What can you conclude about their learning process? Is flying learned or instinctive? (You may want to explain what instinctive actions are.) What conclusions can you draw about the hunting behavior of owls? Why didn't Wol and Weeps become great hunters? Why did Wol choose to hunt mainly skunks?

Make predictions about Wol and Weeps living in the wild. Compare the distinct personalities of the timid Weeps and Wol, the happy tease, to the picture of Wol's mother dive-bombing Mr. Miller in order to protect her nest. What changes would they have to make in their behavior to find adequate food? Could a wild owl have acted as surrogate mother for a newly hatched flock of prairie chickens? Discuss what would happen if a wild owl passed up such food. Have your child judge the decision to keep the birds in human care, remembering that an orphaned baby owl could not survive on its own.

Philip Hall Likes Me I Reckon Maybe. Bette Greene. New York: Dell, 1974. (Gr. 3–6). Lively and full of spirit, Beth Lambert is a gutsy girl, who is the best in the class except for Philip Hall. Philip not only overshadows her at school, he also *allows* her to do his chores after school. But Beth grows steadily in confidence until in the last chapter she is the best in the class, and she wins the 4H calf raising contest. Capturing thieves, earning money, competing fiercely with each other, Beth and Philip tickle the readers' funny bones and will earn your child's admiration.

Before your young reader begins this book, you might want to ask about boy-girl relations in your child's own experience and focus on similar issues in the book. In general, what do boys and girls in your child's school and neighborhood think of each other? Do they like each other? Do they play with each other? Do they compete with each other? Who usually wins? Guess what the girl pictured on the front of the book is like. Will she like Philip Hall? Will Philip Hall like her?

Help your son or daughter understand Beth. Discuss what other characters tell you about Beth and what Beth says about herself. What can you infer about her from what others tell you? Recall incidents that indicate that Beth is more competent than Philip. Especially remember the scene in the dark when Philip thinks he hears Gorilla Man. Talk about Beth's determination in the face of adversity. What does she do when Philip's invitation doesn't arrive, when her allergy acts up with the new puppies, and when the cows trample the vegetable stand? What similarities do her responses have? What generalization can you make about her reaction to disappointments? How would you react if those things happened to you? Which of Beth's qualities would make her a good veterinarian?

Encourage a prediction of Beth's future based on what your child knows about her from her childhood exploits. What problem might make it hard for her to treat animals? How would you evaluate Beth's abilities? Do you predict that she will be successful at what she does?

Girls can enjoy the vicarious pleasure of Beth's victory in the calf-raising contest. The contest does become a boy-versus-girl competition whose end might not please boys. Initiate a conversation on Beth's blue ribbon. Talk about Beth's and Philip's friendship, how it survived the contest, and the attitudes we have on male-female competition. Be sure to contrast Beth's confidence at the end of the book with her confidence at the beginning. When does Beth start to think she can do as well as Philip? Trace the growth of Beth's willingness to stand up to Philip Hall. How does Beth compete when she is more confident? Evaluate how important winning and losing are in the book.

Pigs Might Fly. Dick King-Smith. Puffin, 1980. (Gr. 3–7). *Pigs Might Fly* is an excellent choice for lighthearted fantasy where laughs mock self-satisfied prejudice and ignorance. Daggie Dogfoot is a runt pig (called a dag in the local vernacular) in the tradition of Wilbur in *Charlotte's Web*. Through his courage and determination, along with a little luck and the help of his friends, Daggie escapes the ignoble death suffered by all previous dags, to become a hero admired by his fellow pigs. Humor and fresh perspectives stimulate the reader to think again with an awakened mind.

One source of humor is the author's variations on old sayings that make a young reader aware of how we use cliches. Notice such playful variations as "I'll be butchered if I know" (instead of "I'll be hanged if I know") or "on the other trotter" (instead of "on the other hand"). Point out these expressions to increase awareness of how we use language. What do these expressions really mean?

One of those expressions, the "old sow's tale" that pigs can't swim, is a pivotal element of the story. Ask if Daggie's swimming ability would have been as impressive if the pigs hadn't always believed that pigs can't swim. Could Daggie have become a hero if his ability to swim had not seemed supernatural to the pigs?

Talk about how the pigs reach humorous conclusions because of their inaccurate preconceptions. Because the pigs "know" the Pigman is their servant, they attribute his bending over at the Squire's stall to respect for the Squire rather than to the sloping roof of Squire's stall.

Knowing what the pigs think of the Squire and the Pigman, we are ready to predict their interpretation of the final scene when the Pigman kneels to release the rescue straps around Daggie. Discuss how we find humor in the contrast between the pigs' belief in the Pigman's homage to Daggie and the real causes of his kneeling, which the reader knows were the helicopter blades and the release straps.

The reader can laugh easily at the pigs' faulty reasoning. The pigs, however, might find their ignorance and clouded thinking dangerous. What do you know about the Pigman's meals that the pigs don't know? Compare their ignorance to the despised duck's awareness of the dangers of the Pigman's menu. Consider how their contempt for the Pigman and the duck prevents them from suspecting the truth.

What do you think about the pigs' judgment? Where is the problem in their thinking when they believe Daggie is pulling the helicopter home? What evidence do they consider and what evidence do they ignore? How do emotions affect judgment? Could people make the same mistakes in their thinking that these pigs do?

Rabbit Spring. Tilde Michels. Orlando, FL: Harcourt, Brace, Jovanovich, 1988. (Gr. 2–5). Illustrator Kathi Bhend's drawings of rabbits and hares in their natural habitat will catch any youngsters who love soft, furry animals. *Rabbit Spring* is a bridge between fiction and nonfiction depicting the contrasting lives of rabbit and hare families. Rahn, a young father of new rabbit kittens, enthusiastically builds a nursery for his offspring. His initial pride in his own family trickles away, however, when he discovers newborn hares who are far more advanced than his own blind, deaf, hairless babies. Ask if your child agrees with mother rabbit Silla that all is as it should be, that hares and rabbits simply live differently. To what other areas of life can you and your child apply this generalization?

Lead your child to compare rabbits and hares. Talk about how they seem so similar in many ways, more alike, for instance, than a cocker spaniel and poodle. Yet through Rahn we see many differences. Talk about how their homes are different. How does the isolated life of hares contrast with the large family of rabbits? Talk about their different methods of grooming themselves. How does grooming help us draw conclusions about the hares' isolated life style or the rabbits' community life? Your child will probably notice himself the different ways rabbits and hares escape from danger. How do they watch or signal alarm? How do they escape from predators? How do hares and rabbits differ in physical appearance? Which do you think is the better runner? How does their type of home reflect their physical abilities and their means of protection from enemies? What would happen if hares were like rabbits at birth?

As your child reads about Rahn and his encounter with the hares, he will have to separate the fiction from the non-fiction in Rahn's account. Discuss how much a rabbit or hare can communicate. Can we tell what a rabbit is thinking?

A River Ran Wild. Lynne Cherry. Orlando, FL: Harcourt Brace, 1992. (Gr. 2–5). Lynne Cherry has fashioned a beautiful book with lush illustrations about the Nashua River in Massachusetts in the hopes that her book "inspires her readers to be people who make a difference in the world." Pay attention not only to the full-page illustrations facing the text but also to the border illustrations on the text pages: Wondrous delights reside there, from animals in the Nashua River Valley to Indian supplies and handcrafts to artifacts of the Industrial Revolution, which changed dramatically the lives of the people and the river. Note the maps and time lines on the inside front and back covers for painless history and geography lessons about the Nashua River Valley.

Lynne Cherry tells of the river's evolution through time; of the Native Americans who under Chief Weewa settled in the river valley and named the waterway "River with the Pebbled Bottom"; of the pale-skinned trader who brought new wares; and of the settlers who built fences and plowed fields, who built sawmills and dams, cutting down the towering forests, and who warned the Indians not to trespass. We see the gradual pollution of the great Nashua as the Industrial Revolution sweeps through the country in the name of progress. Soon "The Nashua was slowly dying." We learn of Oweana, a descendant of the original Nashua Indians; Oweana dreams that Chief Weewa returned to weep over the dirty waters and cleansed them. When he told his dream to his friend Marion, together they resolved to do something. Marion traveled the river banks speaking to people about the river's history and getting them to see how beautiful and clean the river could be. People wrote letters to their government leaders, and ultimately laws were passed to prevent further pollution. "Now we walk along its banks and row upon its fragrant waters. Once again the river runs wild through a towering greenway."

A River Ran Wild is a youngster's environmental action book. One discussion that should grow naturally out of your reading is whether or not you and your child can influence the environment in your own community. Talk about the pristine beauty of the river and the surrounding land that the Indians found and nurtured and the river and land as Marion began her crusade. You'll want to discuss the wages of progress with your child. Talk about predicting outcomes: What might the pale-skinned settlers have done to prevent the pollution of the river? What conclusions and generalizations can your child draw from this book? Consider this one: People's actions can make a difference in causing or reversing the land's decline. Or this: Native Americans cared for and respected the land more than Americans today. Also, consider whether progress is achievable without bringing harm to the planet: We don't want children to accept as an absolute that scientific advancement and the earth's well-being are incompatible.

Scorpians. Walter Dean Myers. New York: HarperCollins, 1988. (Gr. 6+). Jamal Hick's world in Harlem is threatening. He worries about his mother's safety as she returns home late at night past the addict below their apartment window. Jamal sees "thrown away people" in the park, people whose lives are wasted by drugs and alcohol, who are frightening because they once were like Jamal—kids living on these streets. When Jamal's older brother Randy sends word from prison that Jamal is to be leader of his gang, the Scorpians, Jamal is flung into rivalry with older kids who want the power and money from drug dealing. Jamal wants safety. The gang seems to provide safety, and the gun he receives impresses the bigger kids who threaten to beat him up. Be sure to discuss the role of the gun with your child. Talk about Jamal's feelings about the gun. Why does he hesitate to throw it away? Weigh its effect in the fight when Jamal was saved from the attacker's knife and its effect in taking away Tito, Jamal's one close friend and confidant.

Help your child become oriented to the setting of this book by talking about the cover. From the picture what can you infer about the boys' attitudes? Are the boys friends? What can you tell about their surroundings? Notice the condition of the steps and railing. What does the graffiti on the doors indicate about the neighborhood?

After your son or daughter has read the book, talk about how Jamal's life is different from your child's. Evaluate the importance of physical violence. What gives kids status in Jamal's neighborhood? How much entertainment comes from after school fights? Talk about the role of school in Jamal's life? Does the school help or hurt him? Review the sequence of Jamal's run-ins with the principal? What can you conclude about the principal's goals and values? What do you predict will be Jamal's future in school? How do you evaluate Jamal's talents and abilities? Does school develop his abilities?

Help your son or daughter evaluate the support Jamal gets from his family. What can you infer about Jamal's mother's dedication to her family? Explore the effect Randy has on the family. Talk about how much Jamal's mother cares about his school work and how little she actually knows about his life at school. What do you predict will be the effect of her not knowing about the pills Jamal is taking? While Jamal finds love in his family, he finds little guidance from his mother, from Randy in prison, or from his absentee father. How will Jamal grow to manhood without guidance in his family? What do you predict for his future?

You may want to introduce this book when your child has gained some maturity and is ready to evaluate the effects of society. Books of this quality that portray Jamal's part of the world are rare. *Scorpians* offers our children a valuable window on our neighbors' lives.

Seminole Diary: Remembrances of a Slave. Dolores Johnson. New York: Macmillan, 1994. (Gr. 3–6). This wonderful tale "of people who risked their lives and homes aiding African-American slaves in their escape to freedom" has a structure akin to a play within a play. We meet Gina, a young black girl who comes upon her mother in the attic examining the contents of an old steamer trunk. Her mother is reading a marvelous work passed on by one of her ancestors, a slave named Libbie, who "left a wealth of precious memories" in her diary.

From Thursday, March 13, 1834 to Monday, June 22, 1835, *Seminole Diary* chronicles the story of Libbie's family and their escape from an abusive slaveholder to South (not North, the usual escape route). Ultimately they join a tribe of Seminole Indians. "The Indians will protect y'all," Silas, an escaped slave declares, "and treat you like brothers even though you'll be their slaves." Slave catchers avoid slaves of the Indians, Libbie's Papa explains after speaking with Chief Running Tiger. We see the black family join the Indian culture—one Seminole woman named Honey Flower takes a strong liking to Libbie's sister Clarissa and the two build a close relationship. When the white men force the Seminoles off their land onto protected Oklahoma Territory and when Papa decides to move his family there with many of the tribesmen, Clarissa vanishes with Honey Flower into the swamps of South Florida "to live on land that even the white man could never want."

There are endless conversational possibilities here to enrich critical reading and thinking. Discuss diaries in general. Why do people keep them? Why did Libbie keep a diary? (Perhaps you can start a diary-keeping project with your son or daughter.) Compare the two lives Libbie had to lead—one as a slave and one as a sister of the Seminoles. What difficulties does Libbie encounter? What problems would any person face in leaving a familiar setting and becoming part of a new culture? What can your child infer about the Seminoles from this book? What kind of people were they? Why would they want to help black families escaping from slavery? How does your child account for Clarissa's willingness to be completely absorbed by another family? Do you think she willingly left with Honey Flower? Why or why not? Why does Clarissa insist on being called Swift Sparrow, the name her Seminole "family" gave her, instead of her own name, which is the name of her dead mother? How does Libbie feel about the Indian boy, Wild Jumper, who holds her interest? Libbie says that Seminole boys don't have time for laughing: "They have to be men," she declares. What does she mean? What conclusions can your child draw about the demands of Seminole life?

The story also allows much opportunity for predicting outcomes, and you can check some of these educated guesses in the library. What does your son or daughter think is the fate of the Oklahoma-bound Seminoles? Dolores Johnson takes much pride in her research for this children's book. In the last two pages Gina's Mom talks about the Second Seminole War (1835–1842) in the Oklahoma Territory, where "Seminole and black warriors chose to stay and fight for their land." These facts flesh out an often neglected moment in American history. Certainly your youngster will have the same kinds of questions Gina asks at the end of the book, and Mom's instructive answers will stimulate further speculation.

The Sign of the Beaver. Elizabeth George Speare. Boston: Houghton Mifflin, 1983. (Gr. 4–7). In the Maine wilderness in 1768, twelve-year-old Matt stays alone to watch over his family's new homestead while his father goes to bring back the rest of the family. Matt soon has a guest—a hungry vagrant who steals the hunting rifle. Talk with your child about how you can infer that Ben, the visitor, is not to be trusted. You and your child might also discuss your judgment of Ben who must have known that Matt was depending on the rifle to get food during his father's absence. Matt, however, soon realizes that he can catch fish for food. What can your child conclude about Matt's resourcefulness?

Contrast Ben with Matt's second visitors, the Indians Saknis and Akkean, who rescue Matt from an attack of swarming bees and who continue to befriend him, bringing him gifts and teaching him Indian hunting skills. What generalizations can you make about each visitor? Who is kind and honest? Who is untruthful?

Woven into Matt's story is the tale of Robinson Crusoe, which you may want to retell for your child although the author has included the bare plot. The similarities and differences between Matt and Robinson Crusoe offer a wealth of comparison-contrast questions. In each book who gave help and who received help? Which situation is more realistic: Crusoe's being shipwrecked with his store of tools and a worshipping native, or Matt's precarious existence in the woods without tools of any sort but with Indian teachers? Noting the sequence of events, discuss Matt's growing awareness of how Robinson Crusoe's fate should have been more like Matt's own with Friday being the teacher in his own land.

Another important comparison is the growth into manhood for both Matt and Akkean. Talk about the meaning of the word "manitou" that your child has learned from reading about Akkean's passage into manhood. When Matt sees Akkean after he has received his manitou, what does Matt infer about Akkean? How has Akkean changed? Matt's movement toward adulthood is more subtle, but careful questioning on your part can make Matt's maturity apparent for your child. Discuss how Matt's parents talked about Matt's achievements on the homestead. Matt's father especially speaks of Matt's doing a man's job.

Finally, Matt earned the respect of his Indian friends when he least expected it—when he decided to wait for his family. With your child explore the values that led Saknis and Akkean to judge Matt worthy of respect. Together evaluate what Matt learned from his experience. Talk about his woodsmanship, his appreciation of another culture, his self-reliance, his courage, and his unusual friendship.

Spectacular Stone Soup. Patricia Reilly Giff. New York: Dell, 1989. (Gr. 1–3). *Spectacular Stone Soup* offers beginning readers familiar scenes and characters that evoke emotions felt by nearly all early elementary children—a desire to please and to be grown up but also a feeling of uncertainty in the new world of the school. The setting is a class unit on helping, which includes a shared stone soup party. Children can identify with normally enthusiastic Stacy who becomes temporarily discouraged trying to fulfill her teacher's image of a good helper.

Talk about the picture you see on the cover when your child is ready to begin this book. What are the children doing? Who do you think the adult is with the spoon? A mother? A teacher? What might be in the big pot? Does the title give you a clue? Can you infer how the children feel by looking at the expressions on their faces? Would you like to be with those children?

Capitalize on an opportunity to relate reading to your child's own experience. Ask whether your son or daughter has ever felt like Stacy. What attempt to help has led to trouble instead? Talk about the fun and feeling of importance that come with participating in a big project.

Show your child how much he can infer about Stacy without being specifically told. Think about how Stacy talks in class. Softly? Boldly? Is she afraid to talk in class, or does she want to speak out? Is Stacy afraid to tell kids what to do in the hall? Would you conclude that Stacy is shy or outgoing? What clues indicate that Stacy likes her teacher, Mrs. Zachary? How old would you guess Stacy is? Are other kids in the school older or younger than Stacy? (For Example, what kids take a snack rather than a lunch?) Can she read the words on the board? How much does Stacy know about hall monitors? Discuss how much your child knows about Stacy's mother who never appears in the story. How is her mother ready to help her? Do you think she talks much with her mother? Find examples of Stacy's repeating her mother's opinions.

A delightful extra in the book is a map of Stacy's classroom. You will want to use it to develop the important skill of map reading. Talk about how Stacy's class is arranged. Compare Stacy's classroom to rooms in your child's school. While reading the story, your child can practice map use by pointing out where the kids are in the classroom.

The Story of Helen Keller. Lorena A. Hickok. New York: Scholastic, 1958. (Gr. 4–7). When Helen's father, in the first chapter, contemplates placing six year old Helen in an institution, be prepared for intense reactions from your child. What conclusion can she draw about Helen's father from his plan? What can she infer about Helen herself? Yet the bleakness of those early years for Helen and her family sets off the achievements that follow. Discuss how the tremendous handicaps Helen faced make possible the great triumph of her life. If Helen had had normal ears and eyes, would she have become famous? Talk with your child about any generalizations you might derive regarding achievement in the face of great obstacles.

The young Helen is frequently compared to a puppy. She eats like a dog, begging handouts at the table, making a sound like a little growl. Then Helen learns language. Compare Helen's personality before and after she learned words. What can you conclude about the effect language had on Helen? What can Helen do once she has words for things?

Could Helen have escaped from her prison of blindness and deafness without help? Have your child explore Teacher's influence. Ask why Helen wanted to write a book about Teacher. Explore the differences and similarities between Helen and Teacher. Consider how Teacher's blindness prepared her to help Helen. What advantages did Helen have that Teacher lacked? Talk about the determination and enthusiasm each posessed.

Helen was more fortunate than Teacher in one way: Helen had a family that loved her. Does it seem strange then that Helen's father considered putting her in an institution? (Remember that institutions in those days were very depressing places.) Did Helen's father love her? What incidents were difficult for him to witness? Did he have much hope that Helen could learn? What happened when Helen started to talk, or sign, with her fingers? What did Helen's parents do to help her? When did they make learning more difficult for her? Lead your child to judge the effect Helen's parents had on her learning.

Contrast Helen's education to the schooling most of us receive. Discuss Teacher's blending of play and learning. How did Helen feel about learning? How much of her learning seemed like a game? Talk about how Helen gained freedom and an entry into a bigger world through her education and how it was fun—at least until the last years of college. Compare her education with our usual feeling that school is more like a prison than a new found freedom. How did Teacher and Helen keep her education from becoming dreary and limiting? Are there ways we might envy Helen?

Tuck Everlasting. Natalie Babbit. New York: Farrar, Straus &

Giroux, 1975. (Gr. 3+). The story starts during the dog days of August, the high point of the year, the static moment that the preceding weeks have been leading to. The following weeks will drop off toward autumn chills. This picture of time frames Winnie Foster's meeting with timelessness, with the possibility of eternal life. Winnie discovers a mysterious spring and the family who once drank its waters eighty-seven years ago. No aging or death threatens their immortality or their youth. From seventeen-year-old Jesse Tuck (or is he 102?) and from his brother and parents, Winnie learns about life lived forever—at one age, without peaks and valleys, without high points and without bonds to other people, for how could they live with those who grow old?

A mysterious stranger has also learned of the peculiar spring. Unlike the Tuck family, who consider the spring a heavy burden holding potential chaos for the world, the stranger plans to publicize the spring and make a fortune from its waters. Why do the Tucks feel the way they do about the spring? Compare the Tucks' life with normal lives and compare their understanding with the stranger's greedy thoughtlessness. Ask your child what the Tucks have learned that the stranger does not consider. Talk about Tuck's words to Winnie in the boat. How is life like the water flowing by the boat? How are the Tucks, who will never die, not really living? How do they exist like a rock?

Ask your child what it would be like to be a child forever? If you were to choose an age to be forever, what age would you be? What problems might you face?

How would your child judge Mae's killing of the stranger? Was she right or wrong? Did she have any other alternatives? Predict what might have happened to the world if the stranger had announced the existence of the spring.

Finally discuss Winnie's decision. Did she make the right decision? When you read the gravestone, do you think Winnie had a full life? Speculate on why she didn't stay with Jesse. Do you think she worried about Jesse's eternal loneliness? Evaluate her choice. Why do you think she chose an ordinary life with its inevitable old age and death? What generalizations can you draw about humans and old age?

Upon the Head of the Goat; A Childhood in Hungary, 1939–1944.
Aranka Siegel. New York: Farrar, Straus, Giroux, 1981. (Gr. 5+). The reader first meets Piri in the Ukraine where war between Hungary and the Ukraine has stranded her on her grandmother's farm. Through the winter Piri lives quietly, but the war sometimes reaches even their remote village. And when the end of

this war allows Piri to return to her own home in Budapest, it is only a respite before the much greater war that will soon envelop them. Piri's autobiographical story resurrects the war years, the hardships, fears, hopes, and daily life of Hungarian Jews.

Do a prereading discussion to help your child benefit from this book. To understand Piri's situation your child may need an explanation of the countries and ethnic groups around Hungary. Also, read together the quote from Leviticus and retell the ancient story of the scapegoat. Discuss why the author referred to the goat in the title?

Because we know the history of World War II, the threat of death lurks throughout the story. Piri's family confronts those fears, but are not overwhelmed by them. Talk about examples from the book showing their ingenuity at finding food. Would you conclude that they are optimistic? Only the first chapter evokes the spectre of death when Piri watches the bodies of Ukrainian soldiers floating down the Rika River. Have your son or daughter reflect on Babi's response that the soldiers are at peace. Talk about Babi's sense of peace. Does it influence the rest of the family?

With your child evaluate the importance of hope for Piri's family. Do you agree that hope could be their salvation? What allows Piri and Judi to enjoy the boys in the ghetto? To what extent do you think they are like kids their age in normal circumstances?

When Piri and her family are taken to the ghetto, Mother's resourcefulness and determination contrast to the despair of the other families. Ask your child how Mother showed the same resourcefulness and determination earlier in the war when living conditions became difficult? Discuss Mother's willingness to help strangers as well as her own family. How is Piri like Mother? What incident shows Piri helping strangers?

Talk about the relations between Jews and non-Jews in the book. What does Mother say about her friends in the city? What do you infer about the difference in social contacts in the city and in the country? Compare Mother's and Babi's attitudes toward non-Jews. How does Mother interpret the silence of her friends when trouble comes? What reasons might Mother's friends have for being distant?

As time runs out in the ghetto some try to organize a rebellion. Help your child judge the consequences of a rebellion. What do you predict the Germans would have done? What emotions did the planning for the rebellion raise in the rebels? Did the rebels feel more worthwhile? Did they feel more human by not submitting? Would the rebellion have been worth the cost?

The Upstairs Room. Johanna Reiss. New York: HarperCollins, 1972. (Gr. 5+). The radio makes Annie lonely. Her father no longer holds her and talks to her; he listens to news about Hitler's Germany, which is just a few miles away from their home in Holland. The day German soldiers parade through the town square, life becomes more difficult for Annie's Jewish family. Unable to get immigration papers, the family goes into hiding. For the rest of the war Annie and her older sister Sini live in a Dutch farm family's upstairs room.

Together with your child try to evaluate what Annie's family lost in addition to their freedom. What can you infer about importance of lost family ties? How had the sisters grown apart when Rachel visited Annie and Sini? What can you generalize about how a family should face a mother's death? What extra loss did their mother suffer dying without her family near? Talk about Annie and Sini's hesitation to leave the Oostervelds' to rejoin their father. What was lost between father and daughters? What material goods did they lose? What can you predict about their financial situation when they return home?

To understand better the difficulty of life lived in the upstairs room, compare Annie's life there to other forms of imprisonment. Brainstorm with your child about ways freedom can be lost: prison, illness, slavery, and so on. Then discuss what global reactions each type of prison would evoke such as anger, guilt, blame, boredom, fear, frustration, and so forth. Which of these reactions is found in Annie's story?

The Oostervelds call themselves plain people. Using factual descriptive details of life in their house, your child can establish what a rugged lifestyle they had. Have your child contrast the Oostervelds' household with Annie's and contrast the educational levels of the families. How great is the difference? Would you expect Annie and Sini to feel at home there? Discuss why such affection grew among them.

Is Johan a dumb farmer as he frequently describes himself? Draw evidence from incidents in the text and from comments in the story about Johan's intelligence. What does Dientje say about him? How does he outsmart the Germans? Is there a sense that Johan enjoys matching wits with the Germans? Despite the many horrors of the war, *The Upstairs Room* is not a pessimistic book. Talk about the bond between the sisters and the Oostervelds. What makes you like and respect the sisters and the Oost-ervelds, ordinary as they all are? Is this a valid generalization to draw from this book: "The kindness of some people can redeem the cruelty of others"? Does your child's experience bear out the truth of this generalization?

The Whipping Boy. Sid Fleischman. Greenwillow, 1986. (Gr. 2–6) Adult readers and children will immediately recognize the poor little rich boy theme in *The Whipping Boy.* Bored and spoiled Prince Horace, or Prince Brat as he is surreptitiously called, takes his whipping boy out for a lark outside the palace walls. Whipping boy Jemmy, whose job is to receive Prince Brat's whippings, unhappily obeys the command to go. Their adventure brings Prince Brat his first taste of the real world, his first experience of friendship, and his first appreciation for the consequences of his own actions.

Your child will want to talk about the changes in Prince Brat. She will probably bring up Prince Brat's new ability to use his brain and his new concern for people besides himself. You can help distinguish less obvious changes such as Prince Brat's new sense of humor. What makes him laugh in the beginning, and what causes him to smile in the final scene with his father? Contrast the way he identifies himself to Billy and Cutwater with the way he introduces himself at the fair. Help your child appreciate the gradual development of Prince Brat's character as well as a sense of the sequence of the story by noting pertinent details along the way. Talk about what Prince Brat has actually learned from watching his whippings given to Jemmy. What have the consequences of his actions been? What conclusions can you draw about the prince's education?

In addition, lead your child to infer the prince's real motives for getting into trouble. What does the prince say about his father? Look at what the king has learned when his son returns. Discuss whether the new understanding between the prince and his father will lead to better behavior from the prince in the future.

Help your son or daughter evaluate who has been the "advantaged" child in the story. Bring her to an appreciation of the two measures in the story, one for outward material advantages and the other for inner moral and intellectual advantages. How do the boys begin at opposite poles and both become more advantaged in the end?

Index